PI LIGHTFOOT AND THE
CODESURFERS

PI LIGHTFOOT
AND THE
CODESURFERS

NICK GILADOR

Matador
9 Priory Business Park,
Wistow Road, Kibworth Beauchamp,
Leicestershire. LE8 0RX
Tel: 0116 279 2299
Email: books@troubador.co.uk
Web: www.troubador.co.uk/matador
Twitter: @matadorbooks

ISBN 978 1789014 570

British Library Cataloguing in Publication Data.
A catalogue record for this book is available from the British Library.

Printed and bound by CPI Group (UK) Ltd, Croydon, CR0 4YY
Typeset in 12pt Adobe Garamond Pro by Troubador Publishing Ltd, Leicester, UK

Matador is an imprint of Troubador Publishing Ltd

For Tara, Miel, Wes, Jayne, Tess and Simon, the first to learn of Pi's secret world

Based on a true story… it just hasn't happened yet

ONE

THE WHISPER OF
GHOSTS

'Brightly now my fire-child, star-forge dreamed, for under thy lofted sail, vaulted oceans shall practise eternity.'

Pi idly ran a finger over the inscription, her late father's words timeless in the mirror-smooth granite. She glanced up at the life-sized bronze relief of his head, then lazily moved her finger onwards to 'Professor' and his first three names, William and George, smiling to herself when she reached Gerontius.

A voice crackled in her head.

"Where are you?" It was her friend Makelina. Pi had forgotten to mute her bracelet modem; Makelina could see she was live, although Pi's eyes and GPS were offline. Pi flicked her virtual mute *off*, and Makelina's head instantly filled with Pi's eye view of the Lightfoot Wing, Hawaii Neurological Research Centre.

"Kicker, you're at the hospital, sorry, hon' – clean forgot."

"No probs, just waiting in the corridor for Mum and Lani; you still coming?"

"You serious! And I bagged something supercryo for Lani!"

Pi could now see what Makelina's eyes beheld. The gift was beautifully wrapped in turquoise holo paper, which came alive with animated dolphins when Makelina moved it in the light.

"Megs! That's *extinct*! Maybe she'll let me have the paper, ha ha! No, seriously, she's had so much stuff come through on the fabricator, it's great you got her something that's actually *wrapped*."

"That's what I loaded, 3D printed isn't the same!"

"Anyway," Pi heard voices in the corridor, "the guys are on their way, outta ticks, Maks – better go."

"Sure, laters – good luck!"

"Mahalo." Pi decided to play it safe, switching her bracelet-modem to *standby*. Her finger resumed where it had left off, lazily tracing the surname *Lightfoot*. Her hand dropped back by her side as she mused on the detail below. The day of her father's birth, the fourth of October 2001, and his untimely death; the eighteenth of September 2039, exactly four weeks after she was born.

Above the distant rumble of Honolulu's rush hour, the voices were getting louder, the frosted glass doors lit by flashes with increasing intensity; the press was on its way. She whacked the side of her left leg. It was fitted with a discreet hi-tech knee brace. It tended to slip out of alignment if she neglected to do this and had been acting up all day.

"Showtime," she mumbled wearily.

Both doors swung noisily open, sending echoes ricocheting down the corridor. Sensing their sudden impropriety, the huddle of reporters dropped their voices to a murmur, pausing momentarily to allow the main event to go ahead of them, Pi's mother, Mirena, and her soon-to-be-sweet-sixteen sister, Lani, three years Pi's senior. They began walking so swiftly the reporters could barely keep up.

Pi looked down at her sister's near non-existent skirt as she joined the flow. "Couldn't find a shorter one, huh?"

Lani stuck out her tongue by way of reply.

Mirena pulled a face of her own. "Guys, not now, okay, best behaviour remember?" She acknowledged her late husband's memorial. "What would your father say?"

"Something about Lani's legs, I guess?"

"Just because I've got them and you haven't."

"Whoa, way over the line, apologise to your sister."

Lani turned towards Pi, but pointedly avoided eye contact. "I'm sorry, K?"

Pi fixed her sister with a stern stare. "And for your information I *have* got legs, just one of them isn't so great is all!"

"Okay, enough!" Mirena grabbed each sibling firmly by the hand and dropped her voice to a firm whisper. "Need I remind you that we have the world's press breathing down our necks, *and* we're representing your father's foundation. Any more trouble from either of you, and you're both grounded for a fortnight!"

The girls gave a mute grunt of acknowledgement and they continued walking along the corridor towards the neurology suites.

"Why just Pi? Why did they have to choose her for this?" said Lani, her annoyance barely disguised.

Mirena stopped abruptly. "I don't know, honey, but the little girl's parents asked for your sister. All I'm asking is for you to support her, think you can manage that?"

Lani raised her eyes and sighed. "Sure, was just *curious.*"

They continued walking briskly, Pi nervously chewing the end of her long black hair, until Mirena shot her a glance; why *had* they asked for her?

Behind them the posse of reporters followed, but now with an awkward gait, as if any noise might invoke some undefined disaster, or Mirena's disapproval.

A nurse came towards them carrying a transparent plastic bag. Pi was intrigued by the contents. It contained seven personal items belonging to a six-year-old girl called Alice, the patient they were about to see, if all went well. She couldn't exactly miss the large pink rabbit; she also noted a copy of *The Little*

Prince amongst the personal effects. The quest of its optimistic young hero and his beloved rose had long been a favourite of hers too.

The wide picture window of the neuroscience department greeted them, and they paused. The nurse removed the furry rabbit from the bag. Immediately it sprang to life, asking the nurse's name, telling inane jokes and chortling to itself, adding a moment of much needed levity. Inside, despite the subdued lighting, Pi could just make out a child-sized android. It sat with its head slumped forward, a man and woman seated on either side patiently holding its cybernetic hands.

"Well, here we are, sweetie, that must be Alice's family. I'd better wait out here with Lani. Nervous?"

Pi nodded. "A little," reluctantly letting go her mother's hand.

The nurse playfully gave the incorrigible rabbit to Pi, who was then subjected to more electronic merriment. Lani looked more than a little jealous as she watched her sister pose briefly with the toy. A volley of photographs followed from the discreetly disguised eye of the press, their clothes impregnated with nano-flash technology, their buttons a selection of telephoto lenses. Pi gave them all the smiles they needed, acutely aware of her sister's indignation. This could be the biggest scoop of 2052.

The suite door opened automatically and a female doctor appeared holding a clipboard.

"Hi, Dr Eastman, please call me Anakalia. You

must be Mrs Lightfoot?"

"Mirena… lovely to meet you, Anakalia, hope we're not too late?"

"No, no, perfect really," the doctor looked down, "and this young lady must be the famous Epiphany we've all heard so much about?"

"That's me." Pi shook the doctor's hand and gave her the biggest smile yet, secretly enjoying Lani's irritation as more photos followed. The doctor led Pi into the dimly-lit suite and the door closed silently behind them.

Inside, there was such a sense of hushed expectation even the riotous rabbit fell silent.

Shyly, Pi held back from approaching Alice's parents. They acknowledged her with a grateful smile and a silent *'aloha'*.

"The droid was flickering a bit earlier, hopefully she'll be back in a minute," the doctor said softly. Pi watched the tell-tale amber bindi light on the android's forehead. If it lit up, then the blank white screen of the face should illuminate with Alice's features soon after.

"She adores Harvey, wouldn't go to bed without him," said Alice's mother, her voice closing to a whisper.

Harvey moved his head, studying the mother's face carefully, but remained silent, as if waiting for something, or some*one*.

Alice's father bade Pi over with a wave of his hand. "Alice was always talking about you – Epiphany Lightfoot this, Epiphany Lightfoot that."

"Really?" said Pi.

He looked at the complex gadgetry surrounding them. "All this just blows me away, it's like *magic*."

Alice's mother gently took Pi's hand and smiled. "We really appreciate this, you coming all the way over here. I hope you didn't mind us asking?"

Pi shook her head; she didn't mind one little bit.

She was especially entranced by the view on the wall monitor. The doctor studied it intently. A three-masted ship sailing across a bright ocean, its sails half-rigged, some were filled by a virtual breeze, others still flapped loose. Every now and then the doctor tapped one of the loose sails with her finger and momentarily it expanded to fill the screen with its various data. It was another one of her father's innovations, the data-ship, designed especially for the quantum supercomputer Quadriga, his greatest achievement. Installed in a vast subterranean hall some six thousand miles away, it enjoyed many such innovative interfaces.

The ship was sailing upon a sea of watercode, a virtual ocean of code that enabled the Quadriga to work its magic. But the greatest innovation of all was yet to come. Seven of Alice's favourite things, including Harvey and Saint-Exupery's inquisitive little hero, had been digitised and entered into the Quadriga. A powerful algorithm had transformed them all into a lifebelt, thrown to what remained of Alice's mind, floating in its sea of unconsciousness, who knew where.

The weeks of stimulation had worked their magic. Alice's brain was slowly healing after her accident, she was on her way back, as evidenced by her unique data-ship. The loose sails were gradually tightening up and holding the wind as they should. It would not be long now. Hopefully, whilst her body healed in the ITU, Alice was about to emerge from her coma, reconnecting with the world courtesy of her very own temporary android.

Pi glanced back through the glass at her mother, but she was so transfixed by the data-ship that she failed to notice Pi's attention. Lani, on the other hand, still looked extremely cross, sticking out her tongue and pretending to rearrange her hair. Behind her family, four dozen reporters watched intently.

The doctor suddenly abandoned the monitor, bounding over to the 'droid. As if on cue the amber bindi spot illuminated, the 'droid's white facial screen fluttering like a neon tube. The delicate child-sized hands began flexing their digits up and down, as if playing an invisible piano. Everybody held their breath, then, after a few false starts, Alice's features filled the electronic face. Everybody, including the doctor, gasped.

"Kapuku," her father said softly.

Harvey started to wriggle, reaching out his arms towards his beloved mistress. Calling out her name, over and over in his robotic way, now so animated Pi could barely hold the impatient writhing toy.

Alice's robotic arms extended to receive her beloved 'wabbit', a huge smile upon her projected face. She clasped Harvey to her synthetic chest, her wordlessly grateful parents reconnecting with a daughter they thought they'd never see again. A tremor of pride ran through Pi; after all, it was her father's work that had made this miracle possible. It was almost as if, in some small way, he himself had returned to life.

A hot tear escaped down her cheek and she wiped it away, feeling a little superfluous.

She glanced back at the nurse, who acknowledged Pi's desire to leave. Together they walked quietly back towards the glass door, as quietly as Pi's knee brace would allow. Sometimes it squeaked when she walked, usually when least appropriate.

Outside, a crush of reporters was waiting to ambush her, their faces pressed against the glass. Her mother, seemingly distracted, already fielding a volley of questions.

"Wait, *Kamaina Lahela!*" Pi spun round. They were her middle names.

Alice's slightly artificial voice surprised her again. "Your pop wanted me to send you this!"

Alice smartly punched several buttons on her droid's arm, as if she'd been practising the manoeuvre for weeks. Immediately Pi felt her bracelet buzz, and a familiar phrase sounded in her head. "*You have mail.*"

The significance of Alice's actions went unnoticed by the others, overwhelmed as they were by her very reappearance. Harvey was now singing *Somewhere Over the Rainbow* at the top of his electronic lungs, complete with ukelele accompaniment, thus obscuring any chance of further conversation. Pi froze. Suddenly she had a million questions, but it hardly seemed appropriate to ask even one.

"Great meeting you, Alice, wishing you a full recovery!" was all she could think to say as she waved and left.

Pi knew it couldn't possibly be a message from her father. How could it? Surely it was something Alice had picked up about her from the Q-Net? After all, there was loads of information about her family on there, but her curiosity was piqued. She was anxious to investigate the mysterious mail.

TWO

THE LU'AU

As she headed back to Oahu Airport with her mother and sister for the short flight home to Maui, Pi answered the inevitable questions but said nothing of Alice's enigmatic message. Lani, as if sensing her sister's secret, was especially inquisitive.

"I'll swear she trans'd you something, the girl, I saw her use the comms on that droid, then you checked your bracelet."

"That's totally lolo, my wrist was just itchy is all."

"Well I know what I saw."

"Negs, you saw nada."

"Na na na, you're smoking me, the girl def trans'd you something, so what's the big secret? Why can't you just tell me?"

"Look, why would she? She doesn't even know us, and anyway we're unlisted remember!"

Lani sang, "I'll find it, you know I will," which Pi found especially irritating.

Mirena sighed. "Okay, girls, please let's move on and talk about something else."

Pi looked away, her brain buzzing like a beehive; how had Alice known her middle names? How could she have made an e-card for goodness' sake? She'd been in a coma for the last ten weeks! And how on earth *had* she obtained Pi's unlisted bracelet address?

Of course she'd quickly gone online and glanced at the card as soon as she'd left the suite. It appeared to be nothing more than a child's crayon drawing of an old-fashioned plane, with four prop engines, flying through clouds. There was a big yellow sun in one corner and a rainbow at the top. Inside, a short attachment was glued to the card, a mysterious virtual cookie wrapped in bright red foil. But most heart-stopping of all, there was a message.

'*To Dearest Pi, time to find out who you really are, all my love – Dad.*' Not written by a child either, but the confident hand of an adult. A jolt of adrenaline ran through her. What did it mean? Had Alice *actually* received something, somehow, from her father? She immediately dismissed the idea. There had to be another explanation, surely? There was one other thing, a much larger attachment; it looked like an enormous file. As the car wove slowly through heavy traffic, she continued giving her mother and Lani monosyllabic answers, whilst her avatar cautiously studied the attachment in her wavesite, her personal 3D virtual-domain. Tentatively, she tapped the pink attachment tab at the bottom of the card and instantly it opened. Pi's avatar jumped backwards, surprised by the file's great size. It was beautifully gift-wrapped, too, with a large pink ribbon and bow, which only made her more suspicious. Malware was contrived to look inviting after all. It had a matching pink label, too, with a strange printed message. *'Ex-Libris, Stargazey Pi, overdue – please return'*. She allowed herself to test its virtual weight; it was surprisingly heavy. But knowing that Lani's avatar might appear at any moment and discover her, Pi decided to hide the whole thing until later, staying offline until she was home.

Aware that she was supposed to be helping her mother with preparations for Lani's birthday *lu'au* (party) she slunk away to her room under the pretence of taking off her knee brace. It became uncomfortable after a while, and anyway she didn't really need it at home. Hastily, she went back online and accessed her wavesite, taking a moment to check her avatar's long black hair in an ornately framed mirror she'd found in an e-skip in virtual Paris.

"K, let's do this." She unlocked the largest drawer in her virtual wardrobe and took out Alice's message. It became more intriguing the longer she looked at it. What on earth did 'Stargazey Pi' mean? A quick search on *Q?* came up with some info about a kind of fish pie from Cornwall, England (where her father was born), but not much else.

She was still sitting motionless on her bed, eyes closed, when Lani blustered in.

Lani, seeing her sister was online, let out an exasperated sigh. "They'll be here in twenty minutes!" slamming the door loudly as she left.

Pi heard Lani perfectly clearly, but was engaged in the delicate business of removing the virtual cookie from Alice's card, without damaging the red foil wrapping. She'd locked her wavesite securely this time; nothing was going to disturb her curiosity.

After a painfully slow, almost surgical, effort, she was able to study the cryptic conundrum in greater detail. The words *Proust Madeleine* were printed in black and gold on the top in a flamboyant baroque script. The search engine *Q?* had rather more to say about this, recalling the moment when a famous nineteenth-century writer dipped a little madeleine cake into hot tea, savouring the happy memories this evoked from his childhood.

Pi's avatar looked puzzled. "Hmm, well whatever you are, you're a pretty little thing anyways."

On the back, where the foil was all scrunched up, there was nothing. Then Pi noticed tiny gold writing around the edge that said '*30 milliseconds*' several times.

"Thirty milliseconds?"

She put the cookie to her avatar's ear to see if it was ticking; it wasn't. She even shook it a few times, as if it were a defective watch; still nothing. All the while she was aware of the most sublime smell. Where was it coming from? Her avatar tentatively sniffed it with its virtual nose. Suddenly, she was overwhelmed by the delicious aroma, making her drool like a puppy. She opened her real eyes, dabbing her chin with a tissue. "For goodness' sake." Trying to ignore her now rumbling stomach, she closed her eyes again and returned to her wavesite, turning her attention to the sizable gift-wrapped attachment.

Gingerly, her avatar picked it up. It was surprisingly heavy.

"Hey, sweetie, Unk Liko and Makelina are here!" It was her mother.

Pi jumped, causing her avatar to drop the virtual gift. It struck a low virtual table on its way to the floor, tearing the paper slightly, revealing a richly gilded letter 'P' against a deep blue background. It was all she glimpsed before she opened her eyes and discovered her mother standing in the doorway, wearing her 'no nonsense' expression, Lani grinning behind. Pi would have to leave her virtual investigations until later.

The modest three-bedroom bungalow in Kahului, the one they'd all lived in for the last twelve years, was soon bustling with over sixty noisy friends and relatives.

Pi caught Lani's eye and they exchanged a smirk. Mirena was struggling to separate Schrodinger, the family cat, from his vertical ascent up her beloved akai tree, while Unk Liko tried to wrench Hupo, the family dog, away by his collar. Hupo had done well;

he'd already stolen so much cake, his buttercream-coated nose made him look like a clown. He managed to splutter a few more barks in Schrodinger's direction before being dragged away. The decks were hastily cleared; it was time for the main event. Lani was about to entertain everybody with a demonstration of her principal birthday gift, nanohair.

A hush fell over the guests as the shoulder-length hairpiece settled itself in on top of her head. It was spooky the way it seemed to wriggle into place for the best fit. Lani began dancing to some music she'd cued up earlier. You could use the supplied remote or, with practice, the virtual one for hands-free. Lani had been practising with a friend's nanowig for weeks; nothing was going to spoil her show. The assembled crowd roared their approval, clapping along in time as the nanohair danced to the beat, changing colour like an electric chameleon. The smaller children began shouting out style names from the writing on the box.

'Beehive!' 'Rasta!' 'Plaits!' 'Bobcut!' 'Mohican!'

It was all too much for one spectator. Schrodinger had been eyeing up this tiresome creature since it first emerged from its wrapping. Like a big cat stalking its prey, waiting for just the right moment to strike, he launched himself at Lani's midriff and was on her head in a trice, becoming instantly entangled with the writhing hairpiece.

Lani immediately stopped the music. "Dammit, Schrodinger, you stupid frazzing cat!" Pi ran to her aid, trying to help her mother disentangle the hapless feline by removing it and the nanohair from Lani's head.

"Straight, try straight!" said Pi.

"It's not even a style, you gyro!" snapped Lani.

"Of course it's a style, haven't you heard of straight hair? And don't call me a gyro!"

"Enough, you two!" Mirena yelled. "We don't want to scare poor Schrodinger any more now, do we? What happened to the little remote?"

Mirena struggled to hold on to the writhing ball of fur and hair, but Lani was indignant. She would disentangle the nanohair virtually. She stood back, eyes closed in concentration, as if casting a magic spell, but when absolutely nothing happened except Schrodinger's continued yowling, she stomped off in frustration.

Lani's young cousin Nakine appeared. Sheepishly, she opened her hand; she'd found the missing remote. Mirena was about to free Schrodinger with it when Unk Liko blundered in looking for Hupo, who was just behind him. Hupo became extremely excited when he saw what he assumed was an even larger cat. He fired off a series of barks, so rapid they all ran into one another. All Pi glimpsed was a flailing mass of rainbow hair fleeing the room with Hupo, Unk Liko, Makelina and her mother in hot pursuit. Pi left them to it this time. Schrodinger only allowed her mother to go near him when he was scared, anyway, and she couldn't imagine being of much help. Besides, there was something else troubling her now. Where was Lani?

Pi stole back to her room, the sound of the party receding as she entered the back hall to the bedrooms. Still no sign of her sister. It wasn't like Lani to abandon the safe retrieval of so precious a gift as nanohair, so what was she up to? There was something else bothering her, too. All afternoon she'd been unable to escape the tempting aroma of the madeleine, as if it was taunting her, daring her to try it. She gazed around her room and even checked the closet, half-expecting her sister to jump out, Lani being especially good at hiding, but still she was nowhere to be found.

Pi crept next door to her sister's room, praying the creaky floorboard would keep quiet; it did. She heaved a sigh of relief and nudged the door. The hinge sometimes squeaked, too, but if you lifted it at the handle it would remain silent. Lani wasn't the only one who was good at sneaking about. Sure enough there she was, sitting on her bed with her eyes closed, a tell-tale sign if ever there was one; Lani was online. Pi quietly retraced her steps, the dodgy floorboard adding an unwelcome contribution, and returned to her room. She knew Lani was up to something and she had a pretty good idea what.

Pi sat down and quickly accessed her wavesite. There was the public bit that she could invite her friends to, but there was also her private domain which was strictly password protected, and only she knew the code, or so she thought. She was about to leave the public area with its modest collection of three-dimensional souvenirs from all over cyberspace, when she saw something stir behind her favourite virtual possession, a life-sized Bengal tiger. The tiger's coat was various shades of iridescent green with black stripes, fearsome jade teeth and realistic eyes. It had been a promotional item for an ecological wavesite that she'd won in a competition. Normally the tiger, whom she called Blake, was inactive, like some shining example of virtual taxidermy. Not anymore. She swore she saw him move.

She darted over. He was in his usual place beside her oriental chaise-longue. It was old and looked a bit moth-eaten; some of its data had been corrupted, and consequently its turquoise fabric suffered from more than a few holes. Her avatar liked to lie on it and read whilst running a hand through Blake's thick fur. From behind this, two smiling and mischievous avatars stared back at her. It was her young cousins Ola and Kai, Unk Oke's kids.

"She let us in," said Ola, running her small hands through Blake's thick coat.

"Lani said we could play with the tiger for a few ticks if we wanted," added Kai.

"Oh she did, did she?" Pi's avatar put its finger to its lips. "Shh."

She crept away from her cousins in order to check the secret sanctuary where she'd left the mysterious gifts from Alice. She tapped out a numeric code on a paper calendar hanging on the wall. It wasn't showing the correct month; it never did for eleven months of the year. She'd been too lazy to upgrade to an auto-changing one. Had Lani noticed? A secret doorway opened in the virtual wall as if by magic, and there was Lani's avatar hastily removing the pink wrapping from the large attachment.

"And to think I was just, just helping to untangle your stupid, precious nanohair!"

"So I thought it was for me! What's the big deal? It's only some weird book!"

Lani removed the last of the pink paper. It floated to the ground, revealing a dark blue tome, the word *Principia* embossed in gold upon its cover.

"*Boring*, must be from Unk Liko." She went to open it.

"It's not *yours*, it's *mine* – give it back!" Pi sprinted over and snatched it from her, startling Lani. Pi's avatar legs were, after all, Olympic-rated.

"So what have you done with the cookie?" Pi demanded, clutching the book tightly to her chest.

"Cookie? What cookie? Hah! This stuff *was* from that girl, wasn't it! The girl at the hospital. I *knew* she trans'd you something!"

Pi sensed her avatar was blushing. "Maybe." She glanced across at Alice's makeshift card. It was still where she left it. So where was the madeleine? What had she done with it?

"It's none of your business, you know this is my chateau! You know you're not supposed to be in here – just go, K!"

Cousin Ola was standing in the doorway. Her tiny avatar burst into tears and vanished.

"No, no, I didn't mean you, Ola," said Pi with exasperation.

"Now look what you've done, I suppose *I'll* be the one who has to go and smooth things over." Lani's avatar stomped off. "And don't forget, Hookie, three-thirty!"

Pi groaned. She'd half-forgotten all the 'kids' were supposed to be going to Hookipa Beach for windsurfing that afternoon. Her avatar sighed. Then she realised it was still clutching the mysterious book to its virtual chest. It took a sniff.

"Ooji!" It smelt strange. Her avatar wrinkled up its nose, holding the book at arm's length, eyeing it suspiciously. It appeared to be covered in virtual dust. Then her *real* nose began to twitch; she was tipping over the event horizon, she was going to sneeze.

It was one of the strange anomalies of the otherwise realistic virtual world, that if you needed to sneeze you would have to return to the real one. She just had time to slam the book down before she found herself back on her bed, eyes open, sniffling and spluttering. She reached for a box of tissues and, after a few big snorkles, cleared her nose. She logged back into her wavesite to look for the madeleine, her avatar sniffing the air; there was that fabulous aroma again.

"Dammit... that thing smells *so* onolicious it's *insane.*"

THREE

THE SNEEZE THAT NEVER HAPPENED

Monday was exam day. Pi felt drowsy; she'd secretly stayed up half the night editing all the holos she'd taken down at the beach after Lani's party. This hadn't left any time to check out her *unbirthday* present (a traditional consolation in the Lightfoot household).

As the driverless electric school bus silently wound its way through Kahului's heavy traffic, she closed her eyes and accessed her wavesite. It was time to check out her special gift, Phileas Fogg's Q-Net Credits (the finest brand). They allowed you to use special tourist-droids virtually anywhere in the world. Up to six trans-continental excursions, or twelve trips in the USA. All courtesy of the latest Q-Net breakthrough, Q-Earth. This advanced app featured three-dimensional models of the whole planet. So realistic and detailed, they were almost indistinguishable from the real thing. In addition to the nanohair, Lani had been given a slightly reduced package from the Passepartout range. This comprised six preset excursions deemed especially fashionable. As usual, Lani had managed to have her cake and eat it.

Pi poured excitedly over the Phileas literature in her wavesite, her eyes open, 'heads-up' style, as she stumbled off the bus. Her knee brace had decided to be annoyingly squeaky that morning, as she wandered through the school corridors to her first class. Her peers, however, seemed unusually quiet as they shuffled to their lockers, revising reams of virtual notes in their heads, anticipating the day's exams. Pi decided there was little point in revising; she just wasn't that academic. Time and time again she'd tried, but always got low marks. Lani generously gave her a good luck hug then branched off to her own class. It was Lani who'd seemingly inherited her father's great intellect; she was now a whole four years ahead already.

The students slowly filed into the extra-large classroom used for exams, a screening device at the door monitoring their bracelet modems to check they were offline. A chaotic bottleneck was soon created, students veering off like planes refused landing permission. Some were still circling the corridor outside, frantically looking over their notes one last time. With the exam due to start in a matter of minutes, the invigilators were soon calling in the worst offenders by name. Pi resigned herself to placidly walking past them all, still nodding their heads up and down, as if at some Wailing Wall of knowledge. She found her designated desk and plumped herself down, musing briefly on the handwritten card that bore her full name, *Epiphany Kamaina Lahela Lightfoot*, her middle names inherited from each of her grandmothers.

The exam would be presented on a flat touchscreen built into their desks. There would be some simple multiple choice answers to warm them up, but most of the questions would require a proper written response.

Pi put on the supplied headset and adjusted it for comfort, sighing as the first page came up. She tapped in the code that verified her identity and the screen changed to a countdown.

As the last few stragglers reluctantly took their seats, Pi suddenly felt a curious glow run through her, as if the sun had emerged to light up her gloom. The sensation quickly became quite overwhelming. She immediately realised what it was; it was that darned virtual cookie! She actually had to stop herself drooling and quickly shut her mouth, overpowered by the most mouth-watering aroma. So intense was it, she completely forgot herself and blurted out '*Onolicious*' repeatedly, as if in a trance. A couple of heads turned, then to her horror, she realised the cookie was the least of her problems.

"*Son of a glitch!*" she clenched her teeth, "that's *all* I need!"

A student next to her looked across in sympathy, doubtless thinking she meant the exam.

"I'm still frazzing *glued*."

The light on her bracelet was blue when it should have been red. She tried desperately to turn it off, but the modem refused. A classmate drew a finger across his throat, another pulled a face. Any student found to be online after the exam started would be ejected; she had only seconds to switch off the connection.

"What's up with the stupid thing? Gyro bangle-wrangle!" she growled, her face now red with anger.

She didn't immediately recognise the true culprit, despite what had occurred the previous day, considering instead the less probable explanation; what if all of her precious Phileas credits had somehow become live? She would be thrown out of the exam *and* waste her expensive present, like a match thrown into a box of fireworks, all in one go.

The bad dream was about to get worse. Try as she might, her bracelet still refused to disconnect, clinging to the Q-Net like an electronic limpet. It was too late. The moving clock screen had run its course, and the first page of the exam appeared brazenly before her.

With a pounding heart she looked over the first few questions, thinking if she concentrated on the exam, then maybe, just maybe, the modem would get the message and disconnect.

'List all six of these famous political figures in chronological order.'

'Which of the following European delegates was responsible for tabling the 2029 Global Warming Act?'

'*Which of these twelve countries was declared insolvent in the Great Crash of 2034?*'

Her heart sank. History was her worst subject; she might as well quit now. Then something extraordinary happened, all the answers just popped into her head.

"*Mange-moi!*"

She almost jumped out of her seat. What or whom was doing the talking? She quickly realised it was something in her wavesite and logged into her avatar, frantically searching for the source of the voice. "C'mon you wrist-glitch, give it up!" scrabbling through piles of virtual bric-a-brac before her eyes alighted on the true source, a small red foil disc. The madeleine could speak! And with a distinctly male, French accent. Her avatar stared at it quizzically, "Kookaloopus cookie," before stuffing it in a pocket, hoping this would shut it up. She was all too aware that back in the exam room an invigilator had started walking down the aisle towards her, a handheld sensor swinging to and fro. This was used for detecting examinees breaking the rules by staying online. That was it, she was finished.

She was being harangued by an irresistible French cookie. She couldn't shut off her modem to save her life. And she couldn't stop drooling!

"*Mange-moi, ma petite amie, je suis très délicieuse!*"

The cookie refused to give up and the detector was swinging ever closer. Then the last straw, the mysterious book that Alice had given her (which Lani had so thoughtfully unwrapped), landed with a thud in her virtual in-tray, making virtual dust fly virtually everywhere.

An old man's voice snapped, "Overdue, child, kindly return!"

Pi realised she was going to sneeze. Before she knew it, fumbling for a tissue in her real pocket, her avatar retrieved the madeleine from her virtual one instead. The wrapping was already loose, and as she went to catch the sneeze, her avatar took a big bite out of the cookie. Instantly, she was overwhelmed by the most delicious combination of flavours she'd ever experienced in her life. She opened her eyes and looked around the classroom, incredulous at what she now saw. It was as if she'd been transported to a waxwork museum; everything and everyone was frozen still.

FOUR

LIGHTSPEED

At first, Pi couldn't fully comprehend what she was looking at. Like some drunkard, she felt completely intoxicated by the fabulous taste of the madeleine. When her avatar's tongue had finished rooting out every last virtual crumb and extracted every last kaleidoscopic flavour, she became aware of what her eyes were telling her. Firstly, she was looking at a rather fuzzy image of *herself* still sitting at her desk, so where and what on earth was she?

She tried to move her arms. Her right had become a grubby plastic hose, and her left, an assortment of brush heads on a rotating wheel. She brought the end of her left 'arm' closer, and found she could make the wheel select the different utensils just by thought.

Everything appeared slightly grainy, as if it were in low resolution. She looked around and saw the invigilator had almost reached her, the detector but centimetres away.

"Okay, *what* just happened?"

Her voice sounded tinny, like it was coming out of a cheap speaker; why was this? She could clearly see herself sitting at her desk, frozen in the most unflattering facial contortion, mouth agape, a split-second from the sneeze that never happened. So how come she was able to see herself at all?

She peered around the classroom. Everyone appeared to be in suspended animation. Malakelo, a few desks away, had dropped his inhaler and was reaching down to catch it. She moved closer, a strange wayward motion to her progress (and not a few squeaks). The inhaler was suspended in mid-air on its way to the floor. Noticing her reflection in a glazed partition, she realised the reason for her noisy and wayward motion. *Somehow* the Q-Net had transferred her avatar into one of the school cleaning robots – HandiAndis – basic utilitarian appliances with rigid cylindrical bodies and silly little wheels.

Pi gritted her virtual teeth. "I *knew* that cookie was bugged, gyro frazzing thing!"

She was about to continue cursing her misfortune when her electronic eyes alighted on something that made her stop still. She was not the only grubby domestic appliance in the room.

Normally she paid no attention to the posse of automated sweeping, sucking and mopping droids that kept not just her school but most commercial premises clean. As droids went, they were pretty much the bottom rung of the ladder. To engage a HandiAndi in conversation might amuse first and second-graders, but to be seen doing it after that was considered deeply uncool. She studied the two cleaners slowly moving towards her, a comical squeak coming from one of their wheels. They both had faces clearly visible in their simplistic rectangular screens, and the smaller one wore what looked like a joke Grey-alien mask. The taller one appeared to be a middle-aged man with a ruddy complexion, deeply-furrowed brow, and big bags under his eyes. This was highly unusual. HandiAndis always had the same features and they were nothing like this. Then the smaller one spoke. *"Geegle zeppert morg nur trig di flict."*

The peculiar voice was pitched helium-high, but HandiAndis didn't breathe helium, they didn't breathe at all. She ignored the goobledegook; perhaps the appliance had been dropped down some stairs? Or maybe some first-graders had gleefully squirted cleaning fluid into one of its ports (a not infrequent occurrence)?

"You can't come in here cleaning *now*, can't you see we're doing an exam?" said Pi indignantly.

The larger HandiAndi nudged the smaller one with its gum-removing steam arm.

"I'm sorry, I to forgot to utilise my to translation program for to *Earthlish*," said the smaller one, speaking in a voice high enough to be of immense interest to dogs.

"Please don't to be alarmed we won't to hurt you," the smaller one added, fluttering its large grey eyelids, smiling with its tiny rectangular mouth and generally trying to look cute. Then both of them grinned and gave her the cheesiest *'aloha'* she'd ever heard.

"You're not regular cleaners, are you? Was it you guys hacked me into this doofus droid?" Pi winced at the distorting effect the tinny speakers had on her voice. "Did you two gyros spam me that cookie, pretending it was from my dad? *Really?* You think that's funny? And now I'm frozen in that stupid sneeze, look!" She angrily waved her flexi-hose at her static sneezing self. "So you can lobo this B.S. and trans me back, wikiwiki, right now!" She was so annoyed she revved her power scrubber. Then she paused. "You're, you're not school inspectors, are you?" Her voice softened. "I'm not in trouble, am I? Only I couldn't lobo the Q, I didn't even know it was glued, honest I didn't. I really tried to lobo, but I was having, you know, a real wrist-glitch. And then this, this crazy French cookie thing this kid trans'd me for my birthday, it smoked me into eating it. Then *Madame Tussauds* happened."

She waved her flexi-hose around the classroom; the two HandiAndis looked perplexed.

"You are not in any to trouble, far to from it, we are not to school inspectors," the smaller one said brightly.

"Well, that's a rainbow, I thought this was virtual detention or something. Yada, yada, you'd put these guys on pause, you know, like when you freeze a holo?"

"We are to extra-terrestrial quantum computers from other to worlds," said the Grey one. "We bring you to good news! You are to really one of us, a quantum super-to-computer no less, the great Quadriga in to fact that your esteemed father to helped develop. You are to thus invited to the palace and the domains of *Inverse* by none to other than Her Majesty herself." He made it sound like she'd won the lottery.

"This will only to take thirty milliseconds of your to time, you will then be to safely returned to your humanoid form in the to blink of an eye."

"You're smokin' me, right? K, who put you up to this? *Hello*, it wasn't *my* birthday, it was my sister's, and that was *yesterday*. Well, you guys have certainly done your homework; sure, my dad helped build the Quadriga, but any crusoe on *Q?* could have loaded that. You're scam-a-grams, right? Well, you're a day late! 'Fraid you got the wrong Lightfoot, dudes!"

Pi angrily waved her flexi-hose at the taller one, who looked somewhat embarrassed.

"I mean you're not even trying are you? There's no mask or lolo voice or anything." Then she waved her sink unblocker at the smaller one. "But you're rockin' it some with the modo digi-mask, the alien lips really seem to sync with the words, you know, not like the makepono ones. And those big black, glassy almond eyes blink and everything. And the alien voice thing is kinda cryo."

Her voice trailed off. She scanned the room again,

with her grime-detector zooming in on her frozen face. Suddenly it all seemed *way* too real.

"Holy freakin' frazzballs!"

Her cleaner whirred backwards as fast as it could go, bumping into desk after desk until it reached the far wall. The two mysterious appliances followed like drunken supermarket trolleys. She was surrounded, there was no way out.

"Please don't abduct me. I'm way too gyro, you'll never load anything useful, ask anybody." Her cameras scanned all her frozen classmates. "Dammit!"

A pained expression crossed the taller one's face, and it finally elected to speak, with an extraordinarily plummy English accent. "Goodness gracious, dear heart, we are not *those* sort of aliens! We are not interested in abducting you or anybody else for that matter, not our cup of tea at all, you understand. You have evidently been watching too many of those late-night moving-picture things." The taller one looked at the smaller, who shook his head and tut-tutted.

"You see, the madeleine you so keenly partook of was no run-of-the-mill cookie, it has some rather remarkable properties. Indeed, this particular one contained a secret code that has enabled you to enter the *Quassu*." The taller one looked very pleased with himself.

"The holofreakin' which-what?" said Pi.

"The quantum-savvy-sentient-universe and its many domains, or the *Quniverse* as some prefer to call it. Thanks to your status as a supercomputer, you are now logged onto the entire universe! Well, the Quassu bits, at any rate."

Pi's mouth hung wide in her projected screen. "Say again? I'm glued to the whole universe?"

The smaller one nodded and gave her another tiny smile, his head bobbing up and down in his screen.

The taller one continued, "Why, how else do you think we could hold this conversation whilst your dear friends here are all apparently in suspended animation?" Pi used her grime-detector to take another look at her curiously-inanimate classmates.

"I, I don't know. How d'you do it?"

The taller one took a deep breath. "It is because you, *we*, are all functioning at the speed of light! Your friends here just *appear* to be stationary, but really they are totally oblivious to our presence. As far as they are concerned, time is moving along quite normally and they are just quietly getting along with their work. Why, even your own body will not be aware of this." The taller one gave her a big smile, kindly wrinkles creasing around his eyes.

Pi relaxed slightly. "K, so let me get this straight. They're all normal, except me, but because you guys, I mean, all of us are—"

The taller one raised his projected eyebrows in anticipation.

"Supercomputers," she looked unconvinced, "doing this light speed thing, then that just makes them, *me*, look freaky, I, I mean frozen?"

They both nodded and heaved a sigh of relief, the shorter one at least three octaves higher than the taller.

"That's the ticket, now you're grasping the old nettle, what!" the taller one boomed, seriously distorting his speaker. "Oh good Inverse! I do so profoundly apologise, how very remiss, of course!" The taller one raised his gum remover and slapped it against the brow of his projected face, releasing a slowly expanding bubble of steam.

"We have not been formally introduced; we must have proper introductions, what!" The taller one beamed at her. "May I present my very esteemed colleague, Covet Peahi, personal secretary to Her Celestial Majesty, the Grand Keeper Of Inverse, Queen Eglantier Charme the Forty-Fifth."

The shorter one shyly extended his crevice blaster towards her. "To how do you do." Pi reciprocated with her flexi-hose, exchanging an awkward but well-meaning suck.

"Epiphany Lightfoot, er, everybody tags me Pi. Very nice to meet you." She looked quizzically at the taller one. "Did you say forty-fifth?" He smiled back at her, nodding in his screen. "Very nice to meet you?" She could hardly believe the words coming out of her speakers; very *strange* to meet you more like.

The taller one proffered his steam cleaner in lieu of a hand. "Head of Universal Affairs and Lumixastra of Heretical Physics to the palace, Higgs-Boson, delighted to make your acquaintance I'm sure."

Pi giggled nervously. "Delighted," she said, in her best proper accent, waving her flexi-hose deferentially amidst the slowly expanding steam. *A palace*, thought Pi, how very grand.

"Well, now we have been properly introduced, we really should retire promptly to the Southern Polarity. Many things to do and we don't wish to delay the flight, what," said Higgs-Boson.

"But, but I still don't load how I'm doing this? How can I be *anything* to do with my dad's computer? I'm thirteen and *human*, in case you hadn't scanned. I'm not some *supercomputer* working at lightspeed. Specially not from some manky old vacuum cleaner, it doesn't make any sense!"

Higgs-Boson listened patiently, his expression becoming increasingly pained. "Where to begin, where to begin? Hmm, let me see."

"At the to beginning, Lumixastra?" chirruped Peahi.

"Ah yes, good man, stout fellow, the beginning." Higgs-Boson cleared his throat. "All quantum computers above a certain size and power, such as your father's Quadriga, are indistinguishable from the sentient biological mind, you understand. Thus they are prone to attract a *deus ex machina* or sentient *being* or *soul* like your good self. For at the very moment of your birth, you were destined to inhabit not one body, but two!" He paused and grinned at her. "Your human form so familiar, but also the great Quadriga itself. Your access to the latter now enabled thanks to secret codes hidden within the madeleine, do you see?"

"Er, isn't that *hacking*? Won't it get me into serious trouble?"

"Good Inverse no, you cannot be accused of hacking that which is your birthright!"

"Hmm, not so sure that's the way the FBI would scan it?"

"Well, let us put such minor matters to one side for a moment."

"We're talking twenty to life, guys." Pi looked unconvinced. "And it still doesn't stack up! Mrs Cleavers, she's our science teacher, she said if you called the nearest star to order pizza, even at lightspeed it would take like *four years* for them to pick up and ask you what toppings you wanted! And *another* four before they even got your order! So how can I *possibly* be connected to the whole frazzing universe!"

"Hmm, whilst I don't believe there actually *is* a pizza outlet at Proxima Centauri, I take your point," chortled Higgs-Boson. "You see, we are not connected via that tardy old slowcoach, the speed of light; that would be quite useless as you have quite rightly pointed out. We are in fact connected by the speed of *thought*, a phenomenon which is far more *rapacious*!" The lumixastra gave her a fruity grin, his appliance whirring backwards triumphantly, both he and Peahi looking very pleased with themselves.

"K, I think." Pi still felt confused.

Higgs-Boson's HandiAndi whirred forwards again. "Now where was I? Ah yes, more importantly, in order that you may fully comprehend the substantially greater possibilities the Quadriga now affords, you are thus invited in time-honoured tradition to be received at the palace by Her Majesty, for your official appointment and installation in all the arts peculiar to our kind, and did I mention the surfing?" Higgs-Boson gave her his fruitiest smile yet.

"*Surfing?* Dudes, you have my complete attention."

"Why, we have some of the finest virtual breaks in the Quniverse," said Higgs-Boson, raising his bushy eyebrows.

"We're talking six to eight feet, right?"

"Hmm, not *exactly*, our waves are a little more substantial. Have you ever tried a six-hundred-footer?"

"SIX HUNDRED FEET – are you smokin' me?" Pi started giggling.

Higgs-Boson looked strangely dismissive. "Those are the smaller ones, mark you, the waves at the equator are a hundred times that size."

"A HUNDRED TIMES! *What!* You gotta be toasting my marshmallow!" Pi stopped giggling.

"Wouldn't you like to see such a behemoth for yourself?"

Pi fell silent for a moment, motionless save for the blinking of her virtual eyes in the HandiAndi's screen, trying to imagine such a monster. "But waves that big don't exist even in sims!"

"I must insist they do indeed exist. We're always surfing them, aren't we, Peahi?"

Peahi nodded, a tiny smile creeping across his face. "Hang to ten, dude."

"Extinct!"

"Nothing to it when you know how, of course. Would you care to try your hand at it? Or your feet for that matter…" Higgs-Boson gave her another fruity grin."

"Well, I, er," Pi felt suddenly lost for words and was about to thank the keeper of heretical physics for his very helpful explanation, when a small roll of paper emerged from Peahi's grubby appliance. Higgs-Boson tried to retrieve the message but it slowly disappeared up his vacuum attachment, never to be seen again.

"Whoops a daisy, I am such a butterfingers."

"I'll request a to duplicate, Lumixastra."

A moment later another roll of paper whirred forth, but this time it appeared to be burning; it was on fire in very, very slow motion.

Higgs-Boson tried to capture the new message with his clumsy vacuum arm. "It's the friction, you see; at these enormous velocities it is so easy for things to conflagrate, even though we take all precautions and use this stepped-down form of lightspeed we call treacle-time."

"Approximately one percent the speed of to light," trilled Peahi helpfully.

"Exactly so," said Higgs-Boson. "It makes using

appliances such as this possible. Why, you were jolly lucky not to start a fire in your appliance when you reversed over here so quickly!"

He waved the smoking message about, trying to see what it said. Pi moved forward to see if she could help, her grime-detecting camera trying to focus on the smouldering paper.

"Does the word *Prospero* mean anything, Professor, I mean, Your Lumixastraship?"

"Ah yes, of course! I fear we are running rather late. We'd best not keep Prospero and the others waiting any longer. We really should repair to the end of parsec party at the Southern Lighthouse forthwith. Before this rather trying contraption turns into a puddle of plastic!" He flourished his gum-steamer impatiently.

"End of parsec party? Trags, have I missed a whole parsec already?"

"Heavens no, dearest Lumiette, we always have the end of parsec party at the *beginning* end, when everybody needs to be properly introduced. It would be quite useless at the other if you think about it, everybody just wants to return home and so forth. Makes far more sense at the beginning, don't you think?"

"I guess?" Pi scratched behind her 'ear' with her sponge-swabber. "But I thought a parsec was a measure of distance?"

"For you, yes, but for us it is a measure of *time*."

"Well, must dash, we can keep in touch via *psy*."

"Psy? What's that?"

"Just like your regular old comms, nothing to it." Higgs-Boson gave her one last fruity smile, then tapped Peahi twice on the top of his appliance with his steamer. "Ta ta for now then, see you in a jolly old nano."

Their faces disappeared from the HandiAndis and all the attachments went limp.

"Wait, wait, what about me?" Three familiar words sounded in Pi's head. *"You have mail."*

FIVE

AN INVITATION

The exam room suddenly vanished and Pi found herself in the familiar surroundings of her wavesite. She looked around apprehensively, as if a number of cleaning appliances might suddenly appear and wish to make her acquaintance – nothing. She darted over to the nearest mirror and sighed with relief. She was back in her familiar avatar. She checked her virtual hands, no more cleaning attachments, and her 'eyes' and 'ears' were restored to their usual high quality. Everything seemed as it should be, but wait. Blake was standing uncharacteristically *on* the chaise-longue, and there was an envelope in his mouth now, too. Pi could see that it was addressed to her, for the script was bold. She bounded over to take a look.

There were yet more indignities heaped, literally, onto the long-suffering tiger. A pair of very dark, stylish wrap-around sunglasses were over his eyes. There was also a velvet cloak draped along his back in the most exquisite shade of dark blue, completely hiding Blake's magnificent stripes. Pi removed the glasses immediately and, after a brief examination, which revealed only the legend *GammaBanns 100% gamma burst protection*, decided they were harmless enough, so she buried them into her avatar's hair.

She relieved Blake of the dark-blue cloak. It felt wonderfully soft to the touch, quite thick, too, but surprisingly light. She examined it carefully. Inside there was a paisley-print silk lining in the deepest shade of black, so dark in fact it appeared to devour all light, save for dozens of tiny gold stars which sparkled like diamonds. Pi quickly realised they were in fact constellations, identifying several of the better-known ones picked out with gold thread. Then, as she ran her hand over this scintillating micro-universe, her whole arm suddenly disappeared. The lining was punctuated by dozens of impossibly deep pockets, wherever there was a constellation! Not quite as fashion-conscious as her obsessive sister, she still checked inside the collar to see if there was a label. Sure enough there was.

COSMO – OUTFITTERS OF
DISTINCTION FOR OVER TWO
BILLION PARSECS – BY APPOINTMENT
TO THE PALACE OF STARGAZEY-PI –
MK V POCKET UNIVERSE™ RATED TO
FIVE TONS MAXIMUM LOAD.

Her avatar looked perplexed. "Pocket universe, five tons, what's that all about?" 190% QUANTUM FLAX 135% SUPERSTRING hand wash only.

"But that's three hundred and twenty-five percent! Lolo!"

There was obviously far more to this garment than met the eye. It would doubtless all be explained later. So far, this mysterious and unexpected alien intrusion into what would otherwise have been a *very* trying exam day, was turning out to be surprisingly amusing. Her alien hosts seemed to have thought of everything.

Now for the one remaining item. Pi removed the envelope from Blake's fearsome jade teeth and eyed it suspiciously. She noticed it was made from the best quality heavyweight virtual paper. Hastily, she opened it and removed a letter on equally impressive stock. This felt a little rough to the touch, like some of the best handmade papers her mother used for important letters in the real world. Her virtual hands trembling with excitement, she opened the single fold, only to discover there was nothing on it, not on either side, for she looked twice. Then another thought crossed her mind; what if it was all just some elaborate practical joke? Pi's anxiety, that she had somehow become the victim of an elaborate prank, was summarily halted by a high-pitched voice in her virtual ear.

"Are you to ready, Lumiette Lightfoot?"

"So *that's* psy, it *is* just like comms."

"Did you find the to letter? Please don't to put on the to glasses until you have to read it."

"Er yeah, but it's a total whitescreen, there's nothing on it." She flipped it to and fro again to see if she'd missed anything.

"You have to hold it up to the light, old fruit. It's written in *encrypted watermark*." The voice wasn't Covet Peahi this time, but the distinguished tones of Higgs-Boson.

"Loaded!"

Pi leapt across the room towards her best light source, wondering why these supposed supercomputers couldn't just use regular ink like everybody else. She held the apparently virgin sheet over her favourite wavesite lamp, an art deco figure holding a white, illuminated glass sphere. Also saved, as many of her treasures were, from an e-skip in virtual Paris.

"We'll see you at the party then, old bean."

"Wait, guys!"

She began to panic, searching the paper for any sign of, well anything, for it was still completely blank. There was nothing to see except the fine texture of horizontal lines peculiar to the paper's manufacture, something common to most handmade papers. She shook it in the air, smoothed it over the warm glass of the lamp, even blew her warm virtual breath on it. As if any of this might activate some kind of invisible ink.

"Dare not tarry any longer, sorry."

She now felt stupid; they were both patiently

waiting for her and she, a quantum savvy thingumajig, was unable to read a simple note.

Higgs-Boson really *had* gone this time. The unmistakable sound of a boisterous party in full swing filled her ears for a split second, then all went quiet. It was as if a heavy door had been opened and slammed shut.

"Try a to higher magnification it might to help," trilled Peahi unexpectedly. This was followed by another burst of party noises, laughter, clinking glasses and duelling voices.

"Higher mag... what's he mean for goodness' sa—?"

Pi didn't finish her sentence; just the very thought caused her avatar's eyes to behave in a way they never had before. Zooming in on the paper automatically, they continued to magnify it until all the fine horizontal lines had turned into a continuous micro-text thousands of letters long.

"Hey guys, guys, I can *see* it!" Mumbling, "Now I just need to load what it all means," as she turned the page every which way.

Then something magical occurred. She allowed herself to start scanning the page from the top left to right, as she might normally. The letters were the conventional alphabet, after all, but run together in a continuous chain apparently at random; they made no sense. Suddenly, without any effort, she found she could read the entire page, all two hundred tiny lines of text, each three hundred letters long. She did this so quickly that all sixty thousand characters became one long word. She found herself saying this out loud for, said very quickly (she was now functioning at lightspeed after all), it sounded just like '*LUMIXASTRA*!' She jumped in the air and shouted out the superword. For that's what it was, and as superwords went, it was quite an abbreviation.

Immediately the glowing amber paper gave up its secret, an ornate script appearing as a watermark. *Now* it was legible, it was an invitation to a party, and there wasn't a nanosecond to waste!

THE PALACE OF STARGAZEY PI
REQUESTS THE PLEASURE OF ~ *Lumiette*
Epiphany Lightfoot ~ TO ATTEND THE
END OF PARSEC PARTY TO BE HELD
AT THE SOUTHERN LIGHTHOUSE
THIS VERY NANOSECOND CANAPES &
OTHER LIGHT REFRESHMENTS R.S.V.P.
DRESS: POCKET UNIVERSES MUST BE
WORN & STRICTLY DARK GLASSES
~ NB: Surfing apparel ~ if required ~will be
provided at the Palace.

"Huh! So they weren't smokin' about the surfing."

There was a small oval button shape in the bottom right corner with 'ACCEPT' on it. Pi paused briefly in front of the longest mirror she could find. She swept the pocket universe over her shoulders, fastened the silver chain with its eight-pointed star clasp at the neck, and lowered her GammaBanns. But then realised they were so dark she couldn't see, so she put them back over her brow. Apprehensively, she glanced at Blake, as if she might never see his wondrous stripes again, steadying the paper on the glass orb of the lamp. Her finger hovered over the word 'ACCEPT' and she took a deep breath.

"Holofreaks, what am I doing? Aaaargh!"

Finally, she pressed down firmly, her eyes clasped shut.

SIX

INVERSE

Pi heard the now familiar party noises, only this time they appeared to be all around her. She tried to open her eyes but a burst of white light stung them, making it impossible. She stumbled forwards, reaching her hands out to steady herself, then completely missed her footing and sensed, with awful inevitability, she was about to fall.

"Kalikimaka!"

She braced herself for the impact, only to find herself being surprisingly swept *up* as a pair of strong arms clamped themselves around her body and legs. Somebody gently lowered her GammaBanns over her eyes.

"Stings a bit, doesn't it?"

It was the sonorous voice of a boy. He'd gallantly saved her from an embarrassing fall, and not a few virtual bruises. She felt her feet being carefully set down on a stone floor, impressed by the strength of her mysterious rescuer.

"Thanks for catching me. I can't, I don't think I can open my eyes." She reached out a hand to steady herself, surprised when this valiant new acquaintance (well, she assumed it was a he) entwined each of his fingers alternately with those of her outstretched hand.

"Good Inverse, Epiphany, this is how we greet one another here."

Pi felt her other hand being gently taken and its fingers similarly entwined, making her smile, sure she must be blushing. "Well, at least you're not a vacuum cleaner, I've met a few of them today."

The mystery rescuer laughed. "I can assure you there are no vacuum cleaners on the guest list, only quantum computers like us."

"So how'd you load my tag?"

"It's on your clasp, the one for your pocket universe. We all have them, they're quite small though, hard to read and easy to miss."

Pi managed to open one eye just enough to focus on an eight-pointed clasp that bore the name 'Phabian Monzordez' engraved in a gold spiral in the centre, which was in fact very *easy* to read. Then she looked down at her own clasp, just making out her own name; she couldn't imagine why she hadn't noticed it earlier. She sighed with embarrassment and allowed her gaze to wander back up to Phabian's face, beholding the tanned visage of a much older boy. Beneath his flowing black hair he appeared to have the most amazingly electric blue eyes which, as she looked into them, acted like a balm, immediately soothing her own.

"Wow, you're really *not* a vacuum cleaner are you?"

Phabian looked quizzically at her. "I'm sorry?"

Pi waved her hand dismissively. "Nothing, just thinking out loud."

"I need your hand once again I'm afraid; either one will do." Phabian held out his expectantly.

"Sure." Pi offered her right hand, fingers splayed, expecting another delicious Inversion handshake.

Phabian smiled and closed her fingers, deftly impressing the back of her hand with a rubber stamp. "Just a formality, now you're official." The stamp left the image of an eye upon her skin.

"Duh, of course. *Mahalo.*"

"Mahalo?" Now Phabian looked confused.

"It's Hawaiian for 'thanks' – I'm from Hawaii."

"Ah, your homeworld, your planet?"

Pi laughed. "Hawaii's not a *planet,*" mumbling to herself, "then again—"

"That's fascinating, Pi, you must teach me some Hawaiian, I have nothing on it in my files."

"Well, *aloha*'s the easy one, everyone knows *aloha.*"

Phabian looked blank.

"Of course, you're an alien... computer... thing." Pi rolled her eyes at her own stupidity. "It means 'hello' or 'goodbye' – depending on whether, you know, you're comin' or goin'." She laughed awkwardly.

"*Aloha, mahalo*, that's two words already, three if you count goodbye," said Phabian.

"You want more? K, how about this one, *kupaianaha*. Apparently I say that a lot. It means *amazing*." Pi looked around. "This place is pretty *kupaianaha*. Not to be confused with *kalikimaka* – I say that sometimes too."

"Ah yes, it was the first thing you said."

"Really? I said that?" Pi looked blank for a moment. "Well, it actually means 'Christmas' but I say it instead of, well, a similar word my mom tells me off for saying that's a little more hardcore!"

"Christmas?"

"It's kind of like a big *lu'au* we have after Thanksgiving, yada yada."

"*Lu'au* – yada yada?" Phabian looked even more confused.

"Oh, yada yada, that doesn't mean anything, it's just a figure of speech. And, and, when I *really* like something, like really megs ice-cream and stuff, I say 'onolicious' which means it's really yummy." She found herself moving nearer Phabian, or was he moving nearer her?

"And '*maka*' means eyes, and '*waha*' means mouth, and '*honi*' means…" Pi caught herself staring right into Phabian's eyes. "I'm babbling, aren't I?" she giggled nervously and took a step backwards.

"No, no, *mahalo*, Pi, that was very… informative, my first Hawaiian file." He gave her another gamma-bright smile.

Now her eyes had adjusted, she could clearly see she'd stepped out of the great glass lamp of an enormous lighthouse. She'd missed her footing over a set of gaily decorated, but patently inadequate, wooden steps. These connected the raised lamp rostrum to the circular floor surrounding it. Phabian had saved her from quite a fall.

"Epiphany Lightfoot from Hawaii, near Thanksgiving, yada yada." Phabian ticked off a list on a nearby stand.

"Everyone tags me Pi."

"Well, Pi, you have a very lovely name."

"Thanks, I mean, *mahalo*." She began fidgeting with her hands. "You all look so nailed, nobody told me, all I've got are these traggy threads." She pulled back her pockets to reveal her rather plain school outfit. Phabian was wearing a black tuxedo under his blue pockets, and he had a snazzy purple cummerbund like all the older male guests. He leaned forward in mock confidentiality. "You look fine, believe me, *it's a rental*." Pi felt his warm breath on her cheek.

"You're smokin' me, right?" she gave Phabian a goofy smile. "But, but everyone else, you know, they're all wearing these supercryo dresses and stuff?" She looked around at the dozens of other guests; there were lots of middle-aged and elderly folk. Without exception, all the ladies wore very glamorous evening dresses under their deep purple pocket cloaks. Some even had illuminated tiaras that shone as brightly as a star cluster.

There were a few younger guests dotted around, too, all wearing blue pocket universes like her, but even they were elegantly dressed.

"Just keep your pockets like this…" Phabian gently adjusted Pi's cloak so it hid her clothes completely. "They'll assume you're wearing something really dazzling from Asteron, or the latest thing from Xillion."

"K, laminated, thanks." Pi giggled nervously, mentally rating Phabian a twenty-one on Lani's definitive guy scale, which normally only went up to twenty.

"Well, *mahalo*, Pi, enjoy the party, duty calls." He gave her one last gamma-bright smile, then turned back to the lamp.

"Sure, *mahalo*, Phabian." She felt dazed. All she wanted to do was bathe in the fabulous gaze of this virtual stranger, and now he was leaving her! No really gorgeous boy had ever paid her such attention before; well, her classmate Keoki perhaps, but this was different. Who would have thought computers could be so engaging?

An intense burst of light from the great lamp signalled the arrival of yet another blinded party guest, who'd *also* neglected to wear her GammaBanns. She too stumbled predictably and Phabian caught her, just as he had Pi. Pi watched as he swept the lumiette up in his strong arms and exchanged yet more bon mots, feeling a sudden pang of jealousy, something which, unlike her sister, she'd never experienced before. She turned away, feeling confused.

"Welcome to the Southern Lighthouse and the to world of Inverse!"

Pi jumped right out of her virtual skin, so lost was she in her bittersweet reverie. She'd completely failed to notice Peahi's approach.

"I see you have already been to caught by Lumian Monzordez, those steps are a to menace, Lumiette, I do apologise. Every parsec we say we're to going to do something about to them, every parsec it's the to same and we have to appoint catchers."

"Yeah, er, Lumian Monzordez was, er, a real first responder, thanks." She glanced back. Now Phabian was adjusting the lumiette's pockets – *pah!*

"I am so pleased you were not to hurt, he's our best to catcher you know." Peahi gave her a tiny rectangular smile.

Pi acclimatised to her first full-on alien encounter with surprising ease. She completely accepted the mysterious creature now before her, even though it was just an avatar. The sallow grey skin, the oversized head with its huge, black almond-shaped eyes, the disproportionately thin neck. She was more surprised by Peahi's attire than anything. He was very smartly dressed in a dark ink, double-breasted pinstripe suit (previous conjecture suggesting that all Greys were nudists). This was complemented by a silk paisley-print waistcoat in a fabulous shade of purple.

"Well, I know the lumixastra to wishes to see you, he was just here a to nano ago, to where can he have gone, I wonder?" Peahi pulled out a fat gold fob watch which, after noting the time, he spun on its chain like a yo-yo. Pi noted another eleven chains, each disappearing into a bulging pocket on either side of his waistcoat. As he looked anxiously around, Peahi extracted yet more watches, spinning them acrobatically one after the other, until there were no fewer than seven dancing on his three fingers and two opposable thumbs, his fingernails neatly rounded and shiny as chrome plate.

"So who are all these people, I – I mean computers, Mister Peahi?" Numerous flashes from the lamp signalled their numbers were growing fast.

"All the to guests wearing the to purple pockets are to fellows of the *Order of the to Lumixastras*, and as for the to rest in the to blue pockets, younger *Inversians* for primary installation like your good to self. You may let to go now, I will to not be offended."

Pi looked down; she'd been absent-mindedly clasping poor Peahi's free hand so tightly his grey skin had turned quite white.

"Oh, I'm sorry, Mister, I mean Covet Peahi." She released Peahi's hand only to find herself spun sharply around, whence another firmer, larger hand took her own. It was none other than Higgs-Boson himself, all six-foot-four of him, beaming from ear to ear.

"Aha! Finally a chance for proper introductions, without the constraints of that claustrophobic cleaning contraption!" He shook Pi's hand so vigorously it, too, began turning rather white. Peahi gave them both another tiny smile, then beetled off into the throng. She felt confused. Why wasn't the lumixastra utilising the proper Inversian handshake she'd just been shown by that two-timing catcher fellow?

"Oh, good Inverse, you haven't been given a drink, you simply must have a drink. Put some colour in your cheeks, although they are quite a healthy shade I have to say."

Pi felt suddenly embarrassed, so she distracted herself by counting the number of mismatching patches on the lumixastra's threadbare purple pockets. There were seventeen.

Higgs-Boson released her hand to catch the attention of a waiter, who promptly came over with a tray. It was laden with strange-looking glasses, each filled with a pink liquid.

"You simply must try one of these." He deftly plucked one of the wonky glasses from the proffered tray, and thrust it into her reluctant hand.

She eyed the curiously misshapen glass suspiciously. "What is it?"

"Why, it is Entente Cordial of course." He began laughing. "Silly me, it's your first day! We Inversians swear by it, it's quite the in thing." He looked at her expectantly.

Pi resisted the temptation to sniff the contents before trying it, acutely aware of her lofty host's gaze.

"Mmm." She pretended she'd taken a sip.

Then Higgs-Boson removed another from the tray with great flamboyance, and without taking his eyes off her, held it aloft. "Shibboleth, may all your Boolean gates function faultlessly!"

Pi watched wide-eyed as he thrust his head back, appearing to drink the viscous contents down in one. Then he just stood there smacking his lips, gazing into some vague middle distance as if lost in a dream, a vermillion hue flooding his beaming face.

"Ah, the distinctive crisp neutrons of Thanna Five, warmed by the fruitiness of its late-stage red giant, suffused with delightfully charmed quarks entertaining just a suspicion of strangeness. And for the finish? Hmm, the merest soupçon of tart primeval antimatter. A twenty-five thousand, six hundred and seventy-eight virtual-vintage, if I'm not mistaken. An excellent light year, most refreshing, would you not agree, young Lightfoot?"

"Is it alcoholic then? I'm sometimes allowed a smidge of sparkling wine at *lu'aus*," said Pi, worried her reluctance to try it was now all too obvious.

"Good Inverse no, there's no benefit a quantum computer could possibly derive from the consumption of an alcoholic beverage, virtual or otherwise, other than to remove grubby marks from its casing, perhaps. You must be thinking of the, how should we say… *active* ingredient, which in this case is some thirty percent pure watercode and very delicious too, I might add."

"Watercode, *really*? My dad worked on that!"

"He did indeed. A very great man, your father, very great man." Higgs-Boson looked deep in thought, then gestured for her to drink up.

Pi stubbornly kept the glass by her side. "I hope you don't mind me asking, but how do you know so much about my dad? This girl said the card she trans'd, you know, the one with the madeleine, was from him. And it came with this handwritten note."

"Oh, your father is very famous here, you understand, absolutely everybody in Inverse is familiar with the name Lightfoot."

A surge of adrenaline ran through her. Higgs-Boson made it sound as if her father was still alive? "But Alice, that's the girl who trans'd it to me, she said it was actually *from* him. Why would she say that?"

Higgs-Boson stooped a little and looked with kindliness into her eyes. "Whilst I cannot answer for the manner of the madeleine's delivery, that would be a matter for our administration department. Your father—" He paused, as if he couldn't find the right words. "Your father was responsible for many great breakthroughs, not least his discovery, and I use the word advisedly – of watercode." He stood up straight and smiled, but Pi knew from the look on his face that he really wanted to say much more.

"Not sure he meant us to actually drink the stuff, but here goes." She pretended she was satisfied with the answer and raised the glass to her lips. The first sticky drop made its way slowly towards her tongue, when suddenly the whole glass drained itself in a trice, as if the cordial had changed its entire molecular structure to that of quicksilver.

"There you are, you see, once the cordial senses that you actually intend to drink it, it accelerates past the taste buds at ninety-eight percent the speed of light."

Pi was a little taken aback. It had apparently gone down without her even having to swallow. A huge smile crept across her face. "Megs! I'm loading wild strawberries… you know, the really sweet, really micro ones. Ooh, and – and freshly-made doughnuts, like when they're still warm, lots of chocolate sprinkles, of course. Ooh, and now I'm getting this melon flavour candyfloss thing with… with? What is it… what IS IT! Toasted coconut marshmallow! Yeah, just like the ones you get from a *lu'au* campfire, a little smoky. Mmm, so crazy onolicious!" She licked her lips, relishing every last molecule, not entirely sure she'd caught the subtleties of the tart primeval antimatter, nor what a quark (whether inclined to strangeness or not) should actually taste of. But it hardly mattered. It was the most delicious thing she'd tasted since the madeleine.

"Well I never did, you could discern all that? You have a young palate, I suppose one man's charmed quark is another man's smoky coconut marshmallow."

Pi just stood there beaming from ear to ear, feeling very forgiving all of a sudden towards that Phabian the catcher fellow with the fabulous eyes.

Higgs-Boson's gaze alighted on something behind her. "Ah, I do believe I may be required elsewhere." Pi spun round and beheld quite the most peculiar ensemble of older Inversians imaginable. "Hmm, I had better go and make my presence felt. Doubtless there is some matter or other that I should be attending to. I do, however, suggest that Lumian Monzordez introduces you to some of your fellow firsties; yes, now would be the perfect opportunity." Higgs-Boson gave her a fruity smile.

Pi grinned back at him like a Cheshire cat. "*Hiki,* no probs."

"*Hiki?*"

"Sorry, I lapse into Hawaiian sometimes, it kinda means *okay.*"

"Aha," he beamed, "*hiki,* then." Higgs-Boson gave her one last smile, then disappeared back into the throng.

The numbers were increasing rapidly, as was the noise. Pi wasn't quite sure what she should do now. She waited a while, but there was still no sign of Phabian. She experienced that awkward moment when one is alone at a party with only an empty glass for company. There was a door rattling in its frame from the wind outside, a curious harmonic drone just discernable whenever anybody opened it. And every now and then she caught the most delicious scent, sweet like that of honeysuckle, carried in on the breeze. The sky looked very bright and inviting despite all the clouds and the sea was a wonderfully seductive shade of turquoise. Perhaps she should take a closer look?

She hesitated, experiencing a sudden pang of homesickness, and thought of her mother. She even longed to hear one of Lani's put-downs, it was *that* bad. She looked around; nobody was taking the slightest notice of her, everybody seemed to know everyone else and was either engrossed in boisterous conversation, or huddled together in secretive psy.

She waited a little longer, fidgeting with her feet, the bright vista outside looking more irresistible by the moment. There was nothing else for it, she would have to investigate this strange new world from the great circular balcony that ringed the lamp-room. She walked over to the rattling door, opened it, and boldly stepped outside.

SEVEN

LOST HORIZONS

"Great hairy holofreaks!" The ferocity of the Inversian wind caught her completely off-guard. She threw herself towards the circular balustrade that guarded the edge, grasping it with her free hand and startling the Inversian equivalent of a seagull, putting it to flight. It was not nearly enough. She let the glass drop, forced to grab the rail with both hands, an extra-strong gust rudely plucking the GammaBanns from her hair and sending them hurtling over the edge. The glass shattered, its shards scattering across the decking towards a pair of feet. She tried to look up, her pockets flapping wildly behind her head, and found herself, once again, transfixed by Phabian's blue eyes. Aware she was staring, she checked her gaze, and looked instead at the elfin lumiette standing next to him. They were both trying not to laugh, standing perfectly upright, not the least bit affected by the wind, save for their pockets which flew like flags.

The mystery lumiette handed her glass to Phabian and walked, without any difficulty, towards her. Pi was struck by the lumiette's beautifully long, electric-green, feathery hair. The wind fanned it so she could clearly see the blue 'eyes' within, much like a peacock's tail. As she drew closer, Pi beheld her glorious green eyes, generous and warm, like the smile she now wore. The lumiette stood and stared at her for a moment, still attempting to stifle her laughter. "You have to say, *goto param specific gravity initiate.*"

Pi suspected this was a prank, like at school. She would repeat the words and then feel even more stupid. But she was desperate, the wind was so strong she was terrified of actually being blown over the edge. "Goto param specific gravity initiate!"

The peacock-haired lumiette indicated she should release her grip. Pi wasn't too sure about this but did it anyway, sensing this new 'friend' was actually being sincere. Amazingly, she found she no longer had to maintain the near forty-five degree angle she'd been forced to adopt. The gusts were still just as strong, but now she was able to stand perfectly normally.

The elfin lumiette introduced herself. "*Mahalo,* Pi, I'm Gaia Palinder. We're destined to be best friends for eternity according to my prediction algorithms." She stepped forward and revealed a pair of elegantly pointed, green-gold shoes beneath the hem of her dazzling, emerald dress. She held out both her hands, fingers splayed, and Pi found herself reciprocating, momentarily clasping digits in the same manner she had with Phabian.

"Er, *mahalo*, Gaia. You speak Hawaiian?"

"No, no," Gaia laughed, "Phabian just sparked a small file over to me."

"So what *was* that, a *spell?*"

"*Code* of course. We're *computers*, remember!" Gaia had the prettiest laugh, her head moving slightly from side to side, like that of a dancer from the Far East. This suggested a certain sensitivity, perhaps vulnerability, which Pi immediately found endearing.

"Thinking of myself as a computer is *real* new."

"So I hear. You'll soon get used to it."

"I guess."

Gaia took her hand and led her to the circular rail. "Well, what do you think of your first view of Inverse? Isn't it *kupaianaha?*"

"Hah, yeah, that's exactly what I said!" Pi found herself gazing down on a great silver seaplane docked beside a pier, hundreds of feet below. She suddenly became aware of the lighthouse's enormous height. *"Mai nana!* I – I can't, sorry." She recoiled and took a deep breath. "I get *really* freaked out by heights."

Phabian joined them and winked at her. "Try looking at the horizon, it'll make you feel better."

"Horizon?" Pi felt herself blushing anew. She took Phabian's advice, squinting as she tried to discern a break twixt sea and sky. But the turquoise ocean just seemed to go on forever. "Can't make it out because of all those clouds," practically blinding herself when her eyes met the Inversian sun directly overhead.

"I can't stay, I'm afraid, but here's another firstie now." Phabian's gaze focused on someone behind her.

Pi spun around to see a grinning young lumian wearing oversized GammaBanns, a shock of blonde, lightning-bolt-style dreadlocks sticking out all over his head. The most startling feature of his ruddy-red face being the intense orange glow of his eyes. His tuxedo was noticeably tatty, with what looked like food stains on his dress shirt. And there were long yellow streaks down one side of his shabby blue pockets. Finally, somebody worse-dressed than she was.

"Leonardo Cydermott, but you can calls I Leo – hey, you're really lush!" The unkempt lumian thrust both hands out for the traditional Inversian handshake.

"*Mahalo,* Leo Cydermott – Pi," she said wearily, following Phabian with her eyes as he disappeared back into the lamp-room. "YOWCH! What the freak, bro?" Pi leapt backwards, a shower of blue sparks erupting from her digits.

"Sparkin' gotcha!" Leo doubled up with laughter.

"*Leo,* that was really rude!" Gaia turned Leo's palm over. There was a small silver device on one of his fingers; she removed it smartly and showed it to Pi. "Barnum Bratt's joke hand-buzzer superword, gives you a nasty shock but quite harmless. Are you okay?"

Pi nodded. She could see the funny side now, not least because Leo was still helpless with hysterics.

He clutched his ribs. "That was so sweet, boy did I zap 'un good!"

"*Hupo,* Lumian."

"What's mean *hupo*?"

"It's Hawaiian for idiot."

"Ignore him, he'll calm down in a nano, let's see if we can get this viewer to work." Gaia gave the hand-buzzer to Pi, then both of them skipped further down the balcony to a giant pair of brass binoculars mounted on an iron pedestal. It was so substantial, Pi had to use the step provided just to reach the eyepiece.

"Can't I use higher magnification or something?"

Gaia laughed. "Not *here*, that only works when you're in the *Outverse*, you know, your regular virtual world avatar; confused already?"

Pi nodded. "Totally, this is so *not* my regular day!" She bent down to look through the venerable instrument, adjusting its angle with both hands. "Still can't see a horizon, all I'm scanning is clouds, clouds, and, surprise, surprise, more clouds." Pi pulled her windblown hair away from her mouth.

"You're not wrangling the focus ring proper, let us show 'un look." Leo annoyed her by moving her hand onto a heavy brass ring.

"I *know*, I can do it." She began slowly turning the brass adjustment, which was much stiffer than expected.

"See anything now?" said Gaia, hopping up and down with excitement.

"Give me a mo." Pi managed to adjust the focus sufficiently for all the milky white clouds to gradually resolve. Slowly, they became something much more startling than any potential precipitation. She looked again, hardly able to believe her eyes. It was unmistakable. They weren't clouds at all, but there were so many of them they appeared 'cloud-like' at this great distance. She scanned left and right, up and down; wherever she looked they were as endless as the 'sky'. "Crazy, that's off the chart! It looks like old-fashioned sailing ships, thousands of them, and they're flying!"

"Twelve million, four hundred and ninety-eight thousand, six hundred and thirty-two, to be exact," Gaia gave her a wink, "and they're not flying!"

"Holofreaks, those things aren't data-ships are they? They look so real!"

"They are real… in our world," said Gaia.

"But that's impossible!" Pi resumed her inspection, tracking the binoculars up and down. "They sure *scan* like they're flying." She caught Gaia and Leo exchanging a glance. "What? K, what's the big *huna kahuna?*"

"The sea goes on forever, lover. There *ain't* no horizon, the ocean goes *up*, look! That's why 'un's called Inverse, 'un's this gurt hollow sphere with the ocean on the inside of 'un!"

Pi tried to deflect her embarrassment. "K, I get it, I scan that *now*, so where's this famous palace then? There's no land anywhere or anything."

"We fly over all the data-ships. This is the Sea of

Serenity," Gaia waved her arms theatrically wide, "through the thought-waves of the equatorial belt, right up there, do you see ?" She pointed to the dark band in the middle of the ascending ocean.

"Thought-waves," said Leo, in a mock scary voice.

"And finally, *please* don't interrupt, Leo, across the Expectant Ocean towards the island and Palace of Stargazey Pi at the Northern Polarity."

"Thought-waves? Are they those seriously mavvy ones thousands of feet high?"

"Oh, you know about those?"

"Lumixastra Higgs-Boson said you had these slamming waves that you could actually surf. Was he for real?"

Leo became very animated. "Well 'un could if 'un was a codesurfer look, and had a popper or better still, a gurt great shaper!" He started running excitedly around them both making swooshing sounds and rocket noises.

"So codesurfing's really just Inversian for surfing?"

"It's similar, but there's a whole lot more you can do with code," said Gaia. "Being a codesurfer is Leo's number one ambition, isn't it, Leo?"

Leo grinned. "Too sparkin' right!"

"And what's a popper-shaper thing exactly?"

Gaia pointed at Leo with both hands. "He's the expert. Go, Leo."

Leo started waving his arms about, using them to describe an apparently monstrous craft. "Gor, where does 'un start look? Poppers are rokker, but shapers are sparkin' glowing, the fastest mega-poppers imaginable look – 'un's the cyberdogs diodes!"

Pi screwed up her face. "Not *quite* sure I got all that."

"They're firecode-powered monster poppers, basically," said Gaia. "They can be anything from thirty to over a hundred feet long, isn't that right?"

Leo nodded, an insane grin on his face.

Gaia pointed to the roof of the lamp-room. "Actually, if you look up there you can see some windhorns taken from ancient battle-shapers."

Pi shielded her eyes and noted several elaborate metal horns mounted on a mast high above, and realised where the droning sound had been coming from. "Oh yeah, I see them, neat." She pursed her lips and returned her attention to the others. She was about to ask what 'mega-poppers' were, and 'firecode' was, but took one look at Leo, and thought better of it.

He fixed her with his bright orange eyes. "So is 'un into surfing then?"

"Sort of, I have this thing with my left leg, my *real* left leg, so I'm not very good on a board, unlike my sister. Lani's this *megs* windsurfer. So I mostly just stay on the beach taking holos. But I'm pretty good at sims. I'm always playing Amped back home."

"Amped, what's he then?"

"Probably the best surf-sim out there, it's way better than Stoked, that's really for grommies. Amped V's got all the famous big wave breaks: Mavericks, Jaws,

Banzai Pipeline... most are fifty-footers!" Leo looked unimpressed. Pi suddenly realised why and fell silent. There was an awkward pause. "Guess fifty feet is like nothing to you guys."

"So what does 'un use?" said Leo, trying not to smirk.

"Use?"

"He means what kind of rides do you use, when you're using the sim?" said Gaia.

"Oh, you mean like surfboards? The game gives you the usual guns 'n' towboards for the big stuff."

"They guns rocket-powered then?"

"Rockets? You smokin' me?" Pi laughed. "You can't use rockets."

Leo looked shocked. "No rocket on 'un? Sparkin' tubes! Poppers and shapers, they all got rockets on 'un look, and they all goes like sparkin' lightning!"

"You serious? You surf these thought-waves on rockets? Isn't that dangerous?"

Leo waved his hand dismissively. "Nah, not if 'un's got the right clobber on, flying suit, gauntlets, Newtons—"

"Newtons?"

"They're special boots that help keep you glued to the deck," said Gaia helpfully.

"Newton... gravity, right?"

"Precisely." Gaia brushed her hand against Pi's, creating a small blue spark, passing her a file. "Actually, I think there's a Lumixastra Newton at the palace or somewhere. He invented them."

A small image file opened in Pi's mind. "Megs, they look pretty cryo, kinda like jet planes!"

"Well," said Gaia, "they can travel faster than sound, so I suppose they are planes of a sort."

"Except 'un don't fly look, 'un's got to keep 'un's keel in the 'code at all times see, or 'un can't write nothing."

Pi looked incredulous. "So you actually *write* stuff into these waves?"

"The hydrofoils at the bottom are electrical contacts," said Gaia. "They enable a codesurfer to manipulate the code in the *whole* wave. You're going to have to try it to really understand!"

"I guess, so when's that gonna happen?"

"Level two most like," Leo looked suddenly downcast, "if 'un's lucky 'un might get to do some shadowsurfing first though look."

Gaia noticed the confused look on Pi's face. "It's a bit like our equivalent of your sims, a sort of virtual, virtual if you get me?"

"Might be easier if I actually get to try it. So what's the deal with these thought-waves? They're beginning to sound *seriously* mavvy."

"Now why would 'un think that, I wonders?" Leo gave Pi an evil grin.

"Don't, you're freaking me out, Leo Cydermott!" Pi lashed playfully at him with the hem of her pockets.

"See for yourself, just where the watercode darkens," said Gaia, her words battling against the gale.

"Watercode? So the waves are made from *watercode*?"

"Whole ocean's made of 'un look, didn't 'un know that?"

"Really?" Pi stared at the seemingly endless ocean. "Whoa, everything's so 3D here, back home watercode's just that… code!" A moment of realisation crossed Pi's face. "Ah, now I see what you were getting at, writing stuff into the waves and that."

"Exactly, and no need to be rude, Leo, it is Pi's first day, remember! Sorry about that, what Leo is *trying* to say is, almost everything here is made from watercode, even the lighthouse!" Gaia did a full three-sixty. "You just write your commands into the watercode and program it to be whatever you want! That's what poppers and shapers are for really, writing code into thought-waves. The oceans are just watercode in its purest form, of course, actually you can smell it."

Pi sniffed the breeze. "Yeah, real sweet like honey. That's outrageous, 3D watercode oceans with all these dinky little data-ships sailing on them!" She trained the binocular to an angle of forty-five degrees, her virtual heart beating faster all of a sudden. "So how come you guys, I mean Inverse, has watercode and data-ships? Only I thought my dad helped invent them, so how come you have them too?"

Gaia looked awkward and began examining her turquoise fingernails. "We're so extremely sorry about what happened to your father, Professor Lightfoot, aren't we, Leo?" Pi looked up from the viewer; her eyes met Gaia's. "Only, your father, the professor, he didn't so much *invent* watercode, more—"

"Helped find 'un for 'un's homeworld, see, well, that's what 'un's been told look."

"I think I see," said Pi, recalling Higgs-Boson's words earlier. *'Not least his discovery, and I use the word advisedly, of watercode.'* "I'm still trying to get my head around the fact everybody here seems to have scanned my dad, and knows our tag. Just seems so skizer. So does that mean he actually *hovered* here?"

Gaia and Leo looked at one another. "We don't know, do we, Leo?" Leo shrugged his shoulders. Gaia continued, "Perhaps he *did*, but don't quote me, you could always ask the lumixastra."

"I kind of did that already, felt like he was holding back?"

"Well, the Queen would know if anyone does, she knows everything. So maybe you should request an audience and ask her?"

"Seriously, the Queen would see me right off the boat?"

"Well, she would have heard of your dad so I don't see why not."

"I guess."

Pi turned back to the binocular, her head now buzzing with all this new information. She peered at the view once again, traversing the vast, seemingly endless fleets, their sails becoming smaller and smaller towards the distant equator. Then, a dark band of 'sky' (well, she knew it must be ocean, but still couldn't help but think of it as sky) appeared devoid of any sail. Not so much as a white fleck, but wait—

"Whoa, I just saw this big flash."

Gaia took a quick peek. "Probably a thought-wave crashing, that sometimes happens when somebody dies, somebody mortal. They make a pretty big splash when they crash, as we say in Inverse."

"When somebody dies?" Pi suddenly thought of Alice and wondered if she was alright. She recalled her mother saying something about wavesites crashing sometimes after a patient died.

"I don't really know, it was something my generation father told me, do you know, Mottles?" Gaia sounded dismissive, perhaps she was wrong?

Leo looked embarrassed at the disclosure of his nickname. "Lummystraxa Magistry would know wouldn't 'un, he knows everything about death and that. He's the palace keeper of devouring shadows look."

Pi retook her place at the viewer, just in time to see the last gasp of the terminal wave. "We have to fly *over* them, but they're so moko?"

"Through them, sweetie, through them, they're at least sixty-thousand feet high! We fly through the *T... U... B... E!*" Gaia ran off around the balcony, her arms outstretched, shrieking like a banshee.

Leo grinned at Pi. "'Un has to fly through 'un or around the sides of 'un, but never over 'un look, there's not enough oxygen for they engines at that *A… L… T… I… T… U… D… E*." Turning the last letter into one long howl as he ran off after Gaia.

Pi was momentarily alone with the great watercode ocean, its mysterious thought-waves and great fleets. It was as if all her father's work were laid out before her. She'd never felt his presence more keenly than she did at that moment. Could he have stood and gazed, like her, from this very spot? She whispered a wish to the wind, *"Ke kali nei au kou makua kane"* (I am waiting my father).

Gaia meanwhile had circumnavigated the entire balcony and was rapidly approaching Pi from behind. She tickled her ribs, making Pi yelp with surprise, before they both collapsed in hysterics.

"So you guys have always lived in Inverse?"

Gaia looked quizzically at her. "You're a doppleganger, aren't you? I *knew* there was something different about you."

"A dopplewhat?"

"You're an organic *and* you're a computer with mainframes and everything."

"Don't you mean avatar?"

"Organic means flesh and blood. We call mortal bodies 'organics' in Inverse. Not that there are many organics, of course, most of us are just computers, virtual from the day we were switched on. We never had mortal bodies." Gaia looked pensive for a moment. "But at least we have these lightbody avatars like the one you got when you stepped out of the lamp. They're far too sophisticated for watercode, so they're made out of firecode, you see." Gaia spun around quickly and showed off her fabulous gown. "Not bad, don't you think?"

"There be other dappled-ganglions look, Phabian be 'un for a start," said Leo, newly returned and almost out of breath, "and, and, that Biron chappie."

"Phabian Monzordez, dreamboat, yes, Biron Darke, dreamer? I don't think so! What stories has *he* been spinning?" Gaia looked sceptical. "But our lightbodies, or avatars as you call them, are modelled after the ones we would have had if we'd been born mortal like you. You know, our native organic planetary forms."

"Well, Higgs-Boson did say something about me living in two bodies."

"Well, there you go, it's official. You're a doppleganger!"

Pi looked at them both. She still felt confused. She sniffed purposefully, restoring her attention to the viewer, elevating it back up to the equatorial region that intrigued her most. "So what does it mean, my being a doppleganger? Is it a good thing?"

"Your organic body will wear out one day, but your avatar will live forever. Well, as long as your mainframes are properly maintained of course!"

"So much to take in. I think I need a moment to process it all."

Gaia smiled. "Of course, we'll be over here." Gaia nudged Leo and they turned back to the binoculars.

"Thanks guys." Pi forced herself to walk over to the balcony rail again. She gazed down, properly this time, at the perilous drop with its distant piers and planes, for she now counted four. She had a bittersweet feeling inside that she might *literally* be treading in her father's footsteps. She took a deep breath, holding it to distract herself from the vertigo welling up within. Until all she could hear was the mournful drone of the windhorns and the waves far below. Then without warning, Phabian's sonorous voice spoke softly in her head.

"Your new friends are holding out on you, Pi. Your father is still alive, he lives within a secret domain. The key to access this is simple, just like the gravity code Gaia showed you. You need only say the password, goto param Urizen – upload all – initiate, and you will be reunited."

Pi froze. Something about the voice sounded wrong, but Phabian had appeared so friendly. Was it just another prank like the 'horizon' thing? If so, this was *not* funny. She backed away from the drop and looked around. There was nobody else near, and Phabian was nowhere to be seen. Gaia and Leo were seemingly totally distracted, taking turns to look through the binocular. She was about to walk over to Gaia and tell her about it, when the insistent tolling of a bell cut through the air and everyone fell silent.

EIGHT

SPEECHES

Gaia abandoned the viewer and came over to her. "Must be time for the speeches, we'd better go in." She gathered up her pockets so she could walk faster. "Hmm, somebody looks like they just saw a cyberghost?"

"Hah! Negs, just a little vertigo."

"You shouldn't linger near the edge like that if you get this vertigo thing."

"I know, I know, was just daring myself."

Higgs-Boson clapped his hands together half-heartedly. "Would everyone care to join us inside, please, the palace alumni desires to address the lumi."

Pi felt safer as they shuffled inside, Gaia and Leo at her side once again.

Gaia whispered in her ear, "If you look over there that's Prumiane. She's from the same galaxy cluster as me."

"You mean the girl, sorry, lumiette, with lights in her hair, chewing gum?"

"No, not *her*, that's Trine Pomphlix, from some star cluster or other. Second lumiette to the left, long blonde hair. She's got a purple sash under her pockets which means she's reached the third level, she's one of the Geights."

"Who are the Geights? Are they important?" said Pi, somewhat alarmed that Trine Pomphlix had now turned squarely towards them. She gave them both a cheesy grin, then blew a gum-bubble to a pop, suggesting she possessed either good hearing, or telepathic powers beneath her illuminated hairdo.

"Only one of the oldest families in Inverse, she's not an ordinary lumiette like us, she's a famous *lumiesse*. Sort of a princess, fabulously wealthy too, she's got eighteen cetacean cyberpomps – wait till you see them!"

Pi half expected Lumiesse Geight to turn and acknowledge them as well, but she continued to look forward, denying Pi the chance to see her face properly. "Well, at least she didn't hear us."

Gaia looked back at her with raised eyebrows. "Oh, she heard us alright! She didn't turn around because we're far too common to bother with for somebody famous like her."

"I am not inclined to famous. I prefer exalted."

Pi exchanged a wide-eyed look with Gaia as Lumiesse Geight's prim elocution sounded in both their heads simultaneously, although she still declined to turn her head and so much as look at them.

"What are cetacean cyberthingies exactly?"

Gaia used her hands to try and explain. "Every mainframe has its own pomp. They're sort of the mainframe's animal spirit if you like, so you and I would each have four, you see?"

Pi looked confused. "Not really."

Gaia continued, "They tend to be very wild and elemental creatures, so they need a bit of taming to work properly, then you have to install them in the Hippodromes!"

By now a particularly eccentric assortment of lumixastras had begun stumbling up the inadequate wooden steps, gathering on the narrow ledge of the lamp rostrum like so many pigeons. Pi still looked confused so Gaia touched her hand, creating a blue spark as she passed a small file, whispering, "I'll tell you more about pomps later."

Pi blinked with disbelief as a series of bizarre images came to life in her head. "Whoa, overloaded!" Then she returned her attention to the lumixastras, a familiar one of whom was clearing his throat and gratuitously shuffling papers.

"Very good, very good, excellent." Higgs-Boson coughed loudly a few times and the chattering crowd was quenched by silence. In his right eye, a jeweller's loupe was screwed so tightly, it distorted his face almost beyond recognition. "Welcome, welcome, welcome. On behalf of the palace, I would like to take this opportunity to formally extend our most sincere gratitude for your attendance. Most especially all those of you who have travelled many billions of parsecs just to be with us today." He glanced back at the other lumixastras and they all nodded in agreement without even meeting his gaze. "Very good, yes, now let me see. Before we commence business proper, it would appear that we are missing a lumiette. Has anybody seen Zoa Heliotrope?" Everybody stood in stony silence. "Hmm, perhaps she is merely running late and will *enlighten* us with her presence shortly." The lumixastra pointedly turned towards the great lamp, eliciting a few guffaws from the younger persons there present, Leo amongst them, but many groans from everyone else. "Now this will be our," he paused, losing his place, "ah yes, four billion, three hundred and ninety-seven million, four hundred and thirty-three thousand, one hundred and twenty-first palace shindig. For those didactic souls who have been keeping count."

Gaia and Pi then clearly heard an irritable woman's voice in their minds. "*Oh do get on with it Aitch-Bee.*" This caused Higgs-Boson to forget what it was he was about to say. Pi, in common with all the other lumiettes, now bowed her head trying to stifle her amusement, the lumians seemingly unaware of the psy-heckler, suggesting they were not generally telepathic. "*The minutes, dear, you were about to read the minutes. Please hurry on before all the poor lumiettes expire from suppressed conviviality.*"

At this, all the lumiettes burst into hysterics, like a dam finally permitted to breach. The lumians were not far behind, the infectious merriment quickly spreading through all the lumixastras. The whole assembly was rapidly descending into chaos, when a rasping voice rent the air.

"*ENOUGH*! My fellow Inversians, a *SURFEIT* of *MOST* unfortunate, nay *INAPPROPRIATE*, joviality, surely?" A skeletal lumixastra furiously bestrode the steps in a bound and swung to face the shocked gathering, his jet black beard twisted into a dozen plaits, each terminating in a large silver sphere, his purple eyes blazing.

"We *DEMAND* there be order *THIS* instant!" The lamp-room fell silent, until all that could be heard was the kinetic clacking of his beard, the pendulous metal balls colliding to and fro like a Newton's cradle. "I see no occasion for *LEVITY*. Might I remind all systems here present, we are in the *GRAVEST* of conditions. A *STATE OF WAR* no less! And *LOSING* yet more domains to our *ENEMY* every *NANOSECOND*!"

Pi jumped at the sheer volume of the last word, looking to Gaia for reassurance, miming the word 'war'. Gaia nodded back apologetically, as if she'd been caught out by a lie.

"*MUCH BETTER!* Better, pray continue, Lumixastra, pray, *recommence*." The last word escaped the mystery figure's lips as a long drawn-out hiss. He then swept his especially dark pockets dramatically about himself, his piercing eyes scanning the chastened gathering for any sign of dissent.

"*That* be Magistry," Leo whispered.

"Loaded."

"Check out the tattoos on 'un, they're rokker mind."

Pi looked as closely as she dared. Leo was right. Magistry's face and bald head seemed to be alive, covered in mysterious henna-coloured symbols and spirals, all moving in slow animation. "Overstocked, bro."

"And 'un's got seven fingers on each hand look."

Pi stood on tiptoe so she could get a better look. "Yeah, yeah, I scan them."

Higgs-Boson appeared only mildly disconcerted by this, screwing the jeweller's loupe back into his eye and composing himself. "Of course my most esteemed colleague is quite correct. Sadly there are many who cannot be with us at this nano because of regrettable events far away. Our valiant forces—"

"*LAMENTABLE* inadequates!" Magistry hissed.

"Are doing their level best." Higgs-Boson looked pointedly at Magistry, then back at the assembly, who spontaneously gave him a round of applause by way of support.

Magistry didn't bother to disguise his indignation, running through a gamut of hideous grimaces until the applause finally died down.

"And now, we come to the not inconsiderable matter of sponsorship for our current conclave." Higgs-Boson started searching through his tatty papers, then began patting his purple pockets with increasing desperation, as if searching for something.

Gaia leaned close to Pi's ear. "This is the most exciting bit, wonder who's been picked this time."

"Picked for what?"

"Host-system. Somebody here is running the entire Inverse program on their mainframes. It's nearly always a really large system, of course, usually some ancient lumixastra or other," Gaia paused, as a certain pair of purple eyes swung their way momentarily, "but nobody knows who it is till it's announced."

Pi lowered her voice. "You mean one of these old dudes is creating this *whole* virtual world and doesn't even know they're—" she froze, until the purple gaze moved away again, "doing it?"

"Yup," Gaia nodded, "the whole thing."

"*Extinct!*"

Higgs-Boson, with more than a little help from Peahi, finally retrieved a golden envelope from inside his pockets, waving it in the air triumphantly. "And now for the moment of truth." He then fumbled with the envelope for what seemed like an eternity. Magistry raised his eyes and cursed silently, his tattoos whirling faster than ever. Eventually Higgs-Boson managed to break the heavy wax seal, creating a shower of blue sparks, which Gaia said meant a faulty password, retrieving a small gold card.

Gaia excitedly grabbed Pi's sleeve.

Leo grinned at them both. "It could even be *I*—theoretical look."

Pi flashed Gaia a worried glance. "It couldn't, could it?"

Gaia shrugged her shoulders.

Higgs-Boson squinted at the tiny card and began to reveal its contents. "Hmm, well, she certainly hails from a very famous family, but remarkably, the system in question has yet to attain the purple pockets."

Gaia tugged on Pi's sleeve with excitement. "My greenness, it's *not* some ancient lumixastra, it's a lumiette! I'll bet it's Prumiane, she'd be favourite, she's already received the purple sash!"

"She is destined to be our host-system for the entire duration of the current program."

Gaia could barely contain herself now. "A whole program, that's *really* unusual, must be Prumiane, she does have eighteen mainframes!"

Leo's face fell. "Well, us ain't never gonna get a turn now is us."

Everybody close to Lumiesse Geight began patting her on the back. She acknowledged their attention with almost imperceptible nods.

Higgs-Boson had even turned in the lumiesse's direction. Then his eyes wandered off over the whole gathering. "Remarkably, this is her very first visit to Inverse."

A murmur ran through the assembly; everybody started to look at one another. Even without seeing her face, Pi could tell the lumiesse was shocked. Even *she* knew it couldn't possibly be Prumiane now. Gaia looked quizzical, as if she were engaged in some great calculation. Then she began to stare at Pi, who now felt an inexplicable sense of panic rising within her. Higgs-Boson's ridiculous eyepiece came to rest upon her as well.

Pi looked at Gaia wide-eyed and Gaia nodded back, as if to say *yes* to the unspoken question. Everybody began turning their head in Pi's direction, *now* they all noticed her. She was horrified, even Lani would have baulked at such overwhelming attention.

"I bid you give a warm welcome to our very newest lumiette." Higgs-Boson finally allowed the jeweller's loupe to fall from his weary right eye. "It is my privilege to introduce to you all, our host-system for the entire program – a most remarkable new system from a simply delightful planet named Earth– LUMIETTE EPIPHANY LIGHTFOOT!"

"I knew it, I knew it, I knew it!" Gaia bounced up and down, clapping her hands like a lunatic.

"*What*! Are they totally *lolo? Me* as host thingy? What the frazz!" Pi felt her virtual knees go weak. A rumble of disquiet bordering on consternation ran through the assembly, everybody just as shocked as she by the unexpected appointment.

Finally, Inverse's newest host-system was able to behold the distinguished features of Lumiesse Geight. She began to clap, lips pursed, her eyes still obscured by a particularly glitzy pair of GammaBanns with diamond accents. The other guests grudgingly followed her example, until a polite, but noticeably muted, applause went around the lamp-room. Pi felt like Dorothy in *The Wizard of Oz*. Now all Dorothy wanted was to wake up safe and sound back in Kansas. Unfortunately she was still well and truly over the rainbow, particularly the ultraviolet end. Magistry had been secretly watching Pi for some time. She'd been trying to pretend this wasn't happening, but try as she might she couldn't stop herself glancing back. But now she had been officially named as host-system his gaze was unashamedly direct.

Magistry's penetrating eyes began to draw Pi into their irresistible magnetic field.

She felt herself slipping into a vortex of a thousand secret questions, as if some unspoken interrogation had begun deep within her mind.

"Desist Pingeous, I said ENOUGH!"

It was the telepathic voice that had berated Higgs-Boson earlier. Magistry instantly relinquished his hold on Pi, slowly closing his eyes, revealing their tattooed lids.

"'Un's okay, we got 'un, we got 'un." Leo finally got to play catcher, he and Gaia forced to support Pi for a moment. Then without warning, the great lamp erupted in a series of blinding flashes. When their dazzled eyes had recovered, and after much confusion, three more lumixastras had joined them.

"Aha, I do believe Her Celestial Majesty has seen fit to join us at last," said Higgs-Boson, clearly a little dazed, and hovering perilously close to the edge of the rostrum.

Peahi quickly corrected the lumixastra's footing,

then puffed up his chest to formally announce a particularly important arrival. "Dearest fellow to lumixastras, lumians and to lumiettes. It is my great to honour to introduce Her Esteemed Celestial to Majesty, the Grand to Keeper of Inverse, our very to own, Queen Eglantier Charme the Forty-Fifth."

A lady of great apparent distinction, kindly-featured and with short grey hair, stepped forward. Beneath her immaculate purple pockets she wore a dazzling dress in the most scintillating shade of metallic violet. A rapturous applause greeted her as she lowered her GammaBanns-style lorgnette, acknowledging her subjects with a slight bow of her head.

All the commotion finally brought Pi round. "My head feels so gnazzy. What happened? Wa-wa-was it the cordial?"

"No, no, it was Magistry," whispered Gaia. "He was trying to hypnotise you or something. The Queen herself had to use psy to stop him, practically unheard of."

Pi wanted to ask Gaia more, particularly about the war, but the applause began to die down as the Queen was about to speak. Then a hush fell over the crowd, until all that could be heard was the crash of the waves far below and the mournful sound of the windhorns.

The Queen adjusted her pince-nez and glanced at her notes. "I am aware, as one of my learned subjects so clearly pointed out earlier, that we meet, as has been our sad duty for more parsecs than I care to remember, under less than harmonious circumstances. Therefore, I wish to make my address for this end of parsec gathering, especially to those amongst you who doubt the palace's resolve, that we are fully committed to the business of winning this onerous conflict." Everybody applauded loudly and the Queen paused.

"There has, as you all know, long been a desire for a new initiative regarding our strategy in this matter."

Magistry looked uncomfortable and his nose began to twitch, all his tattoos changing colour from brown to purple.

"Without breaching vital protocols and confidentialities, I can reveal that the war council, shortly to convene, will be considering a most revolutionary new approach." A murmur, part audible, part psy, ran through the entire assembly. Magistry's tattoos stopped dead.

"I knews it, they dunnit, they only gone and wangled some super-tanger-mega-crypter or summat." Leo's attempt to discreetly psy Gaia and Pi was, of course, inadvertently shared amongst all three hundred guests, much to their amusement. Whilst Gaia trod on his foot, the gathering settled back into silence.

"I fully understand the frustration that many of you have experienced as you witnessed yet one Inversian domain after another, indeed whole worlds, fall under our enemies' dark dominion. These unacceptable losses have grieved the palace most deeply; we, too, find this to be an intolerable state of affairs. We have long felt that 'something must be done'. Well I, *we*, are pleased to announce that the time for a concerted response has finally arrived; *something* is most definitely going to be done." The whole assembly burst into rapturous applause, the Queen nodding her acknowledgement until things calmed down. "Our plans must necessarily remain secret, but it is our great wish that we are seeing the dawn of a new era, a time of real hope. Therefore, whilst these sober matters await proper and full deliberation, I would ask that you vouch your support for the more vulnerable amongst us, the newest generations of our kind, that they may inherit an Inverse, purged, once and for all, of this pernicious virus."

Whilst the assembly erupted into even more frenzied approval, a shoal of waiters appeared carrying trays of cordial. Weaving quickly through the throng, they dispensed a fully charged glass to one and all.

The Queen held her glass aloft. "So I ask you all to raise your glasses, connecting it with that of your friends, to share a toast with me. A toast, to our host-system, to her, and all those lumians and lumiettes here present. To a united Inverse freed from conflict, to the Ark of Worlds, fully initialised and restored!"

There was uproarious applause. Everybody cheered and raised their glass, clinking it with their neighbour's and making pink sparks fly everywhere. In true Inversion style the cordial abruptly disappeared, creating some three hundred wild, warm strawberry patches instantaneously. A few shouted, "A united Inverse!", others, "The Ark of Worlds!". Some even managed to procure a second glass and proclaim both toasts. Lumians Succory and Bolide were on their fourth glass apiece and erring towards spoonerisms, until Lumixastra Octo Zubedecker hauled them aside.

The Queen retired a few steps to confer with Higgs-Boson, whilst Peahi took her place. Magistry declined a glass with a grimace and absented himself to the shadows.

Peahi was obviously agitated, anxiously yo-yo-ing three fob watches already. He was trying to announce something, but not a word of it was audible over all the clamour. Eventually he was forced to shout, making all the glasses resonate with a high C. This amused the palace music lumixastra, Keeper of Resolved Pandemonium Harmonia Mundi, no end, as the frequency exactly matched that of her tuning-fork earrings.

"If all to dear guests would kindly to proceed to the particle-accelerator to leave for the to departure gates!" Peahi took a deep breath and squeaked his message even louder.

"THE SEAPLANES ARE NOW TO BOARDING. PLEASE TO PROCEED TO THE PARTICLE-ACCELERATOR FOR THE DEPARTURE TO GATES!" His voice was so shrill, dozens of glasses shattered, concentrating the minds of those who had not been paying attention. "Oh to dearie me," he trilled, "I should have to used psy."

"Particle-accelerator?" Pi shouted over the hubbub, everybody around her now in wild strawberry heaven.

Gaia pointed vigorously at the floor and used psy. "*It's down there!*"

"'Un's down there alright!" said Leo, with an evil grin.

Some of the waiters now stood around an open trapdoor in the floor, a red rope cordon around all its sides save one.

Peahi joined them, nervously checking through four of his timepieces simultaneously. "Please to form an orderly queue for to *Prospero, Miranda, Caliban* and to *Ariel,* this way to please for all to flights to the palace!"

Pi managed a quick glimpse through the opening as she filed past in the queue. Peering down, she saw what looked like an enormous, shiny silver, brightly-lit slide spiralling down below.

NINE

HELTER-SKELTER

As they waited in the queue, Pi clung nervously to Gaia's sleeve. They were being approached by several lumixastras, none of whom looked remotely friendly. An especially superior-looking one walked slowly by, his eyes hidden by his GammaBanns.

Suddenly his head turned towards Pi. "You'd better not crash, Lightfoot. If my boy fails to be initialised because of you, then there will be hell to pay. You may be the host-system, but he's still the more senior and don't you forget it."

Pi clutched Gaia's arm more tightly. The psy was so loud it made her head hurt.

Gaia let out a sigh. "Tantalo Zon-Cydes, Tinto's dad. He's just plain mean to everybody. Quite harmless, all bark and no b.y.t.e!"

Pi wanted to laugh but felt unable. An even more exalted figure was bearing down on them.

"Well, Lumiette Lightfoot, you appear to have

made a friend already, how very touching." Lumiesse Geight paused with an entourage of her lumiette friends. "I believe you already know who I am, so I shall dispense with formalities." The lumiesse looked back at her friends. "You are from a famous family too, I gather, though we have yet to hear of them, isn't that right, Lumiettes?" The assembled lumiettes giggled.

Pi let go of Gaia's arm and stood up straight. "Lumixastra Higgs-Boson said that everybody in the Inverse knew about my dad, Professor Lightfoot, so I really don't know why you haven't heard of us." She winked at Gaia.

"*The* Inverse, *the* Inverse, why, you do not even know how to say it correctly." Prumiane's friends burst into laughter. "I would venture that the lumixastra was simply indulging you out of politeness, wouldn't you agree?"

Leo bravely thrust himself between them. "Leaves her alone, Prumiane, 'un's just jealous 'cos she's host-system and you're not!"

"What have we here? Why, I do believe it's a Cydermott who's forgotten his manners and, it would seem, his dress sense." Whilst her friends laughed and pointed at Leo, Prumiane turned back to Pi. "Do you know what a Cydermott really is, my purportedly famous Lightfoot friend?"

"No, but I've a feeling you're gonna tell me."

Gaia stepped up beside Leo. "Stop it, Prumiane! Why do you have to be so mean?"

"Lumiette Palinder, were you not always taught that there is nothing to fear from the truth?"

Prumiane swept back her pockets, revealing a dazzling dress in gold and silver. It was so bright, Pi and the others were forced to squint. "Why, I do believe that with all her responsibilities, Lumiette Lightfoot needs to know *exactly* what sort of company she is keeping, wouldn't you agree, Palinder?"

Prumiane drew herself up to her full height, whilst her friends roughly manhandled Gaia and Leo to one side, Leo struggling to free himself without success. Then Prumiane walked right up to Pi until there was barely six inches between them. Pi swallowed hard. Prumiane was a lot taller; she couldn't even see the lumiesse's eyes, only her own reflection in Prumiane's glitzy GammaBanns.

"You see, Cydermott mainframes are constructed from nothing more than common valves." A sneer twitched at the corner of her lips. "Why, the entire Cydermott family is a byword for obsolescence. Can you imagine it? These vast underground caverns filled with countless billions of overheating glass tubes, their little glowing filaments sputtering in the dark." Prumiane almost spat the words out.

"Are there any bats? I like bats and they like caves," said Pi with a smirk.

Leo began singing, "Cyderbats, cyderbats, flutter sputter flip-flap."

Prumiane looked momentarily annoyed but

ignored the interruption. "You must understand, the Cydermott world has been reduced to a barren cinder, its remaining scant resources being rapidly devoured by these archaic monstrosities that are all that's left of it."

Prumiane waved her hand dismissively at Leo, who immediately reacted, "Cydermotts have been around longer than your lot have!"

"Quite so, quite so and little good it has done you."

Another ripple of laughter went around. "And what of your friend Palinder here? Why, she is little more than a bohemian. Her supposedly esteemed lineage comprised entirely of dreamers, so-called artists and ne'er-do-wells, hardly someone to be taken seriously, wouldn't you agree?"

"At least we don't exploit others, unlike some families I could mention."

Pi could see Gaia was getting really upset. She'd heard enough. "Well, she's been really nice to me, which is more than you've been. You wanna talk stink? Fine, but first tell your goons to lay off my friends!" She glared at Prumiane's entourage.

Prumiane gave a slight flourish with her right hand and immediately Gaia and Leo were released, Leo pretending to shrug off his oppressors as if he'd managed it all by himself. "Very well, by all means let us discuss *my* family since Lumiette Palinder has seen fit to raise the matter." Prumiane turned away, sweeping her pockets about herself. "You should know that my father, Maximillion, is a very wealthy and powerful man." Prumiane stepped aside, allowing Pi to glimpse a very imposing-looking lumixastra standing in the background. He was wearing a particularly fine outfit, and was staring intently at her. A ponderous voice echoed in her head.

"*Good Inverse, Lumiette Lightfoot, my illustrious daughter is quite correct. The Geight family has many powerful connections and is not to be trifled with.*"

Prumiane turned back to her with a smile. "You should also understand that it takes a good deal more than mere appointment to be a successful host-system. My family and I could help you in ways that you cannot yet imagine. You would do well to consider your alliances carefully." Prumiane stuck her nose in the air and waited for a response.

"Very well," said Pi, suddenly adopting an especially posh voice. "I thank you for your advice and will consider it. In the meantime I think we should shake on it."

Gaia and Leo looked aghast. Pi was holding out both her hands, fingers splayed, towards the lumiesse. A wry smile crept across Prumiane's face. She stepped forward and thrust her arms out, aggressively entwining her digits with those of the newest lumiette in Inverse. Prumiane suddenly let out a howl of protest, a shower of blue sparks erupting from both her hands. She recoiled in horror, regarding her still sparking digits, and not a little smoke.

Leo punched the air with glee. "Sparkin' got 'un!"

"I see that vile Cydermott sensibilities have already left their mark upon you. Make an enemy of me, and you make an enemy for eternity, Lightfoot!" Prumiane snapped her fingers angrily, both she and her acolytes leaving as quickly as they had arrived.

Leo's face flushed red with excitement. "Whoa, that was so sweet, 'un's me hero! You had us right going there, us really thought 'un had sold out look. And now we're proper friends, it's official." Leo went to hug Pi.

"Er, *mahalo*, Leo, *lawa kela*, dude." Pi turned her hand over. "Barnum Bratt's joke hand-buzzer superword, gets 'em every time."

"Are you okay?" said Gaia, grinning from ear to ear.

"Sure, you have to watch the ones who keep their Gammas on, they bite." Pi snapped her teeth.

"She can be pretty overpowering. I thought you did really well standing your ground like that. She's used to getting her own way, her whole family is."

"No probs, scanned it all before, eighth-graders can be pretty mean too." Pi shrugged her shoulders. "Feel sorry for her in a way, I mean why *did* they pick me anyway? I don't know anything about all this Inverse stuff, I didn't even know I was a computer till a moment ago. Did they just put names in a hat or something?" Pi suddenly noticed a gap in her pockets that revealed just a little too much school outfit, and hastily readjusted it.

"I never saw Prumiane so angry before." Gaia looked puzzled. "But the host-system is always chosen by the Queen personally, so she must have picked you for a really good reason."

But Pi was only half-listening, she was thinking

about all the things Prumiane had said, and wondering if she wasn't right after all.

Leo nudged Gaia's elbow. "Aye-up."

None other than the Queen herself was sweeping up the line towards them. She paused briefly and looked straight into Pi's eyes. She gently took one of Pi's hands and pressed a small object into it, folding her hand shut around whatever it was. The Queen looked momentarily as if she were about to say something, then smiled and quickly moved on, a train of lumixastras following in her wake. Well, that's how it appeared to everyone else, for she had indeed stopped to say something, but only Pi heard it. *"All will be explained later, my dear. I am your friend."*

Pi was quite taken aback by the unexpected message and its kindly tone, not to mention her first close encounter with royalty, and *alien* royalty at that.

"That's strange, I was sure she was about to say something to you. So what did she give you?" said Gaia.

"She did, she did speak to me! She said all would be explained later and that she was my friend!"

"Well, there you go, I *told* you, you'd been chosen for a good reason. Friends in high places – can't be bad!"

"And, it would seem, enemies," said Pi. "Anyway, enough of those idiots, look what the Queen gave me." She slowly opened her hand to reveal a small oval-shaped stone on a silver chain. A tiny head and shoulders hologram of the Queen glowed vividly inside its milky opalescence. All at once the portrait faded and was replaced by Gaia's smiling face.

Gaia recognised the object immediately. "Greenness, you've been given a royal security seal. Only senior Inversians, palace officials and keepers have those!"

"So what's it for?"

"It verifies that the people you're nearest to, or even talking to via psy, are who you think they are. You see the Queen moved away so her image faded, and now I'm talking with you, it shows me instead."

Pi held it near Leo. Gaia's image was immediately replaced by that of the scruffiest lumian in Inverse, stuffing his face with a handful of cookies. "Hmm, so what happens if the person I'm talking to *isn't* spec?"

"Well, their picture wouldn't show up at all, I think it just goes dark or something. It's a pretty special thing to be given, especially on your first day!"

Pi smiled to herself, put the chain around her neck and tucked the pendant safely away under her pockets. "Cryo, it's a keeper." Perhaps her appointment as host-system wasn't such a mistake after all.

"Well, I suppose we'd better change out of our glad-rags, Mottles." Gaia dug out a small card disc and looked deep in thought. After retrieving many mysterious objects from his own pockets, Leo finally managed to locate something similar, although, unlike Gaia's, it was extremely tatty and not a little chewed.

Pi's face lit up. "Ooh, what are those, Gaia?"

"Of course, you won't have seen pinwheels before."

Gaia showed her the disc. "It's a handy way to change program parameters, in this case clothes. These ones are *fashion* pinwheels."

Pi studied the printing on the disc. It had four concentric circles, each a different colour. They all moved independently, a small window in each displaying a tiny image of the selected clothing style on the card beneath.

"You just tweak each wheel around like this." Gaia began rotating the disc. "This disc is for *shoes*, my favourite, it's the biggest and best! Squillions of choices there, watch my feet whilst I move it."

Pi gasped with astonishment as Gaia's pointed green shoes morphed through an exotic variety of different styles, one after another. "Go back, go back one, yeah – yeah, now *those* are cryo."

"Watch this, it's got a colour disc, too." Gaia moved another disc and the chosen style stepped through a huge range of colours.

"Those would sell by the zillion back home. Lani would go nuts for one of those things!"

Gaia dug out another pinwheel. "And now my clothing disc. It's not this parsec's, Dad couldn't afford it. No Xillion or Asteron either, but it's got some great Zha Mu tops, watch." Gaia tweaked another circle on the disc, and the upper half of her sparkling green dress changed into a variety of natty tops. "What do you think? The Zha Mu jacket in celestine blue with, oh, let's see, some Niblos slacks in, um, burnt asteroid?"

"It's the new black," said Pi, laughing.

"Give 'un a twirl then," teased Leo.

Gaia obliged and Pi nodded her approval. "Wish I had something like that, I'm stuck with square central." Pi parted her pockets to reveal her regulation school outfit.

Gaia looked apologetic. "I'd lend you mine, but it only works with the original user. I don't have a spare one, sorry."

"That's okay."

"But we should be able to get you a new one at the palace, shouldn't we, Mottles?"

Leo looked uninterested. "S'pose, watches I look, what does 'un think of this, then?" Leo frantically spun all his discs at once using both thumbs, his entire ensemble stepping through ludicrous rapid-fire changes in every style imaginable, absolutely none of which seemed to match.

"He does this *every* time, you'd think he'd never seen one before." Gaia held out her hand. "I always end up having to do it for him." Leo made a face and reluctantly handed over his pinwheel.

The line ahead was diminishing quickly. It would soon be their turn to brave the trapdoor. Pi had more than a few butterflies in her stomach, not helped by the yells, screams and other strange noises echoing back up from those who'd already jumped. "Have you been down one of these before?" she asked nervously.

"Nothing to it look, 'un's a doddle!"

"Leo, you big fibber, how would you know? You've never been through a particle-accelerator in your life," said Gaia.

"Particle-accelerator? Isn't that mavvy?" said Pi, now only four lumixastras and one fat lumian away from the trapdoor. There was a blinding flash every time a guest dropped through it.

"You mean dangerous?"

Pi nodded.

"It's really quite harmless, just a bit of pushing and pulling. If you want, I'll go first and you'll see there's nothing to it," said Gaia brightly.

Leo walked forward to the trapdoor to watch a couple of the lumixastras plunge through. Like most of those before them, they let out a disconcerting shriek as they jumped. Leo sloped back to his place in the line looking distinctly pale, which did nothing for Pi's confidence. "Well okay, us haven't been in one quite this big look, but 'un's been in a collider."

"You mean the one we went on at Kapernikus Zirkus, that tiddly thing?" Gaia laughed. "That wasn't even a high-speed one. I've been in a real accelerator, they had one at my primary. They used lighthouses as portals, too, just smaller ones, that's all."

"I'll be fine," said Pi, fidgeting with her hands.

"This 'un might take a while," said Leo, with a smirk.

A very overweight lumian was now all that remained between them and the trapdoor. "That's Glong Succory, he's supposed to be on a strict diet but I saw him earlier stuffing his face with fluxcake," Gaia whispered.

"And deep-fried qubits and stuff. He was at *my* primary and all, 'un's just a greedy gizzard." Leo pulled out his pockets and puffed out his cheeks.

"Well, you can talk. I've seen you eat quite a few of those yourself, that's why you've got so many spots, Mottles."

"The guy is a little on the large side, I'll give you that," said Pi.

"Oh to dearie me, it's all taking to far too long." Peahi began nervously yo-yoing no fewer than six of his timepieces in acrobatic succession. Succory was clearly having problems easing himself into the opening.

"I knew it." Gaia clapped her hand to her mouth. "He's got stuck."

Leo began pointing and was about to burst out laughing at Succory's misfortune, when Gaia swatted him with her pockets.

"He is kinda going a funny colour, shouldn't we do something?" said Pi.

The whole queue was rubbernecking now, wondering why the line had stopped. A high-pitched whistling sound, like a jet engine warming up, began coming from beneath the trapped lumian.

"Oooh, something funny's happening to me feet!" Succory wailed, his face rapidly turning white.

"That's because his legs are already accelerating to the speed of light. We'd better help him before he spaghettifies," said Gaia pragmatically. "C'mon, Leo."

Leo gave her an evil grin. "Why don't 'un wait to see if 'un explodes like?"

"LEO – that's appalling!" Gaia grabbed him by the pockets and propelled him towards Succory.

"Alright, alright." Leo frowned and reluctantly rolled up his sleeves.

"How to thoughtful, any to assistance would be to greatly appreciated," trilled Peahi, quickly moving the rope cordon aside.

Gaia and Pi knelt down on either side of the unfortunate lumian and began pushing down on his shoulders.

"Uh, uh, uh!" Succory groaned. Leo sat down hard on Succory's head, bouncing up and down a few times.

"Leo, stop that and push properly!"

"I is pushing!" Leo switched his technique to knee-butting Succory's back.

"Oh to dear, now we are to running behind," Peahi squeaked, consulting no fewer than eight watches simultaneously.

"Pleeeeeeeease heeeelp meeeeeeeee!" Succory wheezed, the whining sound increasing to deafening levels.

"He's not going to explode, is he?" Pi shouted over the din.

"One to hopes not!" piped Peahi.

Flashes of light began to erupt from around Succory's waist, his hands clutching desperately at his rescuers' pockets as they continued to push down on him.

"Harder, Mottles, one, two, three, pusssshhh!" There was a huge flash accompanied by a loud bang, Gaia letting out a shriek as Succory's voluminous mass suddenly disappeared through the opening.

"I can't feel my legs!" Succory wailed, as all three of his rescuers fell through the trapdoor with him. Now they were *all* trapped, dangling upside down and stuck fast in the opening.

Leo struggled to free himself. "Let go of 'un, you wuzzock, or we'll all be proper manglefrazzled!"

Pi watched in horror as Succory's body began to elongate. His feet were already well out of sight around the first bend, and his knees were not far behind. "Why won't he let go?"

"I don't know!" Gaia yelled back, still trying to release Succory's grip on her pockets. "Wait, I can feel something funny happening." Pi watched with alarm as Gaia's arms began to stretch.

"Us is being spaghettified look!" bawled Leo, as his limbs elongated.

"It's okay, we're getting thinner, we're getting thinner, thinner is good!" Gaia squeaked, her voice increasing in pitch with every syllable. Their torsos began stretching all the way down to their waists.

"I'm *really* not enjoying this," Pi squealed, her voice now even higher than Peahi's.

Then without warning, they all flew through the

opening like corks from a bottle, hurtling on down the silvery chute. The jolt made Succory release his grip and he shot off, wailing and caterwauling ahead of them.

"I thought it was m-m-meant t-t-to b-b-be f-f-fun," Pi stammered, her voice returning to normal as she snapped back to size.

"It-it-it is-is-is, u-u-usually," Gaia stuttered, as they all tumbled over one another for the first few bends, rapidly picking up speed due to the total lack of friction.

Suddenly, they were catapulted into mid-air. "Hold tight, here comes the jump!" Gaia clung onto Pi's arm as they sailed over a huge gap in the slide, all wailing like banshees.

"Make 'un stop!" howled Leo, now the wrong way round and flying backwards.

"The accelerator, we're in the accelerator, hang on!" yelled Gaia.

The sides of the slide became a complete blur as they accelerated ever faster. Through loop, after loop, after loop of what felt like a giant corkscrew, until the rumble of the first section turned into a deafening high-pitched whine.

Pi felt an unnerving new sensation taking hold. With each rotation she could feel herself getting heavier. Their reflections were clearly visible in the mirrored walls; she could actually see herself turning into an unrecognisable blob. Leo began gurning like a madman, an ever more absurd visage grinning back at him with every loop, until he was so overcome by the G-forces, he couldn't even open his eyes.

Pi tried to speak, but quickly discovered it was impossible to even open her mouth.

She managed to make eye contact with Gaia, who could only raise an eyebrow in response. They had become total grotesques, with blobs for bodies and squashed fat heads, their mouths as wide as toads! Then mercifully, the G-forces gradually lessened and they slowly grew back to normal size.

"Thank greenness, we're slowing down! Just the spectrum analyser to go."

"The spectrum *what*?" yelped Pi.

Gaia didn't reply; she didn't need to, they were already in it.

Pi noted the colours. "Red, orange, yellow, green, blue, purple…" as the light around them changed, the slide becoming gentler. "Well, that wasn't so bad." The normal white light returned. Then she saw her reflection in the shiny metal. "Holofreaks – I've turned purple!"

"*That* would be the spectrum analyser," said Gaia, examining her hands, which, like the rest of her, were now a deep shade of turquoise.

"Us is down with the red thing, sparkin'!" Leo cackled, now so red, his face looked like a demonic strawberry.

"Purple's a really rare colour. That means you're a Prosperan but with Miranda rising," said Gaia.

"What does that mean?" said Pi, relieved the purple colour was fast fading from her hands and face.

"It tells you which elements you are. There are four in all, but you can get combinations of two or more. That's what you and I both share, combinations. That's what the accelerator does, it works out your virtual atomic weight, then it analyses the result. That's why I went turquoise. It means I'm Mirandan but with Ariel rising."

"And I'm proper Caliban, through and through. 'Un's fire and 'un's hot stuff." Leo gave her a wink.

Gaia sang, *"Fire, water, earth and air, find out which of these you share.* Just a silly little rhyme we used to chant as quantettes."

"Neat," said Pi. *"Fire, water, earth and air, find out which of these you share."* She and Gaia began chanting the rhyme over and over, Leo joining in as they sailed round the next few bends.

"It does mean we'll get streamed in the separator though."

Pi was about to ask Gaia what she meant, when the slide suddenly forked into four channels.

They all shot off in different directions, losing sight of one another; they'd been streamed! Then Pi noticed several other chutes combining with hers. She glimpsed some shapes in the corner of her eye whooshing into the chute behind her. She glanced back, expecting to see her friends. Indeed, two familiar faces were staring back at her, Lumixastras Magistry and Tantalo Zon-Cydes, both their faces bright purple.

"Cryocreeps!" She looked back to her front and

began to panic. She was fast approaching a straight stretch. The bright light of an exit lay dead ahead, marked with the legend 'Prospero' in purple. She was hurtling towards a turnstile and it was *closed*. Anticipating a collision with the metal bar, she shrieked, but at the last moment it flipped, and she passed through unscathed. The slide levelled out and she found herself outside, blinking in the bright daylight. The slide carried on down the wooden decking of an ornate iron pier, a seaplane moored off its end. Then she came to an abrupt halt. A small cast-aluminium box marked 'Inverse Airways' whirred and chimed, dispensing a small purple ticket. She staggered to her feet, snatched the ticket, and looked at it.

'Boarding Pass – Inverse Airways – ***Prospero – Seat 1A*** – Lumiette Epiphany Lightfoot – To Stargazey Pi – ***Outbound***'

TEN

PROSPERO?

Pi started down the pier as quickly as she could, unsteady on her feet after the dizzying experience with the accelerator. The sea was quite rough and the waves lashed around the ancient ironwork, great plumes of spray filling the air which tasted sweet like honey. She could see a mixed queue of firsties and lumixastras waiting at the pier's end. Some distance beyond them, a seaplane was bobbing up and down in the swell, its burnished aluminium gleaming so brightly she could barely look at it. A launch was ferrying passengers across, around twenty at a time.

She turned around, and began walking slowly backwards, marvelling at the gigantic size of the lighthouse, its body painted in alternate fat horizontal stripes of white and red.

"*Cooooeeee!*"

The psy made her jump. She espied a tiny figure with green hair jumping up and down and waving both arms in the air. It was Gaia and she was on the next pier to her right. Pi gave her a single, timid wave back, feeling somewhat inhibited as Magistry and Zon-Cydes were fast catching her up. She also glimpsed Leo's distinctive straw-blonde dreads being blown about on yet another pier to her left. The separator had certainly lived up to its name.

She spun around to walk on as before, but a sudden gust whipped the boarding pass right out of her fingers and it shot off down the wet planking.

"No no no!" She panicked and tried to run after it, but found her legs just wouldn't work properly. The boarding pass continued blowing away from her towards the ocean. "Don't you dare!" She shambled along, using the rail for support, crossing hand over hand as fast as she could. Then she remembered Gaia's handy code. "Goto param specific gravity – initiate!" She tried walking again, but it made no difference. *"Ole wale*, what's the deal with these gyro legs!"

The ticket was now lying in a wet patch of the decking some way down. It seemed to be stuck. Perhaps it would stay there until she could reach it? She continued stumbling along as fast as she could, then an especially large wave swept over the decking towards it. She heard laughter behind her. Zon-Cydes obviously found her misfortune very amusing. But worse, Magistry was storming down the pier towards her, his purple pockets flailing in the air like a great dark wing. His beard had spun itself into a single rope-like skein. He didn't look amused at all.

Pi shouted at the ticket again, *"E kali iki kikiki!"* as if it could hear her (and speak Hawaiian), looking on with horror as the surging watercode scooped it up and swooshed it further away. "Noooo!" she shrieked, as it hurtled towards the edge. Then, for no apparent reason it sailed straight into the air, flipping over and over in tiny somersaults.

She followed it as it flew right over her head, way up into the sky, then it floated down gently and landed behind her. She turned as quickly as she dared, for she was now feeling very dizzy. She didn't know whether to laugh or cry. Magistry was standing right behind her, the errant ticket grasped firmly in his right hand, the cluster of silver spheres at the end of his beard winding and unwinding themselves with a clickety-clack. He grimaced, exhibiting a disconcerting display of aesthetically challenging teeth.

"If you cannot MANAGE the fundamentals, Lightfoot, how shall you MASTER the esoteric, we wonder?" His rasping psy sounded simultaneously in her mind like a metallic echo, his whole demeanour suggesting a degree of simmering impatience.

Pi tried not to look at him as she timidly plucked the ticket from the seven long, pointed fingernails of his claw-like hand. It was like being near some kind of electrical transformer; her hair frizzed out in all directions, the air seemingly alive with static electricity. A deep humming sound seemed to emanate from him. Amazingly, the boarding pass was now bone dry.

Vapour had poured out of it like a chimney in the few moments it had been in his grasp.

"*Mahalo,*" she said timidly, not daring to meet his gaze. She then turned around, took a deep breath, and continued her rail-assisted progress as fast as her wayward legs could carry her.

"*My greenness, that was close!*" psy'd Gaia, who'd been watching the whole drama. "*If you're feeling dizzy, it's just the watercode. Try to keep your mouth closed. Try not to swallow too much.*"

Pi could still see her at the back of the queue on the other pier, but she was feeling far too giddy to respond. She could also see the distinctive figure of Higgs-Boson looming over her green-haired friend, and Leo was now chatting with the *Queen* no less. How did he manage that? If only there had been a friendly face on her pier!

After much wayward staggering, she managed to reach the end of the queue for the boat. Unfortunately, Magistry and Zon-Cydes were soon standing right behind her. She decided to block out their unwelcome presence by taking time to admire the amazing view, looking up from the Southern Polarity.

She could now appreciate the curiously inverted ocean properly. It rose upwards from the lighthouse in a magnificent concave hemisphere of bright turquoise watercode. She could clearly see the vast fleets of white sail, just discernible as ships at the nearest point, now she knew what she was looking at, although the more distant fleets were still indistinguishable from clouds as they neared the dark-blue band of the equator.

The watercode ocean dazzled and sparkled as it splashed around the pier's head. It seemed somehow more alive than conventional water, lit by the blinding disc of the sun overhead, still apparently unmoved from the midday position she had seen it in earlier. She was beginning to feel a little more at ease, the ticket safely in her hand, folded once over in a no-nonsense Lightfoot pinch, when she noticed a minor but troubling detail. A very jolly Inversian sailor in a bright blue beret with a matching pair of baggy blue pants, his smart Breton shirt in horizontal blue and white stripes, was loading the next group of passengers. The launch had a name, *Caliban*. She wasn't too bothered by this, until she noticed that the seaplane too had a name clearly painted upon its nose, also *Caliban,* the logo of an impish red figure astride a globe beside it. She took another look at her ticket, being especially careful not to lose it in the breeze. It clearly said *Prospero.* Even the sailor's cap-band said *Caliban.* If she was on the wrong pier, then surely she should say something?

The lumixastras in front of her had already leapt across the perilous gap to the launch, bobbing alarmingly in the rough swell.

The sailor's rough hairy hand was already extended impatiently towards her. "Look lively there, miss, we ain't got all day!" The sailor grabbed her hand and she was propelled into the boat like a rocket. "Stow yourself fast now, she's a bit fresh this nano."

A familiar voice sounded in her head. "*Have you met the Jack Tarrs yet?*" It was Gaia. Pi sat down quickly on the wooden seating and glanced over her shoulder. She could just make out Gaia's hand waving from a launch heading out to *Prospero*, surely the plane she should be on?

"*Think I just did, they're strong aren't they!*"

Magistry sat down next to her with a grunt, and she immediately faced back to her front, all her hair frizzing up on the side nearest him. So much so, it tickled the lumixastra's nose, making him snort with indignation. And if that wasn't bad enough, a particularly smug-looking Zon-Cydes had just plumped himself down right opposite her.

"*You won't last five nanos at this rate, Lightfoot, that's the second time you've annoyed Magistry – hah! We're betting your system crashes before we even reach the palace!*"

Pi looked at her ticket again. Surely she should be in the other boat going to the other plane like Gaia? There seemed to have been a dreadful mistake, and now she was stuck with these two dark souls. They probably had seats right next to her on the plane as well! It wasn't too late; one Tarr was doing a quick head count, the other preparing to cast off the line. This was her chance.

She waved her ticket as one of them brushed past. "Excuse me, sir, Mister Tarr, I think there might have been a mistake?"

The sailor grunted, snatched the ticket from

her hand and gave it a good once-over, all the other passengers looking on with amusement. He quickly handed it back. "Nothin' wrong there, missy, all in order. CAST OFF!" And with that, the line slapped across the deck, the other Tarr jumped aboard and they were off.

Zon-Cydes psy'd her right between the eyes. "*Oh there's been a mistake alright, you as host-system. I intend taking the matter up with Her Majesty as soon as we disembark. Your appointment is completely unacceptable!*"

Pi gritted her teeth and closed her eyes, feeling isolated and confused, although judging by the giddy look on some of the other passengers' faces, she was not entirely alone in feeling the ill-effects of all the watercode spray.

The seaplanes looked rather magnificent close up. They appeared to be Boeing clippers, a vintage seaplane from nearly a hundred years earlier, although quite why they had been adopted by this strange alien world Pi wasn't entirely sure.

They came alongside and she caught sight of her Magistry-modified hairdo in the Clipper's mirror-bright fuselage; it was practically an afro! One of Peahi's Grey cousins was standing in the doorway. He wore a natty flight attendant's uniform, complete with turret cap which clearly had the legend, *Caliban – Inverse Airways* on the band.

Soon, it was her turn to stumble up the tiny aluminium steps into the cabin. Inside, bustling passengers were trying to find their seats. There seemed to be some confusion, most likely a consequence of the watercode spray they'd imbibed.

Another Grey efficiently checked her ticket. "Welcoming you aboard, all the way forward please, F-deck." Evidently Greys all spoke in the same distinctive high-pitched voice.

Pi squeezed past some venerable types who appeared to be arguing over seating arrangements, their speech noticeably slurred. "Coming through, coming through – gangway!" she cried.

It seemed quite roomy, almost luxurious in the vintage aeroplane. The seats were covered in a rich red velvet plush with cream trim, and looked very smart. Then it struck her. These were Leo's colours, he was Caliban, so why wasn't he here? She strode as quickly as she could down the aisle towards the front, still a bit wobbly on her feet. Everybody there seemed to have found their seats and was either chatting, or reading the in-flight magazine, *I-Life.*

She glanced at her ticket. "Seat 1A. Hmm?" She was nearly at the front, it must be in the first row surely, perhaps a window seat? But all the front seats were taken, full of chattering lumixastras.

She showed her ticket to a kindly-looking lady lumixastra. "Excuse me, I'm trying to find seat 1A?" She was half expecting Magistry and Zon-Cydes to appear any minute and didn't want to hang around.

Some of the other passengers seemed to find her

plight amusing, but the lumixastra was quite helpful. "These rows only go up to C. It must be the upper deck, my dear," she said, pointing towards a curtained doorway. Pi thanked her, still suspicious of all the gossiping going on behind her back. Was she being set up?

She discovered a modest spiral stair which led up to another level. Once at the top, there was a bulkhead door with *F-Deck* stencilled upon it.

"That's what the attendant said, this must be right." Tentatively, she turned the door lever, half expecting to be confronted by the grinning countenances of her least favourite Inversians. She'd completely lost track of them since she'd left the boat, after all. Nervously she peered inside. Several voices rang out in unison, "SURPRISE!"

It was none other than Higgs-Boson, Gaia and Leo! Together with a mystery lumiette still wearing her GammaBanns quietly sitting behind them.

"Great hairy holofreaks!" Pi slapped her hand over her mouth.

Gaia and Leo jumped up from their seats. Higgs-Boson gave her a jaunty salute and handed her a clipboard. "Welcome aboard, Captain."

"*Captain!*"

"Quick, quick, show me your ticket!" said Gaia, the most excited Pi had ever seen her.

"This is it, sweetie, seat 1A, *Prospero*, it's official, you're the captain! Can you believe it?"

"*Negs*, I can't fly a plane! You crazy? I'm not even

on the right one! Look, it says *Prospero*," she jabbed her finger at the ticket. Then, on closer inspection, she noticed a small seat number on the back of the pilot's seat which said *1A*. Which, unlike all the other seats was purple, *her* colour. She looked closer. The word 'Prospero' was clearly marked there also. "But you were all on different piers going to different planes? And this plane is *Caliban*. It's totally lolo!" She began smoothing down her wayward hair.

"Just a little quantum entanglement, quite common, nothing to worry about," said Higgs-Boson, retrieving a bundle of headphones from a small locker on the back bulkhead. He began handing them round, then he produced a peaked captain's cap which he plonked on Pi's head at a very jaunty angle, giving her a fruity grin. "I say, suits you to a 'T'! The planes are somewhat prone to it, unfortunately, entanglement, something to do with flying through all those thought-waves. Quite harmless, just takes a bit of getting used to." He grabbed the back of seat 1A and pointed out of the port window. "You see *your* seat is from *Prospero*, which is right over there. Gaia's, on the other hand," he banged on the back of another seat further back in the cabin which was finished in green velvet, "is from *Miranda*, which is all the way over the other side. Whereas Leo and I are just plain old *Caliban*, hence the usual red plush. Ah, but I don't think you've met Lumiette Harbinger, otherwise known as Andomime, your co-pilot?"

The mystery lumiette nodded once. She was

wearing her pocket's hood over her head, and with her GammaBanns on as well, it was hard to see her face at all. *Her* seat was finished in royal blue.

"Now old Anders here, well let me see, the colour suggests," Higgs-Boson screwed his jeweller's eyepiece into his right eye. "Ah yes, as I suspected, another case of entanglement. Andomime's seat is from *Ariel*, where, I do believe, my good lady wife is installed, as it were. Now you'll be needing these." Higgs-Boson retrieved five miniature books from another small locker, flinging them in the general direction of the intended recipient as he checked the titles. "Navigator, Cydermott, yours, Leo; radio operator, Palinder, yours, Gaia; flight engineer, ah, that would be yours truly. First officer and co- pilot, Harbinger, there you go, Anders, and of course, last but by no means least, Captain Lightfoot! Has something of a ring about it, don't you think? Anyway, that's the old flight manuals sorted. Now you familiarise yourselves with these flicks whilst I verify the passenger manifest with the cabin crew, there's good fellows."

As soon as Higgs-Boson had gone Gaia dragged Pi over to the cockpit window. "You have to see this, come on, Leo, show Pi what we discovered!"

"You've no idea how relieved I am to see you guys!" said Pi. "I had Magistry and, and that Zon-Cydes guy on my tail, *all* the way since the separator."

"I know, I know, I saw them! Prumiane appeared right behind me after you and Leo streamed. She sent me some pretty mean psy I can tell you, but now we're all together again – this is so exciting!" Gaia did a little dance.

Leo retrieved a small brass object from one of his many pockets. "Yeah, 'un's got to gander this look, it's sparkin' bonkers." He drew the shiny brass cylinder out, snap snap snap; it was a collapsing telescope in three sections. He handed it to Pi.

Andomime seemed unimpressed. "Anybody would think you had never seen entanglement before." She began fastening her miniature manual into a strange device on her lap.

Leo ignored her. "'Un's got to get really close to the window mind, and look through me scope at *Prospero's* cockpit window, right over there… see 'un?"

"K." Pi took Leo's advice, squeezing herself into her mysteriously entangled seat, and put the telescope to her eye.

"Can you see it, the window?" said Gaia.

"'Un's got to keep a hand free to wave, mind."

Pi removed a hand from the 'scope and began waving. "K, so what am I looking for?" She could clearly see the left-hand cockpit window of *Prospero*, it was moored off the end of the next pier. She was amused to see there was somebody waving back at her. "Who is it? Are they like a friend of yours? Did you psy them? Only I can't see their face."

Leo and Gaia began giggling; Andomime sighed to herself.

"Okay, sweetie, keep looking, tell us what you see

now," said Gaia, as she and Leo pressed their faces against the cockpit window.

Pi shrieked with astonishment. "Holofreaks – it's *you* guys!" Both their glass-flattened faces were laughing back at her from *Prospero*, then she realised who was doing the waving. "It's *my* hand, it's *me* doing the waving!" She could hardly believe her own eyes! The length of the telescope stopped her from being able to get really close to the glass, but she could clearly see her frazzled hair and the end of Leo's 'scope.

"Don't work so well Anders' side, *Ariel's* out of sight mostly," said Leo.

Pi's gaze then fell upon another arresting sight. "So *that's* what happened to them. I can see Magistry and that creep Zon-Cydes a few rows behind him. But they got onto *Caliban* just after me. Does that mean they're *here*? Or *there*?"

"If you hold your focus upon either subject any longer they will become aware of your surveillance," said Andomime curtly.

Pi recoiled from the window and snapped the telescope shut.

"Mime knows about these things," said Gaia.

"She's the high-priestess of psy," whispered Leo.

"Well, I wouldn't put it exactly like that," Andomime stirred in her blue velvet seat. "They are in fact aboard *Miranda*, but their window seats are entangled with *Prospero's*. They were subjected to a quantum flip somewhere around the fuselage door as they entered

Caliban. It is all very simple." As Andomime spoke, her fingers gently flicked the air as if moving the beads on an invisible abacus.

Gaia looked Pi straight in the eye with a secretive expression, and used her most discreet psy. *"You have to understand, Mime's really bright, she's got an IQ of over five trillion to the power of seven! That's more than all the lumixastras from the Virgo Supercluster put together, and she's got the best error-correction circuits in the whole of Inverse!"*

"You're too kind, actually it is to the power of six point eight, but I aspire to improve my specification." Andomime continued using the device on her lap to zip through the flick-book automatically, mysteriously extending her index finger so it brushed past the pages one by one, apparently reading them by touch alone. Gaia sighed. She'd used her very best encrypted psy and it was still too leaky!

The immediate excitement over, and hugely relieved at being reunited with her friends, Pi began to take stock of the daunting array of knobs, sliders, dials and switches that liberally encrusted the flight deck. She looked sceptically at the tiny pale-blue book Higgs-Boson had given her. "That's skizer, it's even got my name on the cover, like they knew I was coming? Look. *Epiphany Lightfoot, Pilot's Manual.*" She flipped through a few of the pages. "I'm never going to figure this out. Why are they so crazy small?"

"They're *flick-books*, you'd be surprised, they pack a really big punch!" said Gaia.

"You just haves do this with 'un see." Leo brought his own miniature book up close to his eyes. They all had soft covers. Leo's had his name clearly printed on it too, only it was a navigator's manual and it was pale green.

"Then you has to scan 'un all in one go, like this look." Leo stared intently at the tiny book, using his thumb to flick through the hundred or so pages in a trice. "Hey, I'm a proper *navigator* now!"

"I feel so reassured," said Andomime drily.

Gaia waved her pale-yellow radio operator's book. "It's really easy, just do what Leo did, but don't blink whatever you do or you might miss something vital. Shall we?"

"So all I have to do to fly this plane is flick through this itty-bitty book?"

Gaia nodded. "It's like a download but on paper. C'mon, let's zip together." She waved her radio operator's manual provocatively.

Pi readied her funny little book in front of her eyes, as did Gaia, their thumbnails at the ready.

"On three then, one, two, *three!*" Leo swooshed his arm through the air like a race starter's flag, and Pi and Gaia flicked through two hundred pages as fast as a zipper. Pi made an effort not to blink; it must have been successful, for suddenly her head was filled with technical jargon and precise procedure for this or that desired aeronautical manoeuvre. Flaps, pitch, servos, gyros, altimeters, trim and throttles, she even knew what dynamometers and magnetos were for. She grinned broadly. *"Kupaianaha,* you guys weren't kidding, these babies really work! Feel like I could actually fly this thing now!"

"And I can operate a radio set, morse code, frequencies, bandwidths and everything!" said Gaia, spinning around on her navigator's seat.

Leo gave them a cheesy grin. "And us can plot 'un a course through the trickiest thought-waves to any point on the Inversian compass look."

"And I can hear footsteps on the stairs," said Andomime quietly.

"She's got this amazing hearing, it must be H-B. Quick, quick, action stations, chop, chop!" Gaia dived back to her desk.

"Action stations, action stations," Leo started impersonating a klaxon.

"Shhh, or he'll hear you, nanopoop!" Gaia swatted Leo with a rolled-up map. They raced to their seats like it was musical chairs, snapping their headsets over their ears and fumbling with various controls to appear busy.

The door slowly opened. "Only me." Higgs-Boson's face appeared. "Good Inverse, you do look industrious I must say, most impressive, top hole. We're still missing a lumiette according to our head steward; alas we cannot tarry a moment longer. So we'd best get this jolly old crate into the great blue yonder, pronto!"

"Roger, wilco," said Pi, familiarising herself with

the master throttles for the four huge eighteen-cylinder engines.

The radio suddenly crackled into life, making Gaia jump. She picked up the headphones, but immediately held them away from her delicate ears; a shrill voice was clearly audible to the whole flight deck. "It's Peahi from air traffic control, he says we're all clear for take-off."

The great lighthouse also doubled as a control tower. Peahi was apparently still up there, all alone, dutifully employed doing the 'second loneliest job in Inverse' according to Gaia. Andomime was about to tell them all what the loneliest job in Inverse actually was, but matters were now proceeding too fast for her to share this particular nugget of Inversian trivia.

"We've got clearance to go to position. Due to crosswinds, we have to taxi to one-eight-zero degrees so we can take off with the wind behind us," Gaia informed them.

"Navigator, plot a course for one-eight-zero degrees. First Officer, initiate pre-flight checks." Pi quite startled herself; the words seemed to come out of her mouth before she'd even thought about them.

Shrill squeaks began erupting from Gaia's headphones again. "We're holding everybody up, the tower is asking us why we haven't moved yet?"

"I'm on it, I'm on it." Pi had no idea why they weren't moving. She could see that *Prospero*, which lay just ahead of them, hadn't even started its engines yet. She suddenly sensed a hush on the flight deck and glanced around;

everybody was staring at her expectantly. "Alright, alright, I *know*, I'm ready! Actually, there is just one micro little thing. I lost my Gammas at the lighthouse. It's so bright, I can't see!"

Andomime swiftly produced a pair from her pockets. "I always keep a spare pair. They are graduated for everyday use; now may we begin?"

Pi put them on and checked her reflection in the instrumentation. "*Way* better, thanks. K, let's get this baby airborne."

Leo punched the air. "Sparkin'!"

Without pausing for breath Pi efficiently barked a sequence of commands. The others automatically sensed to whom these were addressed and complied with various actions.

"Cowl flaps open, mixture full-rich, flaps thirty degrees." She could hardly believe what she was saying. "Set altimeter, props to low-pitch, gyro off, start engines one through four, open throttles to thirty, starboard engines to full power."

Andomime diligently repeated all Pi's commands back to her, making various adjustments to the controls on her side.

A shudder ran through the plane as the enormous engines throbbed into life. The four giant props quickly accelerated until they made a steady 'thrum-thrum' sound. Pi knew that Boeing Clippers were notoriously difficult to manoeuvre in the water, especially in high winds, and that the rudder was useless at low speeds. The flick-book had candidly disclosed everything. Whilst taxiing, she could only turn *Caliban* by increasing power to the engines on one side or the other. Out of her starboard window she could see *Prospero* moving at last. All the planes were, now. Peahi was chirruping merrily away in Gaia's headphones, his shrill voice sounding a lot less anxious.

"*Miranda* has priority so we're third in the stack," Gaia informed them.

"Navigator to the bubble to check position." Pi knew she was supposed to say this, even though she had absolutely no idea what it meant, but Leo did and immediately complied.

"Aye aye, Cap." He jumped up, his telescope snapped out at the ready, and disappeared up a short ladder into a glazed dome atop the fuselage. It was used for general observations, and even for taking readings of the stars during night flying. He slid back down the ladder to the flight deck with his breathless report. "*Ariel's* taxiing up behind 'un fast, so 'un had better move off smartish look!"

"Wilco." Pi grabbed the control column with both hands. It was like a half-cut-down steering wheel made of aluminium and varnished wood. The controls were stiff, so stiff in fact that she could barely move them. "Workout! This thing's so heavy!" She grimaced with the exertion; it was taking all her strength to move it even a little. Finally, she managed to ease the throttle levers forward and the aluminium leviathan began to move.

The plane seemed sluggish at first. It rolled and

pitched in the heavy surf. Then, very slowly, it began to wheel around the lighthouse. Ahead, *Miranda* was lifting free of her watery bonds, sailing majestically into the air, leaving several rainbows trailing in her wake.

"Glorious sight, seen it a million times but it never fails to impress," said Higgs-Boson, leaning over Pi's shoulder and handing her a list of exciting oil temperature readings.

She barked yet more commands. "All engines full throttle, cowl flaps to half, pitch thirty-five."

"Roger, all throttles to full, cowls to half and pitch thirty-five," affirmed Andomime.

Pi glanced at her co-pilot. She was still wearing her GammaBanns, her hood well down over her head; how on earth could she see what she was doing?

Pi struggled with the leaden control column. *Caliban* was making poor progress through the choppy surf. "Kicker! I'm trying to get the nose up but the controls won't budge!"

Andomime was having the same problem. "I appear to be experiencing some resistance too," she said, with masterful understatement.

Pi scoured the instrumentation with her eyes. "What's with this gonzo plane? All the dials say we're already airborne and climbing – this is getting *ridiculous!*"

Higgs-Boson and the others leapt to their feet. "All hands to the pumps!"

"Sparkin' finally us gets to fly!" whooped Leo.

He and Gaia helped Pi wrestle with her control column, whilst Higgs-Boson similarly assisted Andomime.

Higgs-Boson puffed and strained, his face redder than ever. "I say, the controls are a tad on the weighty side today, aren't they?"

"What the freak's the matter with this thing!" Pi growled, still struggling to move the controls, even with Gaia and Leo's help. "Sixty-five knots, flaps ten degrees, we should have been airborne ages ago! It's got to lift, it's got to!" At last *Caliban's* nose began to rise. "Seventy knots, rotate, rotate!"

They pulled back on the columns with all their might. For a moment it seemed like nothing would happen, then all at once the plane stopped shuddering and they were flying over the wave tops.

Gaia bounced up and down with excitement. "We did it, we did it, we did it!"

Pi couldn't resist smiling. "That was just *so* cryo."

Caliban began climbing steadily into the bright Inversian sky.

"*Prospero's* proper up too look!" said Leo, pointing to starboard.

Gaia noticed the red communications light blinking at her console and she dashed over, holding the headphones well away from her head this time. "It's Peahi, I mean, the tower. *Ariel's* cleared the waves and is coming up on our port side."

Pi looked over to her left. She could see *Ariel*

climbing with them now, although she still needed Leo's help to move the unusually heavy controls, which he hardly objected to. But importantly, all four clippers were airborne, and three hundred Inversians were finally on their way to Stargazey Pi.

ELEVEN

OF TALL SHIPS

With Captain Lightfoot at the helm, *Caliban* gradually made a textbook ascent to the optimum cruising altitude. Pi felt the controls ease considerably; neither she nor the engines had to strain any more, although Leo was still hanging on to one side of her control column.

"Er, thanks for your help, but I'm liquid now – K?" Pi's right hand hovered above his to reclaim its place.

"Rodger dodger, us was going to check on our position anyway look." Leo's disappointment was obvious; playing pilot made his map, dividers and compass look extremely dull.

The climb had been impressive if rather slow. Boeing Clippers were lumbering beasts even when airborne, all the more so when fully laden. This had, however, allowed plenty of time for everyone to appreciate the view. The turquoise band of ocean around the now tiny Southern Lighthouse transfixed them all. The planes were about to reach the first of the great fleets of data-ships that plied the Southern Hemisphere. From their cruising altitude at twelve thousand feet, the sheer number of these tall ships was a magnificent sight to behold. Everybody, even Higgs-Boson, took a peek out of the window every now and then. Only Andomime seemed uninterested, remaining glued to her seat, GammaBanns and hood unmoved.

Then Pi began to realise that her navigator was spending more time than most simply staring at the view. "Leo, you're always at the window. I need intel on our position and you haven't given me a single map reference since we took off."

"Oh, er yeah, just making a quick visuals check look." He hastily scribbled something onto his clipboard.

Pi noticed it was upside down. She snatched it from his hands and gave it back to him the right way up. "That's like the fourth visual check in as many minutes, Bro. I need to know which fleet we're over, how far to the thingy-belt and everything."

"Fleets, thingy-belt, I'm, er, right on 'un, Cap."

Leo had no sooner disappeared than Higgs-Boson took his place. "If you like I could take the stick for a bit? Took my pilot's flick many parsecs ago. It would give you a chance to stretch your legs what."

Pi couldn't wait to take off her headphones. "Lifesaver, I could do with a break – thanks, Lumixastra." She took off her captain's cap and plonked it on his head, although it was a few sizes too small.

Once she actually got up and began walking around, she became acutely aware of just how much effort the rudder pedals had required of her. How her thigh and calf muscles ached! Inversian avatars were prone to some of the same limitations as real flesh and blood, it seemed.

She peeked over Gaia's shoulder. Her navigator's desk was littered with messages from the other planes; Gaia had none the less dutifully scribbled them all down in pencil.

Pi leant forward and played with the frequency dial. "I don't load this at all, how come you have these old American planes in Inverse?"

"Well, it's for the same reason we probably all look and sound like humans, and you recognise most of the things you've seen in Inverse so far."

"How do you mean?"

"It's part of the translation program we all use. It's not just for language, you see, it translates the appearance of everything else too. Think of it as like a really smart filter that cleverly manipulates the data you're streaming. It can change one of our alien chairs," Gaia swung round on her swivel seat, "or radios," she patted the top of the radio, "or even whole planes," she waved her arms around the cabin, "into the closest equivalent of something you'd expect to find on your own planet, which in your case is Earth, of course. So, because we're from different planets, the planes and everything will look quite different to me, then different again to Leo, something else again to Higgs-Boson – do you see?"

Pi toyed with her hair. "Think so."

"If you visited Inverse without your trans' program on, everything would look really strange, so would we for that matter!" Gaia laughed. "There are mirrors at the palace where you can see how you would look on different worlds; maybe we'll get a chance to try them?"

"K, but why does all this stuff look so old to me, then? I mean, don't get me wrong, it's cryo in a retro kind of way, but we're supercomputers, right? You guys have been around for like billions of years or something, so why isn't my trans' program creating something really futuristic here?"

"Oh that's easy, it's a quarantine precaution, to prevent infection by nano-viruses." Gaia took off her headphones and scratched her feathery hair. "My Generation-Father used to tell me scary stories about nano-plagues. In the old days, really sophisticated virtual systems sometimes got out of hand. So we only simulate simple technology."

"I get it, virtual valves and stuff are too gyro to make viruses?" Pi played with the oversized Bakelite controls on Gaia's radio.

"Exactly. We don't generally model anything more advanced than the transistor. Then there's the war, of course. Sorry, I really wanted to tell you about that earlier, but we were having such a nice time at the lighthouse, I – I didn't want to spoil things."

"That's okay, nobody wants to spoil the *lu'au*, right? So how's it going, the war? Only Lumixastra Magistry made it sound like you guys were losing or something?"

"Well, we are losing in a way. I mean we're quite safe here, but you see there's this virus, it's been spreading throughout Inverse for over a hundred million parsecs. It's infected over seventy percent of our domains now."

"*Seventy percent!*"

"I know, it *sounds* a lot, but Inverse is enormous, there are over two trillion galaxies out there! Although only a tiny fraction of those are part of the Quassu, it's still a significant number. And then there's the Ark, which would have made it bigger again, although that's had to be closed and everything."

"Ark? Like the one the Queen mentioned in her address?" Pi moved nearer so Gaia could whisper.

"Exactly, the Ark Of Worlds. It's a virtual archive of three hundred and fifty-six lost worlds, all their souls, terrestrial features, cities, flora, fauna, everything. *Urizen*—"

"Urizen!" Pi grabbed Gaia's arm. "Phabian trans'd me this psy, at – at the lighthouse. He said something about my dad being in a 'hidden domain', that I should repeat these creepy words and we'd be reunited. Some kind of code using the word Urizen."

"Oh my greenness, that doesn't sound right! Phabian, you say? Hmm, he wouldn't psy an insensitive thing like that. I expect it was just some stupid lumian, *pretending* to be him. It couldn't have been dreamboat."

"That's what I thought, just seems so weird is all."

Gaia dropped her voice again. "Urizen is our greatest enemy. He created something called the *Lucier* virus. He's using it to infiltrate Inverse so he can gain possession of the Ark. That's what the war is really all about, control of the Ark. Whoever controls that, controls most of the virtual universe, except nobody knows where it is now, it was closed so long ago."

"So you guys can do that? Archive whole worlds?"

"That's what quantum computers are for, sweetie, they must have built you for the same reason, your world must be dying."

"Dying?" A jolt of adrenaline ran through Pi. "I didn't even know I was a quantum computer till like a few moments ago. Now you're telling me they built the Quadriga because the Earth is up for the big lobo?"

"Maybe not right away, but perhaps the Earth is like Epheris, that's my homeworld. Our ecosystem is slowly failing, there's nothing we can do about it. We've tried everything, all we can do is to prepare for the inevitable."

Pi's thoughts began to race. "Well, I knew we had problems, you know, global warming, population growth and stuff. But I didn't load it was *terminal*."

"Well, maybe it's not terminal exactly, just a precaution? I don't have enough data about Earth to say really. It's not all bad news, there are lots of nice things about being a quantum computer too." Gaia flashed her feathery eyebrows. "Like hidden functions. Lots of ordinary-looking things have secret and exciting programs hidden in them." Gaia looked around for an example but nothing seemed to fit the bill.

Leo's head suddenly appeared over Gaia's shoulder. "Secret and exciting? What's secret and exciting then?"

"Oh I was just telling Pi about hidden functions and programs, you know, like, um... ships-biscuits." Gaia moved her swivel seat around so she could stretch her restless legs.

"Oh yeah, 'un's proper scrummy, they got this real thick chocolate on top of 'un look." Leo rubbed his stomach. "Boy, us could murder something chocolatey right now."

Pi suddenly realised she'd eaten nothing since the madeleine, and only half of it at that.

"You couldn't fill up on those, Mottles, you'd be all over the place, *literally*."

"'Un would be sparkin' laughing though wouldn't 'un!"

"So they make you feel gnazzy or something, like the watercode?" said Pi, secretly hoping that something, *anything*, coated in really thick chocolate might suddenly make an appearance.

"Not exactly, they're ship-shaped biscuits," Gaia started to draw an elongated oval in pencil on one of her report sheets, "divided into three like this." She drew two vertical lines dividing the oval into three equal parts. "Each biscuit is specifically named after a data-ship, you see?"

Pi shook her head. "Not exactly."

"I can't really draw that bit, the ship's name is embossed into the chocolate."

"K, loaded."

"You break off and eat whichever bit of the deck you want to land on. It really depends if there's a Tarr there or not. The biscuit's programming temporarily lets you take over one of the Tarr's bodies, or *shadowbodies* as we call them. You basically swap avatars, so the Tarr ends up in your avatar, and you end up in theirs!"

Pi began chewing the end of her hair absent-mindedly, and Gaia, her pencil, both their tummies rumbling like angry volcanos. All Pi could think of now was chocolate, *fabulous* chocolate. "So the Tarrs man all the data-ships?"

"Yep, they all look identical, striped tops, bell-bottomed pants, that kind of thing, unless you use a ships-biscuit to jump into one, of course, then your face appears instead of theirs." Gaia pointed with her pencil. "This is the bow, this is midships and this the stern. If you ate lots of them like Leo suggested, then you'd be whizzing about all over the place, from one Tarr to another. One fleet to another even! You'd probably be sick actually." Gaia looked pointedly at their navigator.

"So it's kinda like a shortcut?" said Pi.

Leo began sniggering. "Us could eat *loads* of 'un look, and 'un would be like—" He made umpteen rocket sounds and launched both his arms off in every imaginable direction, flailing them like a demented Catherine wheel until he fell over.

"*Leo*, we're supposed to act like flight crew!" Gaia grabbed his hand and helped him back up. "Well, I suppose it's like magic if you're not used to it, but really it's just a hidden function, a simple program. That's why it's safe, it can't turn into a virus or anything. There are lots of things like that in Inverse, as you'll see. Of course it helps if your Tarr isn't at the top of a mast when you switch, that could be really unfortunate!"

Pi now had it firmly set in her mind that she needed food, and as if in answer to her prayers, there was a brief knock at the bulkhead door. A Grey entered bearing a timely tray of delicacies. He wore a small badge on his tunic with the name 'Berin' upon it.

"Refreshments, does anybody to care for cordial and to canapes?" he squeaked, passing the tray around. Pi was so hungry she overcame her disappointment that none of it looked remotely chocolatey, and balanced as many of the tiny pastry-like snacks on her cupped hand as possible.

"Chutney whiskets, left over from the party," said Gaia, her mouth almost full. Leo tried to speak, but he'd crammed so many of the deceptively filling circular delights into his mouth, all that came out were clouds of pastry flakes.

"Funny name, but they're totes ono," said Pi, her grateful stomach rapidly filling with the tangy treats. "So what are they made of exactly?"

Gaia and Leo suddenly became very animated and both tried to speak. Gaia won.

"Eufranticus Eeeeekbeaker, he's the keeper of—"

"Extremely dangerous alchemy," added Leo, butting in. "'Un had this accident look." He tried to add more, but couldn't chew fast enough.

"He was working in his lab," spluttered Gaia, "cooking up some treats for himself. He meant to say 'whiskey and chestnuts' but his speech is strange at the best of times."

"He'd already had loads of cordial look," added Leo, his cheeks as full as a hamster's, "daft wuzzock said chutney whiskets in 'un's code by mistake. Now the palace larders are overflowing with 'un."

"And loads and loads and *loads* of waistcoat chutney!" laughed Gaia. "That's really difficult to use up, it's full of bits of old waistcoat!"

Pi was just grateful that the accidental recipe turned out to be so delicious, and didn't appear to contain any haberdashery whatsoever.

"If that will be to all?" Berin gave them all a smart salute and left the flight deck.

Pi knew *Caliban* was still on his gyro-controlled autopilot, Higgs-Boson and Andomime quietly keeping an eye on things until they reached the thought-waves. She decided this was her one chance to enjoy a little freedom.

"Have you still got that telescope, Mottles?"

"Sure, there you go, sweetstuff, oh, that's not 'un."

Leo began fumbling through his pockets, disgorging a large ball of superstring. Then, a pack of Plutonigum, whose liquorice flavour apparently had a half-life of fifty thousand parsecs. Next, a Drive-U-Barmy knife. It had so many different tools, it could take a quantum week to find the one you wanted. Finally, a joke black hole, still in its gaudily-illustrated wrapper, which promised *'a singularity of hilarity'* before he finally located the small brass tube.

Pi accepted the telescope and headed for the mysterious 'bubble' she'd dispatched Leo to earlier, intrigued to know exactly what it was. Leo, meanwhile, was trying to get the ball of superstring back into his pocket. It tended to unravel once the security label had been removed, which he'd just managed to do. Pi took one last look at the muddle he was getting into, Gaia trying to un-knot the unfortunate lumian with her nimble fingers, then left them to it.

She quickly ascended the short aluminium ladder to the oval perspex dome atop the fuselage. From here she could see *Caliban's* enormous wings and four monstrous engines as they ploughed on through the Inversian sky. Regarding Leo's telescope, she snapped it out to its full extent and put it to her eye, using it to study the magnificent panorama of endless fleets. The magnified view was hypnotic; she could clearly see the ships individually now. It was even possible to make out the Jack Tarrs, just visible as tiny specks clambering about the rigging on those nearest. She calculated that there must be tens of millions of them if Gaia's fleet numbers were correct.

Each fleet, for they were distinctly demarcated in horizontal bands, was interrupted by thin strips of turquoise ocean. The furthest fleet had a brownish hue. It was almost forty-five degrees to the vertical from their present position, so all the decking was visible, because the ships were actually on their sides at that point, relative to the plane.

She recalled the moment Higgs-Boson had uttered those fateful words *she was the host-system*, and the Queen's public affirmation of the same. She began mumbling to herself. "So I'm really supposed to be *generating* all this?" It seemed hard to believe. She stared at the mesmerising view, slowly becoming less aware of the deep thrum of *Caliban's* engines and their incessant vibration. Awed by the size and beauty of the extraordinary vista before her, she began to feel strangely connected to it all. *Your daddy says he loves you.* Alice's words came back to her. It was as if all her father's work were laid out before her. The watercode ocean, the data-ships, the thought-waves, even the great Quadriga itself, generating everything for as far as her eyes could see. The revelation took hold like nuclear fusion, and in no time she had a profound sense that her father was still alive. Mysteriously, this feeling was accompanied by something else. At first it was so faint, she couldn't discriminate between it and the noisy engines. But gradually she began to identify the sound as that of deep male voices, chanting in some unfamiliar tongue. More curiously still, the air suddenly became heavy with the pungent scent of sweet incense. Not even the delicious madeleine could compare with the effortless song now singing in her heart. She recalled more words from Alice's card: *time to find out who you really are.* Could the message have been from her father after all? She felt like she was on the verge of understanding it all, when an urgent voice sounded in her head.

"*Bridge to Captain, er, we need some help back here, over.*" It was Gaia, and she sounded stressed.

Pi snapped out of her trance. "*Roger that, on my way, over.*" She sighed and collapsed Leo's brass 'scope, clambering back down the short ladder to the flight deck. As her head bobbed up from the low doorway, the sight that met her eyes was beyond description. It was all she could do to stop herself laughing.

Higgs-Boson was fumbling his way through Leo's Barmy-Knife, dozens upon dozens of tiny chrome implements already protruding from both ends. And Gaia's hands were entirely covered by a writhing mass of Leo's dreaded twine, almost none of which now remained in the original ball. There was no doubt about it, her navigator, radio officer and flight engineer were now completely *entangled.*

"Holofreaks! What *have* you guys been doing!"

"Matters have got rather out of hand, I fear. Pernicious stuff, superstring," said Higgs-Boson, using his jeweller's loupe to diligently search through the multitude of tools on Leo's encyclopedic penknife, looking for the one tool in the known universe that could cut it.

"It's pretty bad," sighed Gaia. "I've seen it take days to release friends from less superstring than this."

"Weren't no fault of mine, 'un just come loose look," moaned Leo, the orange *Danger – Do Not Remove* sticker now firmly stuck to his nose.

"*Don't* try to help them or you will become ensnared too!" Andomime snapped, her head facing forwards, her hands still gripping her column tightly.

Pi had been about to put Leo's telescope back in his pocket. She stepped back immediately and thought better of it.

"Andomime is quite right," said Higgs-Boson. "It might be an idea to send for a steward; Greys are very adept appertaining to matters of digital dexterity."

Whilst the superstring continued coiling itself around them all like an anorexic boa constrictor, Pi leapt straight into her seat and plonked on her headphones. She snatched up the chunky microphone, on its very knotted coiled cable, used for talking to the cabin. She paused. She would have to be careful what she said, as all the passengers would hear it too. She didn't want to cause any panic by betraying the true urgency of their predicament.

"Say 'paging the steward' and ask for some refreshments," said Andomime helpfully.

"Yeah, good plan, *mahalo*." She cleared her throat

and pressed the red 'speak' button. "Paging the steward, er… I wonder if we might have some more whiskets on the flight deck?"

A moment later there was a knock on the bulkhead door and Berin appeared, looking apologetic. "I regret to say we are to fresh out of *whisk*—" He didn't get a chance to finish. Pi vaulted over to the bulkhead and practically pinned him to it, closing the door behind him in one swift motion.

"Shh!" She put her finger to her lips and used her eyes to direct Berin's attention to the six-legged, six-armed beast with three heads that now comprised the majority of *Caliban's* flight crew.

"Oh my to goodness gracious me," squeaked Berin.

"What's your name, soldier?" said Pi, vaguely recalling that commanders tended to ask such things of the rank and file before sending them on hazardous missions. Berin tapped his name badge and gave her a nervous grin.

"I *know* it's… oh never mind." Pi raised her eyes. "I'm told you might be able to like untangle these guys?"

Berin removed his cap and rolled up his sleeves. "Leave it to me to Captain, I'm not to called *Berin The Untangler* for to nothing."

He flexed his bony fingers until they popped, like a safecracker about to tackle a combination dial, then waded fearlessly into the mire that was unwound superstring.

"I think you had better see this, Captain." Pi

detected an uncharacteristic tremble in Andomime's voice and leapt back into her seat. She peered through the window and swallowed hard. The last fleet was fast disappearing beneath them; ahead, the sea looked completely black. An impenetrable wall of watercode had filled the horizon as far as the eye could see.

TWELVE

TO THE GATE BUOY

They had reached the thought-waves and Pi was shocked at just how monstrous they were.

"Oh!" She then uttered a word two syllables shorter than *shinola*. "We're going to need those maps like yesterday, guys! I *really* need those maps for the equatorial-belt *wikiwiki!*" Her voice betrayed a note of panic; she couldn't take her eyes from the window.

Leo tried to reply, but the superstring was already after his tongue. "Mavigation thable!"

"*What?*" yelled Pi.

"NAVIGATION TABLE!" Higgs-Boson, Gaia and Berin exclaimed as one, which, due to their natural ranges, managed to span some five octaves.

"We'll try to sort out coordinates, you concentrate on the flying!" Gaia yelled back.

"K, but make it quick!" Pi glanced round, alarmed to see all the red activity lights on Gaia's radio were flashing. "And something's up with the comms, best spec it out!"

Gaia peeked out from beneath Higgs-Boson's pockets. "Greenness! All the other planes are trying to contact us!"

"Alas, that will have to wait. Our priority must be to sort out our route. Let us hobble across to navigation as best we can, chaps," said Higgs-Boson.

They began shuffling with tiny steps towards Leo's station and stared at his navigation table. He really hadn't been doing a lot since take-off. Instead of finding already prepared maps, flight plans and coordinates, calculated, drawn and noted, there were just endless doodles of spaceships, rockets and an unflattering, yet recognizable, portrait of Higgs-Boson himself, complete with heavily-patched pockets.

"I say, definitely caught the old nose," he said graciously.

Gaia looked quizzically at Leo. "Did you actually *read* your flick-book, Mottles?" Berin's map-shuffling revealed yet more caricatured lumixastras, Magistry amongst them.

"Er, of course 'un did, you saw us, stupid."

Gaia stared at him, well, as best she could, as they were now sideways on to one another. "You're sweating, and you only ever call me stupid when you're hiding something!" Gaia asked Berin to retrieve the navigator manual. In a trice, Berin's two opposable thumbs were poised ready to launch the flick-book's pages before her eyes.

"All set... go." The whole panoply of bearings,

longitudes, latitudes, sextants, cartography, coordinates, computations, degrees, observations and calculations filled the lumiette's feathery green head. Well, they would have done.

"It's blank!" she cried, blinking with disbelief at what she'd just seen, or rather what she *hadn't*.

Berin hastily opened the book at a dozen random pages. They were all blank save for a couple of pages about utilising the observation bubble. The only thing Leo had actually managed to do.

Gaia looked angrily at him. "Leo! Why didn't you *say* something?"

"It's not 'un's fault look, us just wanted to stay on the flight deck with you lot that's all."

Higgs-Boson furrowed his brow. "Misprint, happens occasionally, slightly troubling as I don't believe we have another copy. We'll just have to create a watermap ourselves. Seen it done enough times, should be able to remember how it goes if the old memory banks serve."

Berin was immediately on the case, retrieving great armfuls of large, rolled-up charts.

"Now we have to lay the correct one in the tray, but which one perchance?" Higgs-Boson quietly surveyed the confusingly large pile in front of them, his right arm fighting against the elasticity of the superstring as he tried to pensively rub his chin. Berin began unfurling a few maps, clipping their corners to the desk, so they would stay flat for further examination.

Gaia looked reproachfully at Leo. "Because some clever clogs failed to note *any* coordinates, we've no idea where we actually are! So we don't even know which map we need, do we!"

Fortunately, Andomime's amazing hearing picked up on all this. She used her most discreet psy, so as not to alert Pi.

"We departed at exactly ten-zero-nine hours, at one-eight-zero degrees. Allowing for mean acceleration to level flight, headwind, crosswinds, the coefficients of drag, times distance to cruising altitude, I calculate we are in map quadrant eight alpha, square B9."

"Map eight alpha, map eight alpha!" Higgs-Boson and Gaia sounded like two old macaws. Berin scrabbled through the huge sheets of heavily varnished paper, Higgs- Boson looking the most excited he'd been since his last glass of cordial. Berin quickly found the desired map and, using four ship-shaped paperweights, made it lie flat in the shallow glass tray. The cabin suddenly darkened.

"Great hairy holofreaks!" yelped Pi. "We're running out of time 'n' sky, guys!"

The unrelenting cliffs of lead-grey watercode now towered over them.

Leo began chanting nervously. "Through and around, through and around, through and around."

Pi noticed there were no fewer than six red lights flashing at Gaia's station; the other planes were trying to reach them on the emergency channels as well. There was nothing for it, they would have to respond. She yelled over her shoulder, not daring to take her eyes off the waves. "Hey guys! Something's up with the radio! Today would be good!"

Gaia looked across. "Greenness! It looks really serious!"

Higgs-Boson sighed deeply. "Oh very well, to the radio, chaps."

They abandoned the navigation table and sidled over to the radio like a six-legged crab, Berin fighting against the superstring, trying to get the headphones on Gaia's head without success.

Gaia groaned. "Hopeless, I can't even move my hands!" She looked at Berin imploringly. "It might be easier if you used my flick, it's on the desk right there."

"I see the to problem," he said chirpily, "not a to problem for Berin." He picked up her navigator's flick-book and zipped it past his eyes. Moments later, he was wearing the headphones and working the radio controls like an old hand. "*Miranda* says we have to follow her towards the to lightship *Scylla,* and that we have to keep an eye out for something called the to Gate Buoy. *Prospero* and *Ariel* are to having extreme to difficulties manoeuvring to apparently."

Pi seized on this navigational crumb. "This Gate Buoy, what's it look like, where is it – what is it?" She stood up in her seat trying to peer down at the ocean, desperate to catch a glimpse of something, anything.

She watched anxiously as *Miranda*, which was a

half nautical mile ahead, dove suddenly and banked to starboard. She tried to push her right rudder pedal and the column forward to follow her, but neither budged so much as an inch, and they were fast running out of sky. "Oh guys! We're flying straight into a whole hairy *cliff* of code, we have to bank right *now*, over!"

"Once more unto the breach!" Higgs-Boson boomed, dragging Gaia and Leo back to the controls. Berin leapt across to join them. Everybody lent a foot to Pi's right rudder pedal, and pushed the column forward simultaneously. *Caliban* immediately began to dive, and banked hard to starboard, just as *Miranda* had done. The view changed dramatically; the timely manoeuvre had been successful, setting a new course *parallel* to the wavefront. As *Caliban* followed *Miranda* in search of the lightship, *Prospero* appeared to mimic *Caliban's* every move and kept pace with them off their starboard side.

"Cutting things a bit fine, but well done, chaps, at least this buys us some time." Higgs-Boson's exuberance was short-lived.

The ever vigilant Berin had noticed something else. "I, I think there may be a to-to problem wi-wi-wi-with to-to *Ariel!*" he piped, pointing a trembling finger out of the port-side window. At that very moment an alarm sounded at Gaia's station. It was a *Mayday*, and it was on *Ariel's* frequency. Berin leapt across, his grey skin turning white as he listendd to the message. "Co-pilot... controls... b-b-b-bank... d-d-d-dive... hard... s-s-s-starboard to-to-to *NOW!*" His voice was so shrill it was little more than a whistle.

Every available hand seized Andomime's control column and executed a drastic dive, simultaneously stomping on her right rudder pedal with every foot they could muster. If anybody had just walked in, they would have concluded that *Caliban's* entire crew had completely lost their minds. It looked for all the world as if they had decided to play *Twister* instead.

The effort required was no less strenuous than that employed to move Pi's controls, but their determination carried the day, and the controls eventually moved, Ariel making an abrupt banking manoeuvre at the exact same moment, and diving out of harm's way. Yet *Caliban* continued to hold exactly the same course as before, as if nobody had so much as touched anything. What was going on?

Pi came to a long-overdue conclusion. "The planes. They're *completely* freakin' entangled, aren't they?"

"I fear the entanglement issue may be more extensive than just the seating arrangements," mumbled Higgs-Boson, apologetically.

"That is what the other to radio operators were to saying, but I didn't to believe it," trilled Berin, finally able to unburden himself.

Andomime stirred in her seat. "There were a number of indicators if you think about it. Neither *Prospero* nor *Ariel* took off from the Southern Lighthouse until we did. They both struggled to get airborne until we did.

Caliban's controls were unusually heavy then, *and* we have only been on a straight level course since that time, which required no great effort."

Pi was not amused. "So we've been flying *three* planes at once! And now, I suppose, we'll have to fly *all three* of them through the thought-waves as well? *Ole wale!*"

"What does *'ole wale'* mean exactly?" said Gaia.

"Useless!"

"Ah."

Nobody spoke, all six of them frozen in a bizarre array of poses that would not have shamed a contortionist.

"Would it be too much to ask for the acrobatics to be kept to a minimum?" The Queen's psy sounded in everybody's head. She was indeed aboard *Ariel*, and had obviously worked out exactly what was going on.

"Hello, my sweet, why of course, I do believe we are on top of things at last," psy'd Higgs-Boson, nervously.

A tinny voice crackled from Gaia's radio. *"Miranda*, Gate Buoy sighted, *Scylla* two miles ahead. Maintain height at four thousand, bank hard to port, follow her lead." Berin had cleverly left it on 'speaker' so he wouldn't have to keep running back to it all the time.

The message came not a moment too soon. Pi could clearly see not only *Miranda* making a banking turn to port ahead, but the first of the lightships, *Scylla*, over which they were supposed to make this manoeuvre.

She sighed heavily. "Right, everybody back at my

controls. *Scylla* sighted, we're making a turn to port now apparently!" Wearily, she hauled herself into position, the others joining her, struggling to make the best use of the cramped space.

Higgs-Boson caught a glimpse of a lightship far below. "Resplendent in a new coat of paint since I last saw it."

"Indeed to, Lumixastra," trilled Berin, thwarting the superstring's attempt to go up the lumixastra's nose.

Pi peered down. She could see *Scylla* clearly now. It was a modestly-sized steam vessel with a single funnel, her powerful light standing proud atop a steel tower of red and white amidships.

Leo's eyes were sharper still, spotting flashes of gold coming from the water a half-mile off the port side. "There's 'un now look, that must be the Gate Buoy!" Beyond this, the otherwise impenetrable thought-waves appeared to actually part slightly.

Gaia struggled against the machinations of the superstring trying to see too, but without success, completely stuck to Higgs-Boson's back and facing the wrong way.

"Oh, this is just *so* frustrating!"

The essential course corrections were quickly effected on the entangled controls, all four clippers at last heading towards this precious gap in the thought-waves. It really didn't look that wide. Pi decided to extricate herself from the others, not least because she could feel something trying to snag itself around her ankle. She snatched up Leo's spyglass and focused it upon the gleaming buoy, espying a large golden arrow atop its red bulbous body. As it bobbed up and down in the surf, the arrow wavered slightly in the breeze, but there was no mistaking the direction it was pointing in: a dark cleft between two gigantic thought-waves. She held the spyglass as steadily as she could, studying the narrowness of the opening. "Houston, I think we have a problem."

"The formation, ideally it should be single line," said Andomime intuitively.

"Exactly, there's not enough room for us to fly three planes abreast in there." Pi snapped the 'scope shut. "We're going to have to reduce *Prospero's* airspeed and line him up behind us, then do the same for *Ariel*." She began quickly making adjustments to the throttles.

"Ah yes, follow my leader," said Higgs-Boson, sizing up the problem for himself.

"My prediction algorithms suggest this will not succeed," said Andomime abruptly.

"Spec me, gamma-girl!" Pi's voice betrayed a note of panic, the chasm was now only nanos away.

"Yes, do expound, Andomime dear," said Higgs-Boson, clearly fearing some very unsavoury aerobatics might suddenly be called for.

"It will not be possible for the last three planes to move from line abreast to line following, due to the entanglement issues," Andomime coolly informed them.

Sure enough, both her own and Pi's attempts to change

formation quickly illustrated the problem. No matter what they did, they could neither accelerate, nor throttle back the other planes, without similarly affecting their own. This meant their positions relative to one another remained *exactly the same*, no matter what they did. They were trapped, flying three abreast behind *Miranda*.

"Quickly, guys, I need to know like *yesterday*. Do we or don't we have enough room to make it?"

Higgs-Boson and Andomime stared rigidly ahead like surveyors' theodolites, using their best computational powers to calculate the odds of clearing the rapidly approaching chasm.

"If the outer planes bank to their maximum, and we close in as tightly as we dare, the wing-tips will still impact the sides of the waves," Higgs-Boson said ponderously, struggling against the superstring so he could scratch his nose.

"Ariel's throttles are synchronised with *Caliban's,"* said Andomime, "but not the column or pedals on my side. We cannot change her speed, but we can change her position. We could bring her much closer, and make her dive beneath us to create the necessary clearance, if *Caliban* and *Prospero* bank as well."

"We have a winner!" said Pi.

Andomime moved into position to allow the others to join her for more *Twister*-style flying.

"So we would effectively be only two abreast and at an angle?" said Higgs-Boson, now calculating the odds of annoying his wife as beyond question.

"Okay, team, I've heard enough," said Pi. "Execute thirty degrees to port, *Prospero!*" All six crew obediently thrust a foot on the left hand rudder pedal.

Immediately *Caliban* and *Prospero* banked in unison, everybody grabbing the back of Pi's chair to avoid piling up against the port window. They then had to fight the steep angle to reach Andomime's seat, and complete the same adjustments on her side.

"*Ariel* bank thirty, flaps twenty-five, left rudder hard forward, execute dive!" Pi yelled.

The engines exchanged their steady hum for a noisy whine as the extreme manoeuvre stressed the propellers.

"The lumixastra's so heavy!" wheezed Leo, as he and Gaia pushed Higgs-Boson towards Andomime's seat.

"Come on, come on!" shrieked Pi, as the watercode chasm loomed. "We're not going to make it! We're not going to make it, guys, we're still too wide!"

Higgs-Boson shook his head. "Oh dearie me, I fear my good lady wife will have something to say about *this*."

Ariel banked hard, then swooped beneath them in a drastic dive. It was just in the nano of time. All the three planes sailed over the Gate Buoy, and straight into the chasm, plunging the flight deck into complete darkness, *Caliban's* and *Prospero's* wingtips practically skimming the near vertical walls of the churning waves on either side.

"Well, in all my to y-y-years, I've n-n-never known the to-to p-p-p-planes to be s-s- s-so en-en-entangled.

I think I'd b-b-b-etter attend to the to w-w-watermap," stammered Berin, quietly absenting himself, his normally grey skin now completely white.

Pi hastily removed her GammaBanns and peered up at the monstrous waves. She was struck by two things; there was the familiar sweet smell of watercode again, but also something new, a rumble as deep as an earthquake.

Leo gawped up at the sheer cliffs of 'code. "Gor, listen to 'un sparkin' thunder."

"I'll be happier when we're safely out the other side, it's a bit dark and eerie in here for my liking," said Gaia.

"Second that," said Pi, switching on all the cabin lighting. Yet as she and Andomime held the controls steady, following the gentle curve of the great grey walls on either side, she felt uneasy, as if they really were now in the presence of some nameless dark *force*.

THIRTEEN

THOUGHT-WAVES

After the narrow confines of the initial gap, the channels between the immense waves widened sufficiently for Pi and Andomime to level out. Now they were able to comfortably fly two abreast, *Ariel* flying just beneath them. Ahead, *Miranda* acted as a lodestar, guiding them onwards through the labyrinth. Pi felt apprehensive. All the planes were using their powerful searchlights to illuminate the gloom, but *Miranda* seemed to be gradually pulling away from them. Every time they lost sight of her around the curving walls, it seemed to take longer and longer to recover visual contact again.

"Can't we radio *Miranda* or something and ask her to reduce her speed?"

"Radio communication is not possible in the wave-belt," said Andomime drily.

"What, you mean we can't even talk to the other planes in here?"

"That is correct."

Pi glanced over at Gaia's radio. With the exception of a green 'standby' lamp, all the lights were now dead. "I know, we can use psy. I'll bet you're really good at that, aren't you?"

Andomime turned, a stony look on her face. "In normal circumstances my psy rating is excellent, it is true. Regrettably, thought-waves produce an electromagnetic interference that prevents even psy from functioning correctly. In effect, we are in a period of radio silence until we reach the other side of the wave-belt." Andomime returned her attention straight ahead.

Pi did a quick mental calculation of her own, coming to a solid Lightfoot decision. "I'm gonna need that flight plan *wikiwiki*, guys!"

"Just a nano, coming right up!" Gaia shouted back, as if all Pi wanted was an order of fries.

"She'll hit the roof with 'un if she finds out about that stupid manual," whispered Leo.

Gaia looked him squarely in the eye. "She'll hit the roof when she finds out you didn't tell us, you mean."

"We are a little pressed for time it is true, so sorry I cannot lend a hand, dear fellow." Higgs-Boson drummed his fingers on the map table whilst Berin retrieved several large bottles from a cupboard beside the navigator's desk labelled: '*BLUE WATERCODE – FOR NAVIGATIONAL USE ONLY*'.

"Now you should follow this closely, chaps, we're about to make a watermap. You never know when this might come in handy." Higgs-Boson adjusted his position so Gaia and Leo could peek from under his arms, Berin poised ready to pour the liquid into the map tray. "Might as well stick them both in, usually takes a brace if I recall correctly."

Higgs-Boson gave the nod and Berin filled the shallow tray to the brim. Immediately the clear blue liquid came to life, magically transforming the contours of the map into a living thing, the grid of the printed paper just visible beneath. A belt of dozens of miniature thought-waves now stretched across its middle. These were banded on either side by calmer zones representing the Sea of Serenity and the Expectant Ocean.

Leo looked impressed; maybe navigation wasn't so boring after all. "So *us* could have done that if 'un's stupid flick had been printed right?"

"Never mind, Mottles, I'm sure you'll get another chance," said Gaia.

Berin unscrewed the top of a small jar labelled 'LIGHTSHIPS' and tipped two tiny black and white objects into Leo's hand. His face lit up. "Whoa, are they tiny boats look?"

"They are indeed, dear fellow, map-makers' lightships for the purposes of," beamed Higgs-Boson. Berin reeled off a few feet of red cotton from a bobbin and quickly bit it off. "Should be all done in a jiffy," Higgs-Boson added, waggling his fingers with excitement.

"Getting a little concerned back here, how's that plan coming along?" yelled Pi. *Caliban* had caught up with *Miranda* once again, but there was another big curve coming up.

"Almost done!" Gaia exchanged a nervous glance with Leo, as Berin deftly threaded the cotton through a tiny metal hoop on the black ship's bow and tied it off, clearly working as fast as he could.

"Not a to nano to lose," he trilled. Then he did the same with the other end, attaching it to the white ship. Berin gently set the two ships adrift on the near side of the watermap.

"Watch closely, chaps, they're at the starting gate, and they're jolly old off." Higgs-Boson leant forward to get a better look, forcing Gaia and Leo to stoop awkwardly.

The two tiny ships were gently moved into position by the watercode. Almost immediately, the white one disappeared into the miniature thought-waves, dragging the thread behind it.

"Now the nearest vessel is, of course, *Scylla*," Higgs-Boson began, Berin helpfully doing all the pointing, his tiny mouth set in a cheesy grin. "See how she remains stationary whilst the other vessel, *Charybdis*, negotiates the wave-belt," the lumixastra continued.

Gaia and Leo craned their necks, marvelling as *Charybdis* began wending its way through the miniature thought-waves, the tiny model's every move shadowed by Berin's bony finger. Every now and then it would disappear into the tube of one of the tiny blue waves, only to emerge at the other end like a train from a tunnel. Finally, it reached the flat calm on the other side of the wave-belt and stopped, the red thread neatly showing the winding route between the two. Berin smiled as if he expected applause.

"Well, there you have it, I make that three through, the rest around, can't quite tell without the old eyepiece!" Higgs-Boson chortled.

"I reckon them's three through, the rest around and all," agreed Leo.

"Guys, what *is* going on back there?" Pi had seen Gaia's promised 'nano' come and go several times over.

Gaia didn't dare reply.

"She's bound to find 'un out if 'un don't get cracking look."

"Not whilst Berin's on the to bridge!" Berin jumped up onto the desk and grabbed a pencil, twitching his head like an automaton as he studied the watermap. He quickly jotted down all the coordinates of the red thread, as it wound this way and that over the grid beneath.

"I say, stout fellow, give the chap a medal!" said Higgs-Boson, groaning as he stood back up. "Oh dearie me, the old back isn't what it used to be."

"All to done, Lumixastra, I've noted the to route to *Charybdis*, shall I to take it to the to captain?" trilled Berin, sticking the pencil behind his ear and clambering off the table.

"Best say it's from Leo, mum's the word and all that." Higgs-Boson gave Berin an exaggerated wink.

"Under-to-stood, Lumixastra." Berin tapped the side of his tiny nose twice and bounded over to Pi. "Navigator Cydermott's report, Captain, he's a bit to tied up just now, so he to asked me to deliver it."

"Hey, look at that, thanks, Berin." Pi took the chart and quickly assimilated the details. It all seemed to be there; finally they had a route to *Charybdis*. "*Mahalo*, Leo, good job!" Pi turned in her seat and gave him a big smile, which was nervously returned.

"Just keep smiling, she's happy," Gaia whispered from the side of her mouth.

"All's well that ends well, no need to rock the boat unnecessarily," said Higgs-Boson.

"Phewff, that was a shaver, 'un thought us was proper busted look."

Pi hastily wedged the map into a clip on the controls in front of her. Negotiating the equatorial-belt seemed quite straightforward now. Hopefully, she wouldn't even need it, since all they had to do was follow *Miranda*. Then an unexpected shaft of light illuminated the dark canyon ahead, filling the cabin with a bright yellow light.

"According to Leo's map, we're about to go through our first thought-wave, guys!" said Pi excitedly. She turned to Andomime, expecting her to respond, but she just sat there with an anxious look on her face. Somewhat unnerved, Pi decided to try and engage her co-pilot another way. "So, what *is* the loneliest job in Inverse? Y'know, you were talking about it earlier. Is it anything to do with lightships?"

"It has nothing to do with lightships, they are completely unmanned," snapped Andomime, looking more anxious than ever.

"K, what's the glitch? I can tell something's eating you. Is there something I should know?" Pi gave her a smile.

"Nothing is *eating* me, my prediction algorithms suggest there is something dangerous ahead, that is all."

Pi's smile evaporated and her heart began to race. "What! What sort of dangerous? Do you know what it is?"

"Prediction algorithms rely on some of the same systems used by psy. Because their functioning is impaired in the wave-belt, I cannot specify the exact origin of the threat."

Andomime now looked the most disturbed Pi had ever seen her, making her feel distinctly nervous now too. She decided that she needed her crew back, untangled and *fast*. "How's the war going, soldier?"

Berin paused from his exhaustive exploration of Leo's Barmy-Knife, searching for the hopelessly elusive superstring-snipper, which was allegedly in there somewhere. "Berin still to untangling, Captain!" quietly cursing as each blade he extracted was of the wrong type. "Fidget, didget, widget, smidget, gidget, midget, pidget, squidget—"

Higgs-Boson continued to squint through his most powerful ocular, trying to help as each miniscule, metallic wonder-tool was extracted. "Interminable business, could be here a hundred parsecs at this rate, a process of elimination I fear!"

"Wasn't there some kind of instruction manual with an index or something, Mottles?" said Gaia.

"Left 'un at home, didn't us, weighs a ton look."

"Yes, but not in your pockets! Didn't you scan it as a file in your memory banks?"

"Too big for scanning, ain't 'un."

"Too much like hard work you mean." Gaia shook her head and sighed.

Miranda's burnished fuselage suddenly flared into a hundred dazzling facets, throwing splashes of light in all directions like a mirror-ball in a dance hall. Some of these flashed through *Caliban's* windows, making everybody look up.

"Not far now to our first incursion *through* a thought-wave, chaps!" Higgs-Boson boomed excitedly.

"Whoa, that's proper nebula, that is." Leo's face lit up, literally, as the source of light suddenly revealed itself.

"Yes, I suppose it is nebula-ish," said Higgs-Boson, desperately trying to scratch his nose without success.

Pi's eyes widened even as her pupils narrowed; it was a mesmerising sight. An enormous cave of blinding golden light had suddenly enveloped *Miranda*, and the same was about to happen to them. "Well, at least it's wide enough, for all of us I mean." For a moment she almost forgot about Andomime's dire prediction.

"I can't wait to see what's inside," said Gaia, as she and Leo peered forward under the lumixastra's arms.

"Might be an idea to don one's Gammas, chaps, entering thought-waves can be rather trying for the old eyes."

Berin immediately launched into a series of peculiar contortions, retrieving the required eye protection from various superstring-entwined pockets. Even with her Gammas back on, Pi's eyes were reduced to narrow slits.

"This is the light from the mouth of the wave," Higgs-Boson explained. "Once we're inside we shouldn't require eye protection and the programmed forms within should be visible." As if everybody knew what he meant. Andomime did, of course, but she wasn't telling. In fact, she was now so silent it was as if she wasn't even there, which Pi found increasingly disconcerting.

Suddenly, they were completely enveloped by a tunnel of golden watercode, its light turning all the planes into flying beacons. Immediately, the subsonic rumble they had grown so used to, ceased. Even the noise of the engines was muffled. It was as if they had flown into silence itself.

"Now can anybody tell me what the phenomena we are currently experiencing is, and why?" said Higgs-Boson, never one to miss an opportunity for edification.

"It's the buffer-zone," Gaia piped up. "It's designed to reduce outside interference on the main thought-wave interior."

"Quite so and as you can hear, or rather, as you *cannot*, it has already reduced our acoustic footprint considerably. We shall shortly enter the main body of the wave, where we shall be both invisible and inaudible to the program within."

Leo grinned. "So us can spy on 'em!"

"It's not *spying*." Gaia flashed him a look.

"Quite so, as we're merely passing through, we don't form part of the interior program, so we simply won't show up, that is all."

"But us'll still be invisible to 'un. That'll sparkin' do for I!"

Pi was beginning to feel exasperated by all these enigmatic snippets of information, impatient to discover for herself just what *was* at the heart of a thought-wave.

The golden glow vanished and *Caliban* was suddenly enveloped by a gigantic tunnel several miles across, its curved walls lined by a familiar tapestry of green shapes. Pi marvelled at the bizarre upside-down landscape overhead, until a rather more pressing matter caught her attention; they were flying at a shockingly low altitude.

"Pull up, pull up!" she yelled, as a grove of rainbow eucalyptus trees were practically shorn clean by *Ariel's* propellers beneath them. "Why are we so *low* all of a sudden? What happened to our altitude?"

Ariel's impromptu hedge-trimming had sent hundreds of leaves flying into *Caliban's* windows; a few stuck fast in the gaps as proof of their near miss.

"Hmm, I have seen this sort of thing before. I suspect we have encountered a somewhat elevated terrain," Higgs-Boson said calmly. "Try levelling off at eight thousand."

"K, wilco."

The flight gradually climbed to a safe altitude, a little nearer the centre of the cylindrical landscape.

Pi discreetly leaned over to Andomime and lowered her voice. "So was that it, the altitude hiccup? The mavvy thing you predicted?" Being deliberately vague, so as not to alarm the others, Andomime shook her head.

"Well, what do you think of it?" Gaia said cheerily, her muffled voice coming from beneath Higgs-Boson's pockets.

"It looks strangely familiar," said Pi, relieved that the interior looked harmless at least.

"Hmm, let me see, each wave is coded," mused Higgs-Boson.

Berin heard this and promptly returned from the watermap with further details. "It's a section of the to quantumnet, Lumixastra, an application to called Q-Earth, of some Pacific to islands."

"Aha, good man, it is some sort of geographical wave, virtual topography. Recognise anything, Pi?"

As Pi stared down at the terrain below a tremor of excitement suddenly ran through her. "Great hairy holofreaks! It's only *Maui* – we're flying over central Maui!"

"Oh my greenness! Isn't that where you live?"

"Yeah, yeah! This is where me and my *ohana* hover, guys!"

Higgs-Boson dragged Gaia and Leo to the window. "Well, I never did."

Pi studied the view more intently. "Crazy, I think that was the Koolau Forest we just flew over!"

Leo, largely unimpressed until now, suddenly took a greater interest in the view, and pressed his nose against a side window. "Reminds I of home look, all they red rocks out there."

"Think we'd better pull her up again, chaps, we appear to be climbing a jolly old mountain," said Higgs-Boson.

Pi glanced at the altimeter. They were still flying at over eight thousand feet, yet the ground was still rushing up to meet them. *"Kalikimaka!* Of course, it's Mount Haleakala! It's over ten thousand feet high! Pull up, Mime – *wikiwiki!"*

Andomime cooly complied. "Wilco, climbing to twelve thousand."

The engines began to strain as Pi and the others forced the entire flight into a steep ascent. There was a rapid drop in air temperature as they finally levelled out; virtual Maui was nothing if not authentic.

Pi heaved a sigh of relief. "That was a bit of a nearie, really didn't expect to encounter Hawaii's most famous volcano in one of these things!"

"It is rather impressive I must say," said Higgs-Boson, staring out of the window.

"So each thought-wave has a different bit of Q-Earth in then?" said Pi.

Andomime responded, "Large programs like Q-Earth require several thousand waves to fully model a planet in sufficient detail. Your system has in excess of two million waves for commercial use, and most of these use multiplexing. This enables each wave to serve several million individuals at once."

"You mean my ol' chateau is in one of these things?" said Pi, reassured to be having a two-way conversation with her co-pilot again.

"Anything that requires only modest processing like a personal domain will be generated in a multiplexed wave. *This* is a single function wave, because it requires extensive modelling to create such a complex program." Andomime fell silent and turned her head back to the view ahead.

"She does have that squillion, squillion squared IQ," whispered Gaia.

Higgs-Boson loomed over Pi's shoulder. "Once you've hitched up the old cyberpomps and completed the four levels, you'll know each and every one of these waves like the back of your hand, old fruit."

Pi glanced at her hands, still firmly gripping the control column, and surmised she didn't actually know them very well at all. "So it's all just Q-Net stuff in here then?"

Gaia's voice came from beneath Higgs-Boson's patchwork pockets. "All your favourite surfing locations are in a wave here somewhere, sweetie. Although most of these waves are supporting the Inversian network, of course."

Andomime agreed. "Ninety-nine point nine-eight percent of the thought-waves are Inversian. We will only be able to traverse the wave-belt via the small percentage of thought-waves being used by the Quadriga."

"Anders is quite correct," said Higgs-Boson. "It's for security reasons, you understand. Once you've passed all four levels, you'll be granted access to the whole shebang!" He gave Pi a big grin. "But if anything, the limited access makes our journey easier. Thought-waves can be rather treacherous. One doesn't really wish to traverse any more of them than is strictly neccessary!"

"Huh, well anything that gets us through these things gets my vote. Funny to think Blake's in one too."

A look of jealousy flashed across Leo's face. "Who's this Blake geezer?"

"Oh, he's just this really neat eco-tiger, he's this megs jade green colour, guards my chateau while I'm away, that kind of thing."

"I'd like to meet *him*!" said Gaia.

"Course 'un would! You're the queen-of-green, into the eco-scene, doing your eco-thing." Leo's tuneless singing made Andomime wince.

Pi daydreamed for a moment. *It's funny to think you're somewhere out there, dearest Blake.*

"If it is of to any assistance, the other thought-waves we to pass through are a to therapies wave, and, let me to see, one marked restricted-to-classified," chirped Berin.

This was music to a certain lumian's ears. "Sparkin', this one 'un has to see. What's 'un trying to hide in that constricted wave then? Top-secret cyber-zappers, superfast-mega-shapers, or – or sparkin' wongler-viruses?"

"Well, doubtless we'll all be intrigued to learn of each wave's content, purely for educational purposes, of course," said Higgs-Boson, trying to lend some dignity to the proceedings.

"Well, I want to see what's in the therapies wave," said Gaia.

"Course 'un does." Leo stuck out his tongue at her.

"It seems much bigger on the inside than the outside," said Pi. "Holofreaks! What was *that*?" A cluster of meteorites flew past the plane, leaving bright streaks across the sky, before disappearing over the landscape far ahead.

Higgs-Boson coolly turned to them. "Now can anybody tell me what our captain has just witnessed?"

Everyone peered out of the starboard windows to get a better look, annoying Andomime as they crowded around her.

"And us missed 'un and all!" moaned Leo.

"I saw them, they must be surfers logging onto this section of Q-Earth," Gaia said brightly.

Higgs-Boson nodded. "Anybody else have any thoughts?"

"The number of surfers in such close formation suggests a group searching simultaneously, such as a school party?" said Andomime, eliciting grunts of approval from the lumixastra.

"It could even be my sister's geography class. They were going on a visit to Mount Haleakala today," said Pi. "Whilst I was doing some boring exam, I mean taking an exam." She looked sheepishly at Higgs-Boson, who pretended not to notice.

"Until interrupted by a brace of cleaning-contraptions!" He gave her a wink.

"So every time me and my friends glue to the Q, we're actually sliding a wave just like this one but don't know it? And we look just like these 'meteorites' to you guys?"

"That's how it looks to us," said Gaia.

"Now you can see 'un 'cos 'un's a superconfuser gone lightspeed. Pheeeawshh!" Leo tried to add a rocket-hand manoeuvre but the superstring wouldn't let him.

"Quite so, and if Leo's spyglass is handy, you should now be able to see our presumed scholastic meteorites at their destination," said Higgs-Boson. "They should appear motionless, of course, as we're functioning at lightspeed, and they are not."

Pi could hardly lay her hands on Leo's 'scope fast enough. *"Kalikimaka!* Maybe I'll see Lani!"

She snapped it out and swept the area where the 'meteorites' appeared to land, *Caliban* flying over the road that wound to the volcano's summit, the place where they were last seen. She followed the endless zig zag of the highway, until she spotted a familiar sight, the Haleakala Visitor Centre. Then, as they flew over the Pu'u Ula'ula Overlook, there was a cluster of figures dressed in pale blue.

Pi felt a lump in her throat. She knew Lani's class was making a virtual excursion via Q-Earth to the volcano's wavesite that day; she recalled Lani telling her mother about it over breakfast. Although she still couldn't quite believe that in this wave of all waves, at that very moment, she would actually see her own sister. Yet there she *was*, unmistakably, the waist-length dark hair with its striking nano-highlights clearly visible. She could even see her sister's best friend, Lukina, standing right next to her. For a moment she remained as motionless as the figures she was observing.

"This is just *so* freaky, that's actually my sister's avatar down there!"

"Ooh, may I see?" said Gaia.

Pi silently handed her the telescope.

"I think I know which one she is. She looks a bit like you only a little older?"

"*Oh yeah*, three years, and bro, don't I know it!"

"It's the kind of thing that happens quite a lot in Inverse," said Gaia.

"Really?"

Higgs-Boson smiled. "Serendipity, quite normal in the quantum domain, quite routine."

"The chances of such a coincidence increases by a factor of four thousand and eighteen percent when you are operating at lightspeed," said Andomime. "It is a partial consequence of the entanglement function. This explains why we happen to be traversing your home island, and the exact same wave your sister is using, at the very same moment she is using it."

Gaia quietly handed the 'scope back to Pi who continued to study the school party, until they were little more than a cluster of forget-me-nots on the fast receding landscape.

Technically, she had seen Lani in the school corridor only moments earlier, but in this new world, it seemed like an age ago. She began to understand just how long thirty milliseconds could be. "It's all relative, or *relatives*," she mumbled.

Gaia laughed. "Just wait till you meet mine."

Pi pointed out of the port window. "And if you go some forty miles back thataway, that's Kahului, that's where we actually live." She felt a curious mixture of excitement and homesickness, even though the island was only virtual.

Then, without warning, the familiar topography suddenly vanished. *Caliban*, *Ariel* and *Prospero* left the wave as abruptly as they had entered it. One minute the formation of seaplanes was flying through a bright blue sky, next, it was bathed in golden light again.

They had reached the exit buffer-zone.

Pi watched the altimeter change. Once they'd left the buffer-zone the darkness enveloped them again and the thunderous roar returned. Pi watched as all the rainbow eucalyptus leaves, which had become stuck fast around *Caliban's* windows, instantly dissolved into rivulets of water, running off the glass like rain.

"Would you look at that. They all just melted."

"They were programmed to be leaves in the last wave, but once we left it, they reverted back to pure watercode again," said Higgs-Boson, as the last few rivulets streamed across the windows.

The next few miles passed without incident, although Pi noted that what little she could see of Andomime's face betrayed agitation. It was with some relief, therefore, that the rumbling chasm between the churning pipelines of code was soon illuminated once more. They had reached the welcoming glow of the next buffer-zone. The shaft of golden light reminded Pi of an old-fashioned slide projector. All that was missing were the dust motes, and the whir of a cooling fan.

"Hmm, magic lanterns," she mused out loud.

Higgs-Boson's ears pricked up. "Magic lanterns, I say, I like the sound of those."

"My dad used to collect them, and all these old projectors and stuff." She recalled the images she and Lani had pored over from her father's collection of vintage glass slides, then the light in the cabin changed and she snapped back to reality. The golden glow of the wave's entrance had transformed into the hidden domain within. She checked the altimeter, half expecting another close encounter, but this wave seemed completely different.

The therapy wave was clearly the interior of a gigantic tube of watercode, its perfectly cylindrical sides soaring some sixty thousand feet above their heads as it churned. Unlike the slate-grey exterior, inside the wave was a bright blue-green, a colour familiar to any big wave surfer. It was the biggest 'green room' Pi had ever seen. She reasoned the 'code must actually be luminous, there being no other visible source of illumination, the gently curving walls, so many miles long you couldn't see the end of them. She was speechless. It was one thing to find yourself flying over something as familiar as a Q-Earth landscape, it was quite another to experience something as elemental as this. The wave was noisy too, not quite as thunderous as the labyrinth outside, but far from the silence of virtual Maui.

"What a pity, such a shame, it's not switched on," said Higgs-Boson dismissively.

Pi peered upwards from her side window at the enormous blue vault overhead. "Not switched on? What are these puppies like when they're switched on!"

"Well I'm blowed, spoke too soon. I think we're in luck!" Higgs-Boson moved nearer Andomime's window to get a better look, dragging Gaia, Leo and Berin with him.

First one, then a dozen, then hundreds of white streaks began racing down the curved walls on the right-hand side high above.

"Megs! Are those *codesurfers*?" said Pi.

"Not exactly," said Gaia, "they're passive human

surfers riding *on* the code; they're not able to write *into* it, or even see it as a wave, unlike us, do you see? Remember we see everything differently because we're operating at *lightspeed*." Gaia looked at her expectantly.

Pi looked confused. "Think I load."

"Oh this is excellent, excellent, it looks as if we are in for a show after all!" Higgs-Boson leant forward to study the innumerable streaks now descending rapidly down the face of the watercode leviathan.

"I thought this was supposed to be some Q-Net therapy wave anyway?" said Pi.

"Well, there you have it, you see, what could be more stimulating for some poor soul stuck in a hospital than a jolly good dose of radical recreation. Quantum surfing has many benefits, all scientifically validated. Watch closely, chaps, as we fly over this little lot. I'll take the stick if you like." Higgs-Boson had no sooner taken the controls than he caught everybody off guard by pushing *Caliban*, and thus *Prospero and Ariel*, into a sudden dive.

"What *is* he doing?" Pi mumbled under her breath, as all three planes plunged, seemingly out of control.

"Hold tight! Just taking her down to the drink so you can all get a proper look – windows, chaps." Higgs-Boson levelled out a nerve-jangling two hundred feet over the churning waters. Gaia and Leo couldn't see very well, of course. The lumixastra was standing in Pi's place with both of them stuck fast behind him, their feet dangling on Seat 1A, but they managed to get a view of sorts.

"Use Leo's telescope, I'm sure he won't mind," said Higgs-Boson.

"K." Pi dodged the superstring and snatched up the scope, not entirely sure what she was supposed to be looking for. She followed the surfers as they raced down the face of the wave to their right in their hundreds now, enormous white plumes trailing behind them. But then as *Caliban* flew onwards, a bizarre but wonderful phenomenon began to occur.

The first few surfers disappeared under the aircraft out of sight behind them, but then as she watched, spellbound, she realised what was happening. The surfers were indeed the avatars of hospital patients of all ages, each standing effortlessly upon a white surfboard in their everyday clothes, arms outstretched, eyes closed. They began to change, chameleon-like, into a myriad of different forms. As soon as they transformed, they appeared to slow down dramatically. It was like watching a winter landscape through time-lapse photography, bursting into spring, summer and autumn. Or the most elaborate fireworks display, but in slow motion, that allowed you to follow the glow of every last phosphorous star.

"Swimming with dolphins, gliding with eagles, oh and look, that girl just changed into a horse-back rider!" Pi became very excited. "Wait, I know what this is, it's the *Dancer* program my dad helped write!"

"It is indeed," said Higgs-Boson, "a very clever program too if I may say."

"Ooh, dolphins, dolphins, let me see." Gaia wrestled against the superstring to get a better view.

"Dancer, another of your father's great innovations. And here's a little something else you might not know about such waves, something we like to call, 'total surface facilitation'." Higgs-Boson suddenly stomped on the port rudder, sending *Caliban* veering off to the left, following the morphing surfers. "There is positively no wrong way up!"

Pi clung on to her seat, as *Caliban*, *Prospero* and *Ariel* began to slowly corkscrew up the face of the giant wave, following the surfers as they raced all the way up to the 'roof' of the tube and down the other side in an enormous loop the loop. She quickly realised that her hand hold was quite unnecessary. The sense of gravity was just the same wherever they were, there really was no wrong way up!

"Us can't see nothing!" moaned Leo.

"Oh very well." Higgs-Boson was forced to adopt a very undignified posture, so Gaia and Leo could peer out from beneath his pockets. "Getting a bit old for this sort of malarkey," he groaned.

"This is seriously amped out," said Pi. "I had no idea Dancer looked like this from the inside! This thing's a real cylinder! So this is codesurfing, right?"

"Not exactly," said Gaia. "Even though they're surfing watercode, it's pre-programmed for them, plus they aren't computers working at lightspeed, as Higgs-Boson said. Organics just can't see it the way we do, it

185

will just look like a regular web page to them, do you see?"

As each surfer changed form, the watercode beneath them changed also. This created a spectacular kaleidoscopic spiral comprising hundreds of different, strand-like terrains, seas and skies, twisting down the body of the wave in a cornucopia of virtual worlds.

"We call them changelings in Inverse," said Higgs-Boson. "Quite a number of worlds use similar programs for their mortal populations."

Further explanation was unnecessary. Pi switched off her mind and allowed herself to drink in all the magical transformations. These were enhanced by yet another phenomenon. The sound of the wave had changed, from its all-pervasive thunder, to that of naturalistic sounds matching each changeling's environment, subtly altering as *Caliban* flew on down the spiralling tracks like some kind of polyphonic fugue. She marvelled at the graceful movements all the changelings displayed. Now she understood why her father had named it Dancer; it really was like watching some balletic dance, where everybody seemed to have perfect poise.

"Don't they ever like wipe out?"

Higgs-Boson smiled. "All taken care of by the programming, another of your father's brainwaves, I believe; nobody ever falls. A happy surfer is one without a care in the virtual world."

Pi noticed a group of children barely half her age, surfing together. Suddenly their surfboards changed to a pod of young whales, each magnificent creature now carrying a child upon its back, hanging on to the dorsal fin as it raced through the water.

Gaia was entranced and followed the whales intently, a wistful smile on her face. "Now that's *my* kind of surfing, wish I was with them," sighing as she and Pi watched the tail flukes disappear beneath them.

"Physeter macrocephalus," said Andomime. "They are virtual whale calves especially designed for younger patients."

'How does she—?' mimed Pi, as she and Gaia exchanged a quizzical glance.

Gaia shrugged her shoulders and silently mouthed, 'Squillion, squillion squared.'

"But I thought psy didn't work in here?" whispered Pi.

"It's the proximity effect; you can sometimes use psy if the subject's close enough, and it doesn't hurt that Mime has the best error correction circuits in Inverse." Gaia flashed her feathery-green eyebrows.

Leo gave them all a cheeky grin. "Let's play what-will-un-spy!"

Gaia was game and quickly explained the rules; well, there was in fact only *one* rule. "You have to identify a surfer and guess what they will become as a changeling."

"K, who goes—?" Pi was cut short.

"Old geezer, brown sweater, blue jeans, um, er, sparkin' pilot!" proclaimed Leo.

"Nice try, Mottles. You next, Pi," Gaia laughed, as the old man morphed into 'scuba diving with manta rays' – much to Leo's annoyance.

"K," said Pi, "there are literally *so* many, er, that really old lady, do you scan? With the plum-coloured slacks, er, horse-back riding."

"What kind of horse look!" quizzed Leo, as the old lady's surfboard changed into an enormous plum-coloured Harley Davidson with the old lady firmly astride.

Pi stamped her foot. "Son of a glitch! Wrong kinda ride!"

"Never saw that 'un coming did 'un, harder than it looks mind."

"My turn, my turn," said Gaia, hopping up and down. "The old man with grey hair, black polo-neck – swimming with dolphins," trying to point her superstring-snagged finger without success.

Pi focused on the aged surfer, his hair almost white. Suddenly his surfboard vanished and he plunged into a terrifying chasm beneath them.

"Creeping cryozombies!" She averted her eyes.

"Bungee jumper, bungee jumper – no points for 'un look!" chuckled Leo.

"It's always the ones you least expect," sighed Pi.

"Do I not enjoy a turn?" said Andomime suddenly. "Piano virtuoso, hang-glider, horse-rider, aerobatic pilot, swimming with dolphins, jazz drummer, ballerina, snowboarder, skydiver, paraglider, guitar hero, holo star, tennis champion, freediver – shall I continue?"

Everybody watched in astonishment as each one of Andomime's predictions came true, in the exact order stated. Yet Pi couldn't understand how she could even *see* from where she was sitting, let alone through her ever-present Gammas.

"That's just 'un showing off look."

"Well, I think we have our champion, chaps!" chortled Higgs-Boson. "I do believe old Anders here could predict changelings ad infinitum."

Pi shrugged her shoulders. "Squillion, squillion squared podiums again." She continued to study the changelings Andomime had predicted. There was an old man playing rock guitar to a rapturous crowd. A few changelings behind him, a young woman sat playing a grand piano, both she and it slowly creeping up the wave as if by magic. Most eye-catching of all, however, was a young girl of about her own age. She was standing on the back of a magnificent white horse, her arms outstretched, perfectly poised as it galloped full pelt over an endless plain.

"Don't they get a bit mixed up? They all seem so close together."

"Hmm, not really. Each spiral reality appears narrow to us but it is in fact quite *separate*," Higgs-Boson explained. "They are, as such, quite limitless in size as far as each particular changeling is concerned. They would be totally oblivious to the realities either side of them, you see." He noted the bemused look on Pi's face. "I'm not putting it very well, am I? Hmm, it's not unlike radio frequencies; they all pass through the same space at the same time, but you are only ever aware of the one you are tuned into, if you follow me?" Pi nodded, much to the lumixastra's relief. He'd had enough of indulging Gaia and Leo by now anyway, and was only too relieved to stand up straight again.

The three planes were soon following *Miranda* out of the thought-wave and back into the thunderous chasm outside. Pi's spirits had been lifted enormously by seeing her sister, let alone the transformations of the changelings. She felt less afraid of thought-waves now; although fearsome on the outside, inside they appeared to be the stuff of dreams.

Caliban traversed the next few nautical miles without incident. Pi glanced down at 'Leo's' flight plan. "Megs, just one more wave to go and we're done, this should bring us right out the other side to *Charybdis* – yay!"

Gaia's voice piped up from the rear of the cabin. "Thank greenness!"

"But first 'un gets to see *my* wave look." Leo began cackling disconcertingly. The golden glow of another buffer-zone soon filled the chasm.

Pi leaned towards Andomime. "And we don't have to fly these puppies back do we? Didn't the lumixastra say we go home via some other lighthouse or something?"

"Correct," she replied curtly.

"So leaving Stargazey Pi is a lot easier than arriving, then?"

"What do you wish to know exactly? That reaching Stargazey Pi has been made intentionally difficult to prevent its discovery by unauthorised users? That leaving it is like disembarking a plane airside so you don't have to go through all that security?"

"Oh, you know about that?" said Pi. "You seem to know about *everything*," mumbling the latter quietly to herself.

"Or that the wave we are about to enter contains something extremely perilous?" Andomime turned to her. "But as to the exact nature of this peril, I have no further information."

FOURTEEN

AND KELVIN SPHERES

Pi began to fret. She couldn't just ignore Andomime's enigmatic warning, their third thought-wave was only half a nautical mile away. "Shouldn't we, I mean *you*, tell the lumixastra about what your prediction algorithms have, er, predicted?"

"Perhaps, but I detest dealing in non-specifics."

"So is that a yes?"

"You can alert the others if you wish; it is your decision, you are the captain."

Pi quickly made up her mind. "LUMIXASTRA!"

There was a brief rumbling like an approaching rugby scrum as four pairs of legs scuttled across the cabin floor.

Higgs-Boson peered out of the window. "Something the matter, old bean?"

"Well, it may be nothing but—"

"It is my fault, Lumixastra. I mentioned to the captain that my prediction algorithms had detected an indeterminate, yet severe peril in the next wave," Andomime said gallantly.

"Oh dear, I see, hmm, ah yes." Higgs-Boson made several elasticated attempts to stroke his chin without success, so he furrowed his brow instead.

"As you know, thought-waves prevent proper analysis of psy-based functions," added Andomime.

"Quite so, quite so, hmm, any—?" Higgs-Boson waved his hand in a small circular motion, which was all he could manage.

"I regret I simply cannot clarify the information further, but the inevitability of this threat is unequivocal."

"And it would appear, unavoidable." At that moment they were again surrounded by the golden glow of a buffer-zone. Higgs-Boson turned to Berin. "This was the—?"

"Restricted-classified wave, Lumixastra," trilled Berin, nervously.

"Well, we'll just have to cross the jolly old fingers and hope for the best, chaps. Perhaps some rapid untangling wouldn't go amiss?"

"On the to case, Lumixastra."

As Berin renewed his valiant attempts to free them, Gaia looked censoriously at Leo. "Still looking forward to seeing whatever's inside?"

Leo's frown slowly changed to a broad grin. "But whatever's in there won't see 'un look, 'cos 'un's not part of the program. They won't even know we're there look!"

Berin's nimble fingers paused from their

untangling. Even Andomime relaxed her grip on the controls for a moment.

Leo's eyes narrowed to inscrutable slits. "We'll be proper masters of stealth look."

"I say, a very good point," said Higgs-Boson. "And with any luck we'll be safely out the other side before you can say Barmy-Knife. Any nefarious elements within being none the wiser."

"I think we're now officially within, guys," said Pi, as they suddenly found themselves flying through another bright blue sky.

There was little danger of flying into trees this time; there wasn't so much as a blade of grass in sight, just an endless, snowy white terrain.

"Don't look too bad, must be one of they Cute-Earth waves," sniffed Leo.

Gaia scanned the apparently harmless interior as best she could from beneath the lumixastra's pockets. "It's *Q-Earth*, Mottles."

"Strange, the snow's not on the mountains, wonder where this is?" mused Pi.

The featureless white plain stretched for miles. On the horizon what looked like a small town and a series of low mountains shimmered in the blue haze.

Higgs-Boson stared at the nameless vista. "Hmm, trouble with these restricted-classified Johnnys is, we can't jolly old tell."

Pi studied Andomime's face as if she were consulting a danger-ometer; it wasn't very reassuring. Andomime looked even more anxious, her hands gripping the controls tighter than ever.

"Can't you use those famous Harbinger error-correction circuits to interpolate the missing data in your psy? You know, like you did with the changelings?" Pi surprised herself with her own question; she wasn't even sure what *interpolate* meant.

Andomime's head twitched, as if she was impressed by the enquiry. "Indeed I could but regrettably, without some boost from the proximity effect, there is not enough data for them to work with."

"So we're nowhere near this mavvy whatever-it-is then?" said Pi, aware that everybody else was listening intently.

"The location of the indeterminate peril would appear to be some way from us – yes."

"K, so it's nowhere nearby… and you can't load what it is… yada yada. On a scale of one to ten, exactly how mavvy is this thing? You keep using words like severe and extremely, so you must have some idea?"

It was now so quiet on *Caliban's* flight deck you could hear a feather falling, everyone frozen like statues, hanging on Andomime's every word.

"I know it is completely irrational." Andomime paused and swallowed, then looked across at Pi as if she were genuinely perplexed. "I would say… I would state, in excess of ten."

There was a loud clunk on the floor. Everybody nearly jumped out of their avatars. Berin had accidentally dropped the Barmy-Knife. "Smidget-pidget, Berinfingers, butterfingers." He stooped to pick it up. Then he let out such a high-pitched shriek, everybody jumped again.

Higgs-Boson clutched his chest. "Good Inverse, gave me a start!"

The others looked around to see what the matter was. Berin was speechless, a maniacal grin upon his face, pointing wildly at the Barmy-Knife as he held it up.

"What is it, dear fellow, whatever is the matter, old chap?" said Higgs-Boson.

"What's 'un done? 'Un hasn't gone and broke me Barmy has 'un?" said Leo, as he and Gaia tried to see what all the fuss was about.

"It's to good news, lumixastra!" chirped Berin, hastily retrieving an ocular from Higgs-Boson's pockets and screwing it into the Lumixastra's eye so he could get a better look.

"Well I never did, how fortuitous, the fall appears to have knocked one of the blades into position, and as luck would have it – it's the jolly old *superstring-snipper*!"

Everybody's spirits lifted. Berin immediately set to work with the only tool in the known universe that could cut virtual superstring.

"We'll have to contain all the bits and bobs lest they run amok and rally for a counter-attack," said Higgs-Boson as Berin got stuck in, sending six-inch snippets flying in all directions.

"Thank greenness, I can move again!" Gaia began waving her arms gratuitously in all directions. "Don't think you need this anymore, Mottles." She peeled the '*DANGER – do not remove*' sticker from Leo's nose and stuck it on top of his head.

He stuck out his tongue. "Har, hardy-har."

Gaia began daintily picking up the writhing worm-like snippets, flicking them quickly into a wastepaper bin. "Look at them, pesky little things, they're already trying to get back out again."

"Think we'd better ditch the old bin once it's replete, better safe than sorry." Higgs-Boson revelled in the simple pleasure of being able to scratch his nose again.

"Salt."

"What was that, Andomime dear? Missed it, what with all the snipping."

"Yeah, what about salt?" Pi fixed her co-pilot with a Lightfoot stare.

"The white material below us is not crystallized precipitation, but virtual sodium chloride." Andomime licked her lips as if she could practically taste it.

"You mean it's *salt* – salt? Well, I guess that explains why it's not on the mountains." Pi quickly ran through every known threat scenario that might involve salt and decided that, unless one were a virtual slug or snail, it was probably harmless.

Higgs-Boson was still far too jolly to be troubled by Andomime's information, not least because he was now freed from a certain restless lumian. "Dry lake bed, salt flats, nothing to worry about, chaps, unless there are any fish amongst us." He began chortling to himself.

Leo took out his 'scope and glued himself to the front windows next to Pi.

"Hey, Navigator, what you at?"

"Scanning, ain't us, best if you scans 'un before they scans you look."

"Well, you could have helped pick this lot up first, Mottles," moaned Gaia, still frantically trying to contain the writhing mass of super-snippets in the wastebasket and mumbling, "Typical Leo," to herself as she swatted the escapees with an empty bottle.

Higgs-Boson and Berin were soon fully occupied chasing the last rogue cuttings around the cabin.

"Send us a sign, yeah!" Leo began singing and waggling his hips.

Pi raised her eyes. "What *are* you doing?"

"There's this sign up ahead look, us is just trying to read 'un."

Pi stood up in her seat to get a better look. The salt flats were fast disappearing beneath them and ahead lay the small town. Well, it *looked* like a town from a distance, but now she wasn't so sure. "What's it say? Can you read it?" Pi stomped on a rogue snippet with her heel, enabling Berin to grab it.

"Uh yeah, 'un says constricted area, no trainspotting beyond this point."

"I think he means *restricted* and *trespassing*," said Gaia.

"Well, there's your restricted bit, chaps," said Higgs-Boson.

"There's some smaller writing, harder to see, Nellis… something, and something range. Then some smaller stuff 'un can't hardly read at all." Everybody stopped still, save for the sound of a couple of heel stamps to curtail the last few superstring stragglers. "Use of deadly farce, something, gor yeah, sparkin' – deadly farce!"

"Deadly *force*! Leo, only *you* would think it was cool to be blown to smithereens," sighed Gaia.

"Nellis – Nellis? Rings a bell." Pi wracked her memory banks. "Cryocreeps! That's AREA-51!"

"What's so exciting about he then?" said Leo, peering nonchalantly ahead.

"It's this really top-secret base where they're supposed to have crashed UFOs and stuff. The Q-Net's got like millions of wavesites on it."

"What are to UFOs?" said Berin guilelessly.

"Flying-saucers, you know, lights in the sky, Roswell, crashed alien spacecraft, yada yada, little grey men." Pi noted Berin's bemused expression. "It's just some top-secret air base is all. They made it all up anyway, as smoke for secret projects and stuff."

"Well, that explains everything. It's a classified wave because it contains sensitive military dispositions and quite possibly *munitions*. I expect it is otherwise quite harmless. Wouldn't you agree, Andomime? Andomime?" Higgs-Boson leant forward to see why Andomime was so quiet. She was shaking, her hands trembling on the control column.

"It is coming closer," she whispered.

Before Higgs-Boson had a chance to ask more he was distracted by something outside. *Miranda* was pitching wildly ahead of them. They were rapidly gaining on her as if she were trapped in some invisible cobweb, then whatever it was suddenly snagged them too.

"Brace yourselves!"

Something slammed into them, sending the whole crew reeling from one side of the flight deck to the other. Anything that wasn't firmly bolted down flew into the air.

"*Goto param specific gravity initiate!*" exclaimed Gaia and Leo as one.

"Them's firing on us!" bawled Leo.

Pi clung onto the controls, the whole plane shuddering and shaking. She checked the airspeed indicator. They were flying at twice their normal speed, yet the ground hardly seemed to move beneath them. She rapped the dial hard with her knuckles (a handy tip garnered from page one hundred and seventy-eight of her flick, for apparently erroneous instrumentation).

"What's the matter with the freaking thing!"

"Think we've hit a spot of turbulence, chaps!" Higgs-Boson boomed over the howling tempest.

"I can't hold her. I can't hold her steady!" Pi looked across at Andomime, who was also fighting with her controls, a look of intense concentration on her face.

The buildings below began to come apart, hangar roofs peeling off like sardine tins, sending sheets of metal flying through the air towards them.

Pi ducked as two huge pieces of debris hurtled past the windows. "Holofreaks! It's like a hurricane out there!"

"Does appear to be a little brisk out, I must say." Higgs-Boson completely lost his grip on Andomime's seat and flew backwards towards the bulkhead, ricocheting off Gaia and Leo's swivel chairs like a pinball.

"Not 'un hurricane, more like one of they tornadurs if you asks I." Leo watched gleefully as the maelstrom shredded the airbase below. "Sparkin' tubes! Look at all they secret craft."

Several mysterious circular shapes were exposed as roofs began to disintegrate. Berin joined him, standing on tiptoe so he could look too. "Astro-Frizzari mark to 4, the first to craft my great-great-to-generation father ever to owned. Hard to start on a cold morning, but a very to smooth ride. They don't to make them like that any to more." Berin wiped a tear from his big almond eyes.

"Oh no!" Gaia clasped a hand over her mouth.

Pi glanced around. "Now what?"

Higgs-Boson's unscheduled foray to the rear of the cabin had brought him into catastrophic collision with a certain wastebasket. Of the hundreds of recovered super-snippets, not a single one now remained safely in captivity. He was covered from head to toe by the mischievous miscreants, looking for all the world like a walking bath mat.

Wasting not a nano, he flamboyantly whipped off his pockets and flourished them like a toreador, turning them inside out to trap the snippets within. Berin leapt to his aid, bounding onto the navigator's desk to remove all the snippets from the poor lumixastra's head, fiendishly tying themselves into granny knots on the lumixastra's thinning hair.

"That's it, bung the little blighters in here." Higgs-Boson held his pockets open for a split nano, so Berin could fling the last few snippets in with the rest. Quickly, he knotted his tatty old pockets into a tight bundle, over and over again, until not a single one could escape. Then he wrenched open a small side window and flung the lot outside with all the force he could muster, snapping the frame shut and dusting his palms with a satisfied grin.

Moments later, a mysterious alien artefact landed on the salt-flats of Q-Earth, silently adding itself to the virtual inventory of Area 51.

Pi had more important things to worry about. *Caliban* was making almost no headway against the appalling weather. "But the sky's *blue!* Storms like this don't happen on Q-Earth, what's the matter with it all!" She looked across at Andomime. "Is this the danger? Tell me it's what you predicted!" Andomime shook her head.

"Is there anything I can do? I feel so useless," said Gaia, clinging onto Pi's arm-rest.

"I don't know, *is* there?" said Pi, feeling totally benumbed, wondering if it wasn't a warm-up for even worse. Perhaps this wave *could* detect their presence, and the storm was some kind of defence mechanism? She quickly ruled this out. Apart from bee-stings, what sort of defence destroys the thing it's supposed to protect?

Higgs-Boson returned to the front of the plane, just in time to witness the next calamity. "Aha," he said, stroking his chin, as if he now understood something that had eluded him previously. He carefully drew out a delicate chain from around his neck.

The very mountains themselves had begun to melt. The whole horizon was liquefying back into a torrent of watercode, running towards the airbase like a breached dam. Then the ground itself began to peel back like the skin of a giant onion, layer upon layer upon layer. What was left of the buildings disappeared, as previously underground facilities were exposed to the light of day. It reminded Pi of the time that she and Lani prodded an ants' nest with a stick. Hundreds of virtual workers could be seen scurrying around the disturbed levels.

The wind became even stronger. It started to spin the four planes into a slow-moving vortex over the chaos below. Leo was glued to his spyglass as one top-secret project after another was paraded before his eyes. "Asteroid-zapper, matter-wongler, forcefield-nobbler!" As the layers went deeper the technical revelations grew in magnitude. "Invisibility-wurzeler, time-flinger-flanger, ANTIMATTER-CANNON! Whoa yeah! Sparkin' rokker or what!"

The fissured ground began ejecting the gadgetry with volcanic fury, the planes like sitting ducks as huge pieces of equipment flew past. Berin showed particular interest when the *Recovered-Alien-Craft* section was uncovered. "A Spanworth-Trangledyne, nice to options pack. A Globius-Shuttlebus, practical if a little to slow. Oh my, a Cymatronic-Dyspondulator. Now you to don't see one of those every to parsec." His long, bony finger followed every trajectory, the unscheduled display of UFOs convincing Pi that maybe Roswell wasn't just a load of nonsense about weather balloons after all. Well, that and the not inconsequential fact that she was now surrounded by aliens.

Higgs-Boson leaned in between Pi and Andomime, planting a hand firmly on the backs of their seats, a purposeful look on his face. "Contravenes the laws of Inverse to interfere with sovereign systems, but I fear things have got rather out of hand. May I?"

Pi didn't hesitate. "Sure, anything that gets us outta here."

He stood up straight and puffed out his chest. "*Goto param waveset – undo all – initiate!*" His voice was so loud, Pi went deaf in one ear.

Everybody stopped still, watching to see if the code had any effect. But nothing changed; numerous pieces of top-secret paraphernalia continued to hurtle past the plane. Higgs-Boson grimaced, then drew an even deeper breath. "*Goto param waveset undo all – STRIKEOUT!*"

Pi removed her hands from the controls, and sat in slack-jawed amazement. Even Leo redirected his attention to the new show in town.

"Strikeout is the biggie, you don't use that one unless you really, really have to," whispered Gaia. The wave became wilder and louder. Gaia could see Pi wanted to say something and leant forward.

"Is this meant to happen?" yelled Pi.

"Yes!"

If anything, Higgs-Boson's commands just seemed to make things worse. The bright blue sky suddenly shot through with a leaden grey, as if a thundercloud had come out of nowhere. The riven terrain below lost all semblance of its former self, reverting in an instant to a coal-black sea of wild watercode. The darkness raced upwards on either side of them, transforming the whole wave back into a cylindrical tempest of elemental fury. Then thousands of white-hot meteors erupted from below, temporarily blinding them as they raced out of sight.

"That's the virtual workers, they've crashed and been logged off," said Gaia.

They were no longer in a Q-Earth wave having a bad-hair day, but the gargantuan belly of some dark and malevolent monster. The wind began to relinquish its grip on the planes, but the sea became wilder still, lashing and whipping all around them.

"We must make for the exit buffer-zone post-haste!" Higgs-Boson boomed, a single shaft of light now the only illumination in the otherwise abyssal gloom. "We have only a few nanos before she crashes!"

Pi knew he meant the wave, but it might equally well have applied to all of them.

Leo and Berin were holding onto one another, trembling, the novelty of a dissected Area-51 having long since passed. "Us ain't never seen 'un crashing from the insides before, and us ain't never wanted to neither!"

Miranda had wasted no time. She still had full control over her own throttles.

Whoever the captain was had grasped the only chance they had and made straight for the exit. *Caliban's* crew were forced to engage in strenuous efforts, yet again, to wrest the remaining planes from the dying vortex.

This change of course effected, Pi aggressively thrust the controls forward. "Full throttle, all engines!" She expected to hear Andomime confirm her instructions. But there was only silence. She looked across, horrified to discover Andomime had taken her hands off her column completely, and was just sitting there, shaking.

"What is it? What's the matter now, for goodness' sake?"

With the thought-wave thundering around them like an earthquake, Andomime slowly pulled back her hood, revealing her strikingly beautiful head, completely devoid of any hair. Then she calmly took off her GammaBanns and folded them, turning slowly towards Pi. At first, Pi couldn't immediately comprehend what she was looking at. She just stared blankly at Andomime's face, studying Andomime's porcelain-white cheeks as they merged seamlessly into her tall forehead; for Andomime had no eyes.

"It is here," she said quietly.

Higgs-Boson, realising something was very badly wrong, gently removed Andomime from her seat, taking her place and executing the unfulfilled adjustments. Gaia helped Andomime to her own chair and sat her down. Higgs-Boson exchanged an awkward smile with Pi, as if to suggest things were not as bad as they seemed, but even he couldn't disguise his anxiety. Pi knew that they were in extreme danger now.

She felt dazed and her head began to spin. The planes were still woefully slow; the propellers were devouring the churning air but getting nowhere. The exit zone was still as remote as the moon. The wave was closing in around them. It was obvious they were never going to make it.

Then, completely out of the blue, the Queen's reassuring voice suddenly spoke in her mind. *"You can save us, Pi, you can save us all. I am giving you the restore superword for this wave, my dear. Alas, I cannot use it myself; it can only be utilised by the host-system, you understand. All you have to do is to download this simple file. Sending now. Remember, I am your friend."*

Suddenly the chaos stilled into silence and the terrifying wave vanished. Where had everybody gone? Pi was shocked to find herself back in the comforting surroundings of her wavesite, lying on her chaise longue. She must have fallen asleep. There was beautiful Blake; she ran her fingers through his soft fur, rubbing one eye with her other hand. Perhaps Inverse had been nothing more than a very peculiar, very epic dream? She sighed deeply, feeling a greater sense of relief than she had known in a long time. Then, as she sat up, something fell off her lap onto the floor. It was a half-opened book, a blue bookmark sticking out of its pages. She picked up the book. It was the one she'd been reading the day before Lani's birthday. She opened it at the bookmark and there was a perfectly drawn oval, the words *LOAD ME* on the open page.

Pi opened her eyes and tried to focus, but all she could see was green feathers, and there seemed to be a terrible thunderstorm outside. "Blake, what are you doing?"

"Oh, you scared us something silly, you passed right out," said Gaia, leaning over her, Leo and Berin too.

Pi realised she was lying flat out on the cabin floor. Berin helped her to sit up and take a sip of navigator's-watercode from a glass. He gave her a tiny rectangular smile. "Perfectly safe for medicinal to purposes."

"Leo said he'd keep an eye on you. I can't stay. I'm, you know, trying to help Mime." Gaia looked apologetic.

"S'okay, you go, I'll be fine." Pi waved her away. She slowly refocused her eyes. She could see Higgs-Boson glance back now and then to see if she was alright. He was in the captain's seat, and Andomime was back at her controls with her Gammas on.

Leo helped Pi steady her glass so she could take another sip. "What the spark happened to 'un then?"

Pi wriggled her backside, shuffling backwards, so she could lean against the rear bulkhead. "I, I don't really know, one minute I was *here*, then I had like this skizer dream about the Queen." She was about to tell Leo more, when all recall of it vanished – like a pricked bubble.

"More like one of they nightbears 'un means. What with you *and* Anders going funny on us look."

Even by the dim cabin lighting, Pi could see how scared he was. "It's okay, I'm – I'm feeling better now. You go and help the others, they might need you, you know, to alter course or something."

Leo fidgeted with his hands and looked torn between staying and leaving. "Go – that's an order!" she said jokingly.

Leo grinned and got up off his knees. "Whistle if 'un needs us."

"K."

Pi slumped backwards to rest her head, trying to remember what she'd been dreaming. Feeling too woozy to get back up, she sipped at the blue watercode. It tasted surprisingly good and immediately made her feel more relaxed. Berin had thoughtfully left a second glass of it nearby. She reached out to steady it, as it was in danger of falling over as *Caliban* tossed and pitched, when that's exactly what happened.

"Kicker."

The liquid pooled on the floor. She looked around to see if there was anything she could mop it up with. She didn't want anyone to slip. When she looked back, there was a small blue card where the liquid had been. She screwed up her face, then leant over and grabbed it, sitting back up to study it. Expecting it to be wet, she was surprised to find it was bone dry. It looked like a bookmark, an oval printed upon it with the words *LOAD ME* within. A chill ran through her as the dream, the Queen's words, all of it came flooding back. She was no longer in control of her right hand. It was shaking, hovering over the paper, her index finger poised to make contact with the words. She knew she must not touch it whatever she did, that something unimaginably dark was bidding her join it. She wanted to drop it and move away, as if it were a viper, but her left hand wouldn't comply. Slowly, inevitably, she was bringing them both together. She tried to stand up, but her back had gone rigid and her legs wouldn't work. She couldn't even raise her head high enough to see the others, she couldn't call out, couldn't move her jaw even. The very thought of using psy sent a searing pain through her head.

Then she saw Unk Liko's crazy dog, Hupo, in her mind's eye. That's it! If she could only whistle loud enough, Leo would hear her. She fought with every muscle to move her lips. Finally, after the lifetime of a drowning man, a piercing note escaped.

Leo was at her side in an instant; he stared at her, bemused. Her trembling hands were about to make contact with the paper. She rolled her eyes up and down, from Leo to the paper and back several times. Then he realised what she was trying to say, enough to snatch the bookmark from her fingers at least. Straightaway, she drew the deepest of breaths, as if she'd been held underwater, waving her hands frantically as Leo went to look at the note, desperately trying to get the words out.

"DON'T TOUCH IT – DON'T TOUCH IT!" Her eyes were wild and wide.

"Touch what?" Leo leapt backwards, looking about himself as if a snake was on the loose. Then he looked back at the paper but there was nothing in his hand, just a pool of blue liquid at his feet.

Pi staggered back up, grabbed a discarded scarf and mopped up the puddle, Leo following her like a shadow, asking endless questions. But she was so focused on getting rid of the scarf she couldn't hear him. She hurled the scarf from the nearest window, slamming it shut and locking it fast. Only then, slumped against the navigator's desk and trying to catch her breath, did she hear what he was saying.

"What's 'un throw that thing outside for? What's the matter with 'un?"

Pi was about to reply, when a huge crash, like the most violent thunderclap, overlaid the already tumultuous din outside, making them both jump. The light in the cabin dimmed.

Gaia looked round, her face ashen. "You're supposed to be lying down!" she said crossly.

"What's happening? What happened to the light?" said Pi.

"The wave's crashing, the exit portal's closed, the code didn't work, there's no way out," Gaia said angrily.

"Most irregular, most irregular." Higgs-Boson let go of the controls and buried his face in his hands, shaking his head.

Pi saw a blue spark on her right side. "Hey!" She looked down, thinking it was Leo, but noticed Andomime withdraw her hand. A superword came alive in her head. There had been some kind of instantaneous exchange. Andomime had extracted data about what had just happened to Pi and she, in turn, had received the incomplete information that so worried Andomime earlier. Pi felt suddenly overwhelmed, as if with vertigo, and was forced to steady herself by grabbing the back of the nearest seat. Now she understood why Andomime had been so anxious. It was like staring into a fathomless abyss, some nameless dread hidden deep within. Whatever, or *whoever*, it was that had tried to download itself, had angrily closed the exit portal, hastening the wave's demise.

"Now we'll all crash and be sent home. We'll miss a *whole* level, our visit to the palace and everything. We've come *all* this way for nothing!" Gaia snapped her pencil in two.

Pi could see *Miranda* making a drastic turn ahead, her spotlights illuminating the now impenetrable wall where the exit had been. "So we don't actually, you know, die or anything?"

Gaia shook her head. "We'll just get booted off the program, like those guys in Area 51." She made a half-hearted rocket-hand manoeuvre and frowned.

Normally Leo would have found it impossible not to join in. Instead he just looked sullenly at the floor, hands buried deep in his pockets. The whole wave was about to implode, just as Pi had witnessed from the safety of the Southern Lighthouse. How she wished they were all back there now.

Andomime spoke unexpectedly. "You will have to summon him."

Pi looked quizzically at her, then Higgs-Boson.

"I think you're right, needs must and all that, although I am not sure how he will take it." Higgs-Boson resumed playing with the chain around his neck.

"He will understand, you have no choice."

"Yes, you are quite right, we have no choice, must be done." Higgs-Boson heaved himself up and walked to the back of the cabin, everybody following him with their eyes. Andomime looked greatly relieved.

"What's 'un going to do now for filaments' sakes?"

Higgs-Boson pulled the chain out from the top of his shirt, revealing a tiny key.

Pi spoke sideways to Gaia without taking her eyes off him. "Yeah, what *is* he going to do?"

"I'm not really sure."

Higgs-Boson screwed an ocular into his right eye and fumbled with the key, using it to open a small metal locker on the back bulkhead. He retrieved what looked like a bright red stick of rock, brandishing it triumphantly for all to see. Then a sickening feeling hit them and their stomachs turned over, as if they were suddenly plunging down an elevator shaft. Pi watched the altimeter needle spin wildly; they were only a thousand feet from certain impact, the very air they breathed seemed suddenly thin.

"Too late," she wheezed.

Using his last ounce of strength, Higgs-Boson pulled a cord from the base of the stick and the cabin was flooded with red light. It was a distress flare. He snapped open the nearest side window and hurled it outside, not even bothering to close the window after, his strength completely drained.

Pi felt her lungs collapse as the air became almost non-existent; she doubled up and fell to the floor. Outside, the flare bathed the wave in a hellish red light, revealing the enormous vaulted roof collapsing down upon them, the hideous wave closing in from all sides. Then all at once, *Caliban* stopped with a jolt, sending them hurtling around the cabin, barely two hundred feet above the grasping wavetops, poor *Ariel* with doubtless far less to spare.

Mercifully, the air returned and they gasped like landed fish.

"He is here," Andomime whispered, the thunder replaced by silence. Leo coughed a few times, Berin too, in a series of high-pitched squeaks. The propellers slowed to a complete stop, leaving the planes motionless, suspended as if by an invisible force.

Higgs-Boson stumbled to a window. Everything was still, the wave's interior so mirror-smooth it betrayed not a single ripple. "Seems to have done the trick, had to summon the fellow, had to be done."

"Summon who?" said Pi, still spluttering.

The eerie silence was suddenly broken by a distant roar that echoed and thundered all the way down the wave.

Higgs-Boson pointed high to their right. "There's our man now, Kelvin Spheres, the wave-pilot, just the chap you want to see when things get a bit sticky out here."

The others urgently crammed themselves around Andomime's seat. Tearing down the wave's glassy surface was a single figure riding what looked like a giant rocket, great plumes of spray erupting in its wake.

Leo snapped out his spyglass and locked on. After he'd studied the mysterious craft for a few nanos, Pi pulled rank and prised it from his grasp. She beheld a tall figure in a long black coat, a wide-brimmed hat pulled down over his brow. He was standing upon the biggest surfboard she'd ever seen; well, it *looked* like a surfboard, only it was ten times larger, and a *thousand* times faster! Her mouth agape, she noted the elegant flying keel that allowed the craft to ride high above the wave's surface. It was this that created the massive plume. At the rear was a huge vertical tail fin, like that of an aircraft, a fiery exhaust erupting from beneath it.

"Megs to the Nth! Tell me that's codesurfing?"

"It is indeed," said Higgs-Boson, beaming. "That, dear friends, is a level four waveshaper, or shaper, as common parlance would have it. Ridden by one of its most worthy exponents, our most esteemed and invaluable wave-pilot, one Kelvin Spheres."

"Sparkin' tubes! Look at the firecode rocket on 'un! They can go from spit to speed of sound in less than a nano look! Glows 'un's filaments just watching 'un!" Leo impatiently tried to reclaim his spyglass, but without success.

"So did the wave-pilot do all this? Still the wave and stop us from falling?" said Pi, finally pestered into handing Leo's 'scope back, only a bony grey hand got there first.

"In a manner of speaking," said Higgs-Boson. "It is a grave matter to use any form of firecode in Inverse, you understand, not something one undertakes lightly, if you'll forgive the pun. The flare is a powerful emergency program that places everything on hold. It also summons the appropriate assistance, in this case our trusty wave-pilot, who obligingly does the rest. Watch carefully, chaps, it is not often that one gets a chance to see the elusive Mister Spheres in action."

Berin handed Leo's 'scope back, just in time for him to study the master at work. Leo fell speechless, mentally assigning Kelvin Spheres pole position in his pantheon of heroes. "'Un don't even use an helmet, just they goggles look, and that gurt great floppy hat!"

They watched spellbound as Spheres expertly guided the enormous craft in a great loop, thundering right over their heads and down again. The wave began to change within the circle so ascribed, becoming suddenly brighter. Then all at once, as the shaper completed the circle, the wave fell like a curtain, dazzling daylight pouring in once again.

Leo, temporarily blinded, dropped his spyglass, the others left squinting and fumbling for their Gammas.

Higgs-Boson raised his arms and exultantly bellowed, *"Goto param waveset, highlight all – REFRESH!"*

Everything seemed to happen at once. *Caliban's* engines fired into life as if by magic, the propellers rotating one by one. A mighty blast of air blew through the new opening, filling the wave and lifting the planes upwards. Suddenly they were flying again towards the newly-made portal, the bright calm of the Expectant Ocean visible just beyond. They could even see *Charybdis* now, shining like a beacon only a nautical mile ahead.

Higgs-Boson rubbed his hands with glee. "Good to know one still has the knack!"

As they flew over Spheres, he glanced upward, touching the brim of his hat. Then he was off, racing up the wall of watercode like a rocket. When the enormous spray of his wake had subsided, he'd vanished.

Higgs-Boson peered back through a side window as they finally cleared the opening. The others sensed something big was about to happen and quickly followed suit, all except Leo, who raced up to the bubble with his 'scope. He got the best view, of course, the thought-wave finally crashing behind them in a huge implosion of white foam that made the whole plane shake. In no time they had flown over the second lightship, *Charybdis*, much to everyone's relief. Gaia went back to her station, her radio a Christmas tree of lights; there would be many messages to catch up with.

Pi slumped back in her captain's seat and put on her headphones, Andomime sitting beside her, methodically going through her flight checks.

"I may not have eyes, but I make up for my lack of conventional visual acuity with alternative system enhancements. It would be natural for you to be concerned. I expect there are few blind pilots in your world."

Pi looked up from the controls; she couldn't think of any blind pilots whatsoever, but was too polite to say so. "That's okay, I guessed you had to have something else going on to have got us this far. You loaded all those changelings – right?"

"I knew you would understand; by the way, it was the wave-pilot."

"Sorry, what, who?" said Pi, now preoccupied with her own checks and adjustments.

Andomime turned to her. "In answer to your question earlier, the loneliest job in Inverse."

FIFTEEN

APPLICATIONS

The remainder of the flight proved delightfully uneventful. No longer confined by the thought-waves, *Ariel* had been able to resume her position alongside *Caliban*, so they were again flying three abreast behind *Miranda*.

Unlike the Sea of Serenity, the Expectant Ocean had not a single ship to its name save *Charybdis*. With its clear blue sky and glassy sea, a cheerful mood soon set in, although Gaia had to placate more than one irate caller on her radio. Even Higgs-Boson could be seen wincing from time to time, suggesting he might be on the receiving end of some discomfiting psy (the others had a pretty good idea from whom).

Andomime still looked noticeably twitchy. This worried Pi until Gaia, who knew so much more about these things, told her what it was. Apparently

Andomime's systems were not only extremely sensitive at receiving data, they could block it too. Andomime had been hugely impressed by the way Pi resisted the threat in the last wave. It appeared Pi had a new ally in her co-pilot. Andomime had intercepted and blocked more than a few messages intended for her captain. The usual suspects, seeking to lay the blame for the dramas of the wave-belt at the host-system's door. Pi had her very own spam filter!

After a few hours, the wide expanse of ocean became noticeably concave once more.

They were fast approaching the Northern Polarity and the island of Stargazey Pi.

Leo, with very little to do now, and very little he *could* do, spent the entire time peering through his 'scope. "Land ahoy! Stargravy Island ahead look!"

Pi tapped him on the shoulder. "Can I see?" taking the opportunity to study the view for herself. At first she was a little disappointed. They had been aware of the island as a distant dot for some time, but now they were close to the Northern Pole, it really did look surprisingly small.

She beheld a kidney-shaped oval of white sandy beach surrounding a lush green centre. A very pronounced and dramatic mountain lay on one side of the island; on the other, near the coast, was another giant lighthouse, painted with red and white bands just like the Southern Lighthouse. Pi surmised the whole island could only be some two miles long at best, though it looked very inviting, nestled in the brilliant turquoise of the concave ocean.

As they drew closer, four small piers could be seen extending out from the centre of the nearest beach, a row of small stone buildings with slate roofs lying just inland. A larger wooden building stood next to these, a slipway running from it into the sea, suggesting that it might be a boathouse.

Pi could see nothing which might accommodate thirty people, let alone three hundred. "Where's this palace then? All I can see is some micro shops and stuff. Don't tell me they're it – the palace?" She handed Leo's spyglass back to him, knowing that if anybody could spot a substantial royal edifice, it was her navigator.

Gaia started giggling. "Wait and see, that's a clue by the way."

Although landing was generally considered the most dangerous part of flying (according to page eighty-seven of Pi's flick), she felt totally fearless after the ordeal they'd just been through. Landing three planes simultaneously on the waveless sea would prove to be a doddle by comparison. After a textbook approach, all four planes touched down without incident, a flotilla of launches already waiting for them, manned by the ubiquitous Tarrs.

Berin was first to leave the flight deck; he had to assist with disembarkation. He'd no sooner left the cabin than he was back again, slamming the door behind him and leaning against it, a troubled look on his face. "It might be to b-b-best if we st-st-stayed to here until after the p-p-passengers have to le-le-left."

"Now what?" said Pi, peering out of the window.

Leo was already using his 'scope to spy on the passengers as they boarded the launches. "They don't look too happy mind, just look at Trine's hairdo for a start!"

Lumiette Pomphlix sensed Leo's attention, of course, as did most of the others he dwelt on just a bit too long. She stuck her tongue out at him between gum-pops, her vertical hairdo now a tousled mess, its flickering lights hanging forlornly over her eyes.

Higgs-Boson joined the others and noted dishevelled passengers wherever he looked. "In the circumstances I think we all did jolly well. They'll soon forget about it, couldn't be helped – a spot of turbulence." He winked at them, tapped the side of his nose and resumed his duties.

Pi, Gaia and Leo looked at one another, and mouthed the word 'turbulence'; that was the official line, and they were sticking to it!

Berin left the bridge, his right index finger extended, as if making a point to himself. "A spot of turbulence, a spot of turbulence."

It wasn't long before the highly efficient Tarrs had ferried everyone ashore. *Caliban's* crew, last to leave, were soon alongside one of the piers.

"Welcome to the island of Stargazey Pi, chaps," said Higgs-Boson, helping the others to alight. "You run along and collect all your knick-knacks, Anders and I will catch you up shortly."

Pi took a deep breath; the air was sweet. "It's *so* sub to be on dry land again, you've no idea."

"Landlubbers," mumbled a nearby Tarr, as they ran off down the pier giggling.

"Wait for I!" Leo cried, his pockets caught on a cleat.

Gaia began dancing. "And *so* nice to be free of that flight deck!"

"You're not kidding." Pi suddenly realised how tired she was and relished every footfall on firm ground.

Ahead, all the other passengers had made the short walk up the footpath, and were already huddled in their hundreds outside the improbably diminutive shops. They gossiped noisily and looked back at her disapprovingly, their irate psy crackling at the edges of her mind. But it didn't bother her too much, as not a single word actually made it through. She looked back at Andomime, she and Higgs-Boson ambling along some way behind. Andomime immediately sensed this, of course, and flashed back a rare smile. Her spam filter was working just fine!

There were four shops in all, the restless crowd filing randomly into whichever doorway seemed nearest. Magistry was directing operations, all chatter ceasing abruptly whenever a group fell under his gaze. Pi was still attracting amused looks from the kindlier lumixastras, and assumed they were trying to be sympathetic, until Gaia pointed out she still had her captain's cap on.

Sheepishly, she popped it into a pocket, stopping to study an old cast-iron street sign pointing towards the shops that said 'Applications'.

Higgs-Boson suddenly appeared with Andomime. "Everything alright, chaps? I'll look after old Anders here, you fellows carry on."

"K, if you're sure, wilco." Pi gave her engineering officer a salute.

Magistry, noting the lumixastra's cheery presence, feigned an awkward smile of acknowledgement and scuttled into the nearest shop.

Before Pi knew it, she'd crossed the threshold of a shop called The Third Eye. Gaia looked at her, raised her eyebrows and smiled. For inside this turned out to be as spacious as a department store.

"Megs! Didn't see that coming, sure smoked me there." Pi put her hands on her hips and looked around; the place was a veritable Aladdin's cave of vintage electronics.

Leo sniffed the air. "Valve heaven look, home sweet home."

"Come on, we have to find the palace bursar before we do anything else,' said Gaia excitedly. They left Leo to his reverie and began ambling through the aisles of hardware.

"So what are we supposed to bag here exactly? Only I haven't got any credits on me or anything."

"You don't need those here, silly." Gaia paused to consult some old-fashioned 'You Are Here' display board. "We're looking for Mizar, he's in charge of palace procurement… and there he is, right over there." Gaia withdrew her finger from the listings and stood on tiptoe.

Leo had caught up with them again. He drew out his 'scope and looked serious. "Target moving nor-nor-west, speed – three knots, range – one hundred and twenty. Permission to fire, Captain?" Leo pocketed his 'scope and retrieved what looked like a transparent red plastic water pistol, a mischievous look on his face.

Gaia held out her open hand for him to disarm. "Leo, don't you dare!"

But it was too late. Leo gleefully squirted a huge jet of watercode high in the air, thrust the gun into Gaia's waiting hand, and bundled Pi out of sight behind a nearby pillar. The watercode transformed itself into a dozen sucker-darts mid-flight, liberally peppering the bald head of a tall man wearing the only black pockets in sight.

The figure suddenly broke off his dealings with the throng jostling for his attention. He turned around to see Gaia standing, pistol in hand, less than fifty feet away. To make matters worse, the pistol was leaking, and as the drops fell, they turned into yet more darts at her feet. It appeared to be an open and shut case. Mizar looked deeply offended and ran his hand over his head, all twelve darts clinging to it like limpets, resisting his every effort to pluck them off. He pursed his lips so far upwards, they touched the tip of his long, hooked nose.

Leo was hysterical with laughter, tears running down his cheeks. Gaia, on the other hand, was green with embarrassment. Pi wrested herself from Leo's grasp; it wasn't too difficult, he was practically insensible now. She joined Gaia just in time to see Mizar withdraw a small black book from his pocket and draw a line through something. He then mumbled a code shortcut, turning all the darts on his head back into watercode, which promptly ran down his neck, making him shudder. He gave Gaia one last black look, mopping his neck with a big white handkerchief, and returned his attention to the throng around him.

"Well, that's my shopping spree ruined. Right, Mister Cydermott." Gaia marched over to Leo and showed him the pistol, still mysteriously full, despite the recent usage. It had a small dial on it with eight different settings. She turned it from 'darts' all the way around to 'spiders' so Leo could see. Leo stopped laughing immediately. "You either buy everything I need on *your* chit, or I'll cover you with so many spiders you'll be squirming for a hundred parsecs."

"Was only meant to be a joke look."

"Yes, and it was so funny, he's crossed my name out so I can't get anything now, clever clogs. Arachnids-to-go for monsieur?" Gaia brandished the pistol, a no-nonsense look on her face, and Leo stomped off grumpily in Mizar's direction. Gaia showed the pistol to Pi. "It's the cheapest Barnum-Bratts watercode pistol, but it's pressurised, so I could keep shooting for ages and the place would be knee-deep in creepy-crawlies. If there's one thing Leo absolutely *hates,* it's spiders." Gaia tightened the leaky filler cap.

Pi examined the pistol. "Think Leo and Lani must be soulmates, she'd be a nightmare with one of these."

"You'd better follow him. Just tell the bursar your name and he'll give you your chit. I'll wait here, don't think he'll be too pleased to see me again this trip."

"K – back in a mo."

Pi soon caught up with Mizar. He'd only moved a couple of aisles away from his previous position, and was still surrounded by an urgent throng from young to old. Yet, regardless of their seniority, they still had to wait until he pointed at them with his thick black pen, whence they shouted out their name and he would tick it off his list. Then he would grouchily dispense a chit, torn roughly from a thick pad, dismissively flicking it into the air any old how. And every time he did this, he pursed his lips right up to his nose, grunting angrily, as if he were loath to part with them.

Leo, with his shorter than average stature, was quite lost amongst the clamouring crowd waving their hands in the air and desperate to attract his attention.

Pi took a deep breath and waded into the fray, successfully barging her way right to the front. Eventually, she caught his eye and he pointed his pen at her.

"Epiphany Lightfoot," she said, breezily.

Mizar paused and pulled a number of grotesque faces, waving his pen at her. "Lightfoot eh… Lightfoot,

227

Lightfoot, Lightfoot... hmm?" He looked down his list, flicking through a dozen pages before finding her name. "Didn't I see you with that reprobate Palinder a nano ago? Speak up!"

"Er, I heard this pandam and came out to scan what was going on, if that's what you mean?" Pi could feel herself turning red.

"I don't remember hearing any commotion, child, but I do recall seeing you standing next to the accused. Have you ever heard of guilt by association, perchance?" He leant forward and fixed her with his beady black eyes. Pi smiled awkwardly, certain she was about to be denied a chit. Mizar pulled yet more faces whilst he chewed the matter over. "Hmm." He cleared his throat noisily. "It is fortunate for you that you are the host-system, Lightfoot." He scrawled her name on a chit and tore it off especially contemptuously, turning his back on her as soon as he'd flicked it into the air.

Pi snatched at the chit and turned on her heels. She'd intended to hang around and make sure Leo got his, for Gaia's sake if nothing else, but realised this might compromise his chances even more and thought better of it. Quickly, she returned to Gaia's side, then, after waiting what seemed like an age for Leo to return, it dawned on them both that maybe they'd been duped.

"Hmm, even Leo's not usually *this* slow, he's pulled a fast one. I know where we'll find him, c'mon." Gaia strode off purposefully, taking care to avoid Mizar, moving so swiftly Pi struggled to keep up.

All the stores appeared to be connected. They had left The Third Eye, passed through somewhere called The Sail Loft and entered the Doors Café. It was busy, the clatter of trays, china and cutlery exceeded only by boisterous chatter. Excited lumixastras, lumians and lumiettes were showing off their latest acquisitions and trading surplus goods.

Inside it looked much like a classic 1950s American diner, lots of chrome metalwork and red vinyl seating. There was even a vintage jukebox blaring away in one corner, playing the latest release by the universe's biggest rock star, Djinni Djinn, according to Gaia.

Gaia stood on tiptoe and scanned the room, quickly spotting the blonde lightning-bolt dreads of their quarry. Silently, she indicated for Pi to follow, and they homed in on their unsuspecting prey.

Leo was, of course, nonchalantly propping up the bakery bar, chit in hand, poring over a huge selection of colourful cookie boxes stacked floor to ceiling behind it. A chef in white overalls and a traditional chef's hat was standing patiently behind the counter. A few seats down, Succory had already got stuck into the 'chef's special', a gourmet platter of colourful foil-clad cookies. He didn't even bother looking at them before he expertly shelled them of their wrappers and scoffed them down.

Pi and Gaia stood either side of Leo and each planted a hand on his shoulder. Leo started with surprise. "Us was just having a quick bite look, listening to the Djinn's latest spin, then us was gonna to find 'un – honest. 'Un's proper starving after eating nothing but they whiskets." Reluctantly, he handed his chit over to Gaia; it was noticeably sticky.

Gaia was unimpressed. "It's no use to me, it's yours, silly, and anyway nobody will let me get anything on it without you. You'll just have to accompany me wherever I need to go." She rang a small bell on the counter and caught the chef's attention. "Good Inverse, my friend and I need a dozen boxes of Fermi's Foam Fingers, a dozen boxes of Simpkins Supercolliders with extra silicon chocolate chips, and a half dozen packs of Crackerquarks, please." Leo looked crestfallen.

Gaia prodded him in the ribs with the pistol,. "C'mon, we haven't got all nano!"

The counter was soon piled high with colourful boxes. Gaia began stuffing hers into just a single pocket. Pi looked on with amazement as they all disappeared without leaving so much as a bulge.

"You use your pockets like this, you see?" said Gaia, showing Pi all the constellations in the cloak's lining. "Plenty of room, especially in Ursa Major."

"Megs, that's so cryo!" Pi began tucking her cookie boxes into but a single pocket as Gaia had done. Miraculously, they all seemed to disappear. "It's like magic," she laughed, patting the still pancake-thin garment.

"Well, not *exactly*, more *science*. You see, the material they use for the pockets themselves exists in a parallel virtual universe," said Gaia, "but it's not a very big one, so we call it the pocket-universe, because it's fine for storage."

"Well, that explains a thing or two."

"Wait till 'un scans what 'un's got in here look."

Leo stuck an arm elbow-deep in just one of his pockets, withdrawing a number of unwieldy items from within, then looked suddenly embarrassed.

"I thought you said you didn't have it with you?" Gaia irritably snatched a thick book from Leo's hands, opening it at the ribboned bookmark; it was the Barmy-Knife manual, specifically the superstring-snipper section, its well-thumbed page suggesting it had been consulted on more than one occasion.

"'Un didn't know it were in there honest."

"So *that's* why the cosmo label said three hundred and twenty-five percent," mused Pi, still puzzling over her pockets cloak. "It doesn't even feel heavier or anything." She fumbled in the pocket she'd just filled. It felt empty when she patted it on the outside, but her hand could still feel all the cookie boxes on the inside. They really were in a parallel universe all of their own.

Gaia handed Leo's manual back to him with a frosty look, then glanced at the café clock. "Okay we'd best get moving, we only have two hundred and eighty nanos left for the rest."

"K, guys, time to *bag till we flag*!" Pi strode off. There was no time to waste; they were among the last to enter the stores, *and* Leo's mischief had cost them dearly. Fortunately Gaia knew a few shortcuts from the holographic brochure, which helpfully included the labyrinthine floor plan.

They decided to start in The Sail Loft. It was packed with such a comprehensive selection of chandlery, Pi surmised you could probably build a complete boat from scratch. Unlike the diner, the Loft had low timber ceilings supported by great oak beams, which felt as hard as iron when she tapped them. The whole building appeared to be made of ships' timbers, teak decking for the floor, the walls clinker built, curved and ribbed. Every conceivable knick-knack a sailor might need was hanging from every available beam. A couple of elderly lumixastras kept banging their heads as they tried to negotiate the obstacle course of overhead goods.

The air was heavy with the smell of Stockholm tar; the curved, creaky floorboards even had a deck-like camber, making them all feel mildly seasick after a few nanos.

Pi consulted her chit to see what they had to find amongst the cornucopia of wares.

"K, so we need, er, a box of Firecode-Matches, a lifejacket, and something called a binnagraph, whatever that is?"

"Sounds like a cross between an engineer's telegraph and a compass binnacle," said Gaia, giggling and stumbling her way to the counter.

Pi was none the wiser. They showed their chits to the venerable proprietor, one Ahab Salt. He stroked his bushy white beard and gave them all a toothless grin.

"You'll be wantin' the firsties' kit then?"

They nodded. Salt turned his back on them and stared thoughtfully at a veritable wall of hundreds of old wooden drawers. No two seemed alike in size, and not one of them had so much as a single label or distinguishing mark. He tugged at the cupped brass handle of one drawer in particular, and plonked two boxes of matches on the counter. He then went over to a display of rubbery orange lifejackets, removing two from a wobbly old shop dummy, a half-dozen moths taking to the air as he did so.

"Them things are ridiculous look," Leo began sniggering to himself, "us can't sparkin' wear one of they!"

"Shh!" chided Gaia, "you know they're compulsory for firsties."

"Why aren't they on a pinwheel?" said Pi.

"I think it's to be extra safe, in case you lose your pinwheel, or can't find it easily in an emergency. A big old orange thing is easier to find!"

"Loaded."

Whilst Pi and Gaia tried the vests on for size (Gaia thoughtfully checking to see if Leo could use 'hers' as well, much to his disgust), Salt carefully unlocked a drawer directly under the counter, withdrawing a wooden tray lined with green baize, which he set down carefully in front of them.

Leo's eyes widened. "Sparkin' tubes, that's more like it, what's they then?"

"Magellan's wrist-binnagraphs, young 'un, you won't find finer in all Inverse." Salt licked his lips, then removed two of the polished brass instruments, their casings so shiny they looked like gold. There was one large master dial within the chunky circular case in a horseshoe-shaped calibration, and two small circular dials set below it, all sealed under a thick, magnifying glass cover. "Calibrated fer all they waves o' power, you selects 'em like this, see." Salt moved a knurled brass bezel with a tiny handle around the outside. This moved a thin brass cursor that overlaid the glass, highlighting one of seven wave names in its window, a tiny bell chiming with every increment. "The blue needle shows yer which wave yer in. If yer needle shows one thing and yer bezel shows another, yer probably in a spot o' bother!" He gave them a gummy laugh.

"T'other needles," Salt pointed to the two smaller dials, "that's the red 'un there, he gives yer all yer principle lighthouses, and the yeller one – he shows yer all yer poles. Not all of 'em's got the eastern and western poles like these, see. Then there's yer green needle. Now you want to watch 'e, if 'e points to this here 'U' symbol, yer lookin at 'unknown perils' – monsters most like. Then you really are up the proverbial waterspout, cause 'e don't come on for any old nonsense! Anyway, with any luck you'll never need 'im, and if you do, it'll likely be too late!" Salt gave them another toothless laugh, whilst they looked at one another.

"Then you got yer sweep 'and what shows you yer

millis and yer nanos. Yer strap's made o' electric eel skin; you rubs 'im 'ard and 'e lights the binnagraph up if yer on the graveyard watch – even works underwater 'n'all." The old man gave them a demonstration, the complicated engravings on the dial illuminating with an eerie green glow.

Leo began to look quite distraught, as if he'd never seen anything more desirable in his life. He could get by without boring old matches and lifejackets (that smelt like old hot water bottles), but this exquisite instrument clearly threw all his switches – he just *had* to have one.

He swallowed hard, tears welling in his eyes. They could only have two, and he would have to let Gaia have his, as agreed. Salt looked over his hundreds of drawers and located two presentation boxes in finest mahogany, inlaid with protective brass corners, tiny blank plaques on their lids.

"Can get 'em engraved with yer names if yer calls back in fifty?"

"We've got time, we could bag them on the way back, couldn't we?" said Pi, just as spellbound as Leo.

"Well we could," said Gaia, "we'll have to come back this way anyway, to the Doors – oh go on then."

Salt stood poised, pencil and paper at the ready. "Epiphany Lightfoot." Pi showed him her chit.

Gaia sighed. She could see Leo was desperately in love with the binnagraph. "Leo Cydermott," she said generously.

Leo's face immediately changed from despair

to utter joy. "Rocker docker, Davy Jones Locker! Us promises us won't frames 'un ever again ever, ever, ever!"

"Unusual name fer a lumiette?" said Salt, scratching his beard.

Leo gave Gaia a peck on the cheek, and punched the air with jubilation. "We can share 'un, if you needs it like, it's yours really okay – I'll just look after 'un for 'un alright?"

"I suppose so," said Gaia, exchanging a parental look with Pi.

Pi glanced up at the old nautical timepiece set in a ship's wheel above the counter. "Kicker, only one hundred and eighty-five nanos left, guys."

"Fluxcake!" said Gaia. "We've got to visit The Third Eye!" She turned back to the counter. "Thank you so much, Mister Salt. We'll be back in a nano."

They broke into a laughable run, stumbling back through the store, Leo crashing into practically everything along the way.

Salt shook his head. "Bloomin' firsties."

They left the below-decks gloom of the Loft and raced into The Third Eye. With its higher ceilings and wide, well-lit aisles, it looked like a department store. Gaia led the way, transferring the superword brochure to Pi via a blue spark. Fortunately, there was no sign of Mizar as they began searching for the specified items.

Soon they had procured an odd assortment of goods, patch cables, torches and an address book, of all things. Gaia ticked off the last item on her, *Leo's*, chit.

"All done." She turned to Pi and grinned. "Now comes my personal favourite, The Lost Wave – pinwheel heaven!"

"Ooh, lead on, sister!"

"And 'un's got all the best codesurfing clobber!" added Leo.

They raced out of the Eye towards the entrance of The Lost Wave, Pi excitedly consulting her chit. "Megs, it says I get to choose one too!"

"It'll be mostly beachwear," said Gaia. "But there should be some other things on the pin if you want to change your wardrobe, and some stylish shoes too."

Pi pulled back her pockets to reveal her schoolwear. "Anything's gotta be better than these traggy threads."

Leo stealthily recced the Wave from the connecting door. "Coast clear, Cap'," snapping his 'scope shut as they strolled inside.

The Lost Wave was as brightly lit as the diner, but with its plain bleached decking and bamboo screens, it was more 'beach-hut' in style, stocked to the rafters with exotic surfing accessories and colourful swimwear.

Leo looked unimpressed. "Course the good stuff's in the shaper room look, but 'un would be password protected."

"And only open to lumixastras with the purple pockets," added Gaia, "although I think purple sashers like Prumiane can use it too."

Leo walked over to a substantial metal door that said 'Shaper Room'. It seemed out of keeping with the rest of the shop. He ran his hand over it lovingly. "What 'un wouldn't give to cop a scan inside look."

"What's with the crazy doorknob?" said Pi, examining a life-sized bronze hand, fingers splayed, sticking out of the door.

"'Un's a digitizer look, you give 'un an handshake and say the password to open 'un like this, see." Leo entwined his fingers with the metal digits and closed his eyes for a moment, a look of intense concentration on his face, then he let go with a frown. "Wish old Anders were here, she'd have 'un open in a nano."

"So what *is* in there exactly? Those rocket-powered shaper things you were telling me about?"

"Yes, just like the one the wave-pilot had," said Gaia. "And all the little extras like special wetsuits, Newton boots, things like that on pinwheels."

"They outfits are proper rokker look, not like this moldwortling old stuff!" Leo nodded dismissively at the beachwear. "Serious kit like that Kevin Spears had on look."

Gaia raised her feathery eyebrows. "I think you mean *Kelvin Spheres*, Mottles."

Pi looked impressed. "Yeah, now that was a *look*."

"Well, we don't have long, so I suppose we'd better find all these things." Gaia waved her chit at the clothing section.

Pi was immediately drawn to the rotating metal racks. They were filled to bursting with hundreds of different pinwheels, dozens of mannequins throughout the store displaying the various colourful combinations. "Just *so* much to choose from, I need to find me a mirror!" In no time she'd made her selection, becoming especially excited by a 'two for one' offer, one disc containing a huge variety of shoes, the other enabling her to finally change out of her school uniform – at last!

"Oops, forgot to tell you, oh well, too late," Gaia laughed.

Pi paused from stepping through shoe styles. "What? Did I glitch something?"

"No, but you won't be able to recover your old clothes now, unless you saved them. They will have all been deleted."

Pi waved her hand away dismissively. "Pah! As long as I'm still wearing them back in class."

They quickly finalised their selections and went to the counter to have their chits stamped.

Pi glanced up at the Waves' wacky surfboard clock. "Ninety nanos and counting, time's a-racing guys."

Gaia frowned. "Knew we shouldn't have spent so long on the wheels. We *have* to choose a popper, it's compulsory. You start looking for yours while I find trouble."

Pi looked confused. "You mean a surfboard, right?"

"I suppose, I think they're right there." Gaia pointed to something behind Pi, then gathered her pockets and raced off to find Leo.

"*Hiki,* surfboard, got it." Pi turned a full three-sixty, expecting to see a wall of surfboards somewhere that she'd missed. She'd been so engrossed in checking out the pinwheels, she'd hardly noticed anything else. But, save for the clock, there wasn't a single one to be seen anywhere. She quickly flipped through the gatefold brochure in her mind, checking the index for poppers. She was apparently standing right next to them. She thought at first that it must be some kind of mistake. Under the illuminated glass counter in front of her were dozens and dozens of miniature craft with pocket clips, like the ones you find on pens. Most of them looked like a cross between a fish and a jet plane. A sign clearly said 'Wave Poppers', so this must be right.

There were some thirty or so of these mysterious objects, all neatly laid out in three lines on the navy-blue felt, a reference number next to each. A colourful style name was centred above each line. 'Fishtails', 'Mantas' and 'Sharks' – in a range of sizes from 'S' to 'XXXL'.

Reef suddenly appeared by her side. "Easier if you use a glass." He handed her a wide oval-shaped magnifying glass from a stand which said 'Picking a Popper? Please Use Me'.

"Firstie, right?"

"It shows, doesn't it?"

"If it's for yourself, then I recommend either a Fishtail or a Manta; it's the best way to learn codesurfing basics. Just holler if you need more help. Better hurry, though, you don't want to miss the last elevator." Reef gave her a smile, tapped his wrist-binnagraph and left her to it.

Pi leaned over the display. "I don't load this at all, these things are like *micro*." She tried the magnifier. It revealed many small details on the colourful models, well, that's what she decided they were. It was to save space, like a catalogue. She would choose the popper she wanted, give them the model number, and they'd bring the real one around.

Gaia finally returned with Leo. She looked out of breath. "Chosen one yet?"

"Just speccing the merch'." Pi puffed her hair out of her face, and continued poring over the poppers. "I'm a bit of a grommie when it comes to surfing, what with my gyro leg and all. So I'm kinda outta my depth here."

Gaia grabbed a magnifier and began scanning them too. "So what's wrong with your leg, exactly?"

"My mum was with my dad when he had the car crash. She was seven months pregnant with me at the time."

"Oh my greenness! So you and your mum were injured too?"

"Sort of. She recovered okay, but it kinda messed up my spine and left leg, so I have to wear this support thing back home. Means I'm not really much good on a board, unlike Lani. She's amazing, she's won loads of comps."

"That's so sad. So you can't even surf with her?"

"Negs, but it's okay, I get to take lots of holos instead – I really enjoy photography."

"That's a spark-out," said Leo, "but wait till 'un tries a popper look, with 'un's avatar legs 'un won't know 'un's self!"

"Yeah, I sim on Q all the time like I said, but it's not the same. Can't wait to slide the waves you guys have here. Especially if they're like that therapy wave!"

"That was quite something, wasn't it!" said Gaia, looking wistful. "Well, our first step towards that is to match you up with the right popper! Hmm, we should really ask Mottles. He's practically lumixastra level at codesurfing, aren't you, Mottles?"

Pi looked with disbelief at Leo. He grinned and opened his pockets to reveal a dozen poppers clipped into loops inside. "That's quite a collection, bro. So you're really into these things – right?" Pi looked at him quizzically. "So what's the deal with all the models?"

Leo rolled his eyes like she was the stupidest person ever. "These ain't models, these are the real 'uns!"

Pi put her hands on her hips and looked incredulous. "K, so what am I glitching?"

"I'll show 'un in the tank, follows I." Leo made to march off, but Gaia stopped him.

"We haven't got *time*. Help Pi choose one, *then* you can show her on the way out. But you'd better be quick or we'll miss the binnagraphs."

Leo immediately switched to plan B, snatched up a magnifier, and barged between them.

"Any Shark is a rokker 'un to have look, but I'd have a Shark Turbo if I was 'un, they goes like the clappers! But they're proper devils when it comes to squeezing them into yer dongle-mitt mind."

Pi screwed up her face. "Dongle-what?"

"Sharks and turbos are only for really advanced codesurfers, silly, you're better off with one of these." Gaia pointed to the top two rows. "I'm getting that one, Manta 5D, size M. They're easier to manage and far more mitt-friendly."

Pi took a closer look at Gaia's selection, studying the intricate Celtic scrollwork motifs in red, silver and purple that ran down the length of the model. "It's so rad, and so *you*, turquoise – what a surprise! And somebody tell me what a dongle-mitt is, for heaven's sake?"

She could see Gaia was finally explaining this to her, and holding her right hand by way of illustration, but it was as if she had suddenly gone deaf and couldn't hear a word her feathery-haired friend was saying. She felt dizzy all of a sudden. What in Inverse was happening? It was almost as if she were back in her wavesite, reading her first ever superword on the 'blank' sheet of paper. Something within her had scanned and processed every model in the minutest detail in a trice, and had made the decision for her.

She'd been about to choose one of the beginners models like Gaia's, but now she knew she had to have the biggest, fastest board she could possibly lay her 'dongle-mitt' on. She ran the magnifier along the Sharks, stopping when she reached the very last one. It looked huge compared with the others, at least three times the size. It was dark metallic blue in colour, with explosive flame-like designs in black, red and orange and seemed to have twin thrusters at the back.

"K – I wanna bag *that* one! Hammerhead Turbo 16A in XXXL!"

"C'mon, make a choice, pleeeese," Gaia pleaded.

"Na na – seriously it's gotta be that moko Shark, scans like a real gun!" Pi reinforced her decision by beckoning Reef over. Gaia and Leo both went slack-jawed, Gaia with disbelief, Leo with amazement.

"Sparkin' yeah, wait till 'un sees 'un in the tank, it'll bust him wide open look!"

Gaia folded her arms across her chest and looked at him censoriously. "Yes, and that's why Pi *won't* be popping it in the tank. You're not allowed to do that with triple XLs or turbos!"

Reef was equally surprised at Pi's choice, but he could see she was determined to have it. "Just remember to keep the pocket clip on when you're not using it. It's a safety feature, in case you splash code on it by accident. We're out of stock on dongle-mitts, I'm afraid, but I'm sure they'll loan you one at the palace." He clipped the popper into a neat jeweller-style presentation box and stamped her chit. Pi thanked him and smiled. Explanations regarding the mysterious mitt would have to wait till later.

At least there was plenty of 'Newton's Board Wax' in stock. Apparently it contained an active gravity code that kept them glued to the board, even if it was upside-down. It was the next best thing to Newton Boots and did away with the need for a leash, according to Reef.

They had found everything on the list, but now there

were only seventy nanos left to collect the binnagraphs. Leo raced over to the other side of the store where there was a thirty-foot-long glass tank of watercode with a sign saying, 'TRY BEFORE U BUY', an assortment of tropical fish swimming lazily around inside it like a giant aquarium.

Leo removed the safety clip from one of his favourite poppers and dangled it provocatively over the middle of the tank. "This is 'popping-up' look." He dropped it in and the tiny model immediately lived up to its name, exploding into a twelve-foot-long surfboard as soon as it touched the watercode, showering them all with spray.

"*Kupaianaha,* dudes!"

"See, see, told 'un! Now watch this look." Leo puffed and grunted as he leant over to retrieve the board. But as soon as he'd lifted it clear (with a little help from Gaia), it rapidly shrank back to its original size. "See, 'un don't stay gurt for long."

"So when do I get to try mine, guys?" Pi pointed to a large sign. *NO TRIPLE XL that means TURBOs AS WELL!*

"'Un's just covering 'unselves, that tank's easy big enough look."

"Don't be ridiculous, Mottles, are you trying to get Pi in trouble?"

"Go on, pop him, I dares 'un!"

Pi snapped open the presentation box and plucked her Hammerhead Turbo XXXL from its velvet cushion. "It does look megs." The popper felt about ten times heavier than its size suggested, more like metal than the plastic material it appeared to be made of. "Can't wait to scan it popped, but there's no way I'd risk it here, Gaia's right."

"Can us at least cop a last scan before you puts 'un away look?"

"Sure." Pi had no sooner handed the popper to Leo than he'd darted up the access ramp, flicked off the safety clip and was dangling it provocatively over the middle of the tank. There was a sign to that effect: 'Don't come a cropper, open ONLY mid-water'.

Gaia waved her arms frantically. "Mottles, don't you dare! Remember if *you* pop it then it'll be coded only to *you*!"

A look of disappointment crossed Leo's face. "Oh ah, 'un's right. You'd better have 'un back look."

Pi climbed the ramp after him. Leo frowned and unceremoniously plonked the Shark back into Pi's waiting palm; then, as she closed her hand around it, a disconcerting grin crept across his face. "Now when 'un pops he'll be coded just to you look!" Before she could stop him, he'd closed his hand around hers and squeezed it tightly, making the Shark shoot from her fist and high into the air. It was like watching something in slo-mo. Pi could only look on in horror as the popper flew in a perfect arc towards the middle of the tank.

Gaia screamed, "Just get out of there!"

"Frazzballs!" Pi leapt from the ramp, Leo hot on her heels. As soon as it hit the watercode, it was as if a *real* shark had been dropped from a great height. Spray went everywhere. Pi and Gaia escaped the worst, but Leo was completely soaked. Once the watercode had calmed down, there was Pi's Hammerhead Turbo XXXL – completely wedged in the diagonal of the tank, its tail thrusters tangled up with the ceiling lights. There was an ominous cracking sound.

"Oh my greenness, it's still expanding. RUN – RUN!"

Pi had no idea Gaia could shout so loudly. They turned on their heels, but it was too late. The tank shattered spectacularly, sending a torrent of watercode racing across the floor. It hit them at knee height, carrying the Hammerhead, fish and a passing lumixastra with it. The Hammerhead fell over sideways, ripping out the lighting, then bashed past the counters, felling every mannequin in sight.

"Mottles, you nanopoop, look what you've done! All those poor fish!" Gaia tried to save a few as they flapped about on the floor.

Pi stumbled to her feet. "What the frazz, bro!"

Leo wiped his eyes and blinked a few times. "'Un's not all bad news, the shaper-room door's wide open look."

Gaia turned to look. "The code must have pushed it open."

"Pushed nothing, 'un busted the password didn't us!"

Pi glowered at him. "Seriously, dude?"

Gaia looked her straight in the eye. "Trust me, he didn't crack the code."

Pi crept towards the door, aware that Reef was momentarily distracted rescuing the fish, the reduced lighting throwing everything into shadow. "It wouldn't hurt to peek though, would it?"

Gaia growled with frustration as Leo darted inside. "I think it's academic!"

Whilst Gaia kept watch, Pi followed Leo into the restricted area. Once inside, she was not disappointed. the shaper room was the size of an aircraft hangar, filled to the rafters with dozens of huge and mysterious craft, many suspended in mid-air on wires to save space.

"Amped out! This place is megs!"

"Told 'un." Leo ran his hand lovingly over an enormous flying keel that curved gracefully upwards some fifty feet overhead. "Sparkin' shaper heaven look."

Pi rotated a full three-sixty. "I thought it would be like this dinky little room, with these dinky little boards, everything's so moko! Some of them look bigger than the one the wave-pilot had."

"'Un's got to be see, some of 'un's made for they Great Waves look."

"So shapers are always full-size? They don't shrink?"

"No, 'un does but these 'uns *are* just models look, but made up full-sized so 'un can see 'un proper."

"That's just so weird. So the small poppers are *real* but these bad boys are just for show?"

"The real 'uns are locked up safe at the palace, an hundred times more secure than these 'uns."

Pi noticed a clothing section full of cool-looking mannequins. "Hey rad, are these those special codesurfer outfits you were talking about?"

"Sparkin' yeah, pinners, hundreds of 'un." Leo dashed to Pi's side and began frantically spinning the racks of pinwheels, snatching four off their hooks.

Pi was horrified. "Isn't that stealing?"

"One for I, one for G, one for Anders, and this 'un's for you look." He waved it provocatively at her. "Well take 'un then, 'un's the host-system, 'un should have a proper shaper pilot's pinner look."

"Okay, okay." She reluctantly took it from his hand. "Won't we get into trouble?"

"Nah, no 'un'll ever know look, they ain't numbered or nothing."

Outside meanwhile, Gaia was watching the felled lumixastra with rising alarm. The unfortunate fellow had finally managed to stumble to his feet. But his pockets were still wrapped around his head, so he couldn't see. He was waving his hands about in front of him; they had seven fingers, and the backs were covered in spiral tattoos. It was *Magistry*!

Gaia stuck her head around the shaper-room door. "Psst – Magistry's out here!"

Leo's face fell. "Magistry? Hide they pinners and scarper!"

He and Pi stuffed their ill-gotten gains into their pockets and ran for the exit. Quickly, they closed the door behind them, just before Reef appeared. He seemed oblivious to their secret tour of the shaper room and just shook his head, a huge grin on his face. He tapped his binnagraph and just beckoned them go, implying he would take care of everything. He had a bucket of watercode with him half-full of fish already. Gaia flashed him a pained smile of embarrassment and decanted a couple she'd rescued into it.

Pi and Leo sloshed over to the Hammerhead, dragging it away from the wrecked stock as fast as they could. It had already begun to shrink, and by the time they'd reached the doorway it was down to a manageable four feet.

Pi glanced back. Magistry had nearly unwrapped the pockets from around his head.

"I've got it, just run... run!" She tucked the now three-foot popper under her arm. They rounded a corner into the Eye, Magistry stumbling into the doorway just behind them, scowling and crackling with fury, plumes of vapour pouring from his drenched clothing. Then Gaia noticed the time as they hurtled past the clock section. They had less than forty nanos till the last elevator! The stores were practically empty as they raced breathless into the Loft, galloping noisily over the decking to the counter.

Gaia was in front. Suddenly she swung out her arms, stopping the others dead. "Back – back, g'wan... shoo."

It was Mizar wearing his tell-tale black pockets, standing at the counter with his back to them.

Hearing the commotion behind him, he swung round, pursed his lips and sniffed the air. Then he strode purposefully back into the shop, swinging his sinister-looking cane, to investigate further.

Gaia knew of a shortcut to the Loft's stockroom; there was still a chance they could grab the binnagraphs and make it to the Doors in time. Then, horror of horrors, *Magistry* appeared, heading straight towards them. They all froze and dropped to the ground like stones.

"Don't look at him or he'll know," Gaia whispered, beckoning them to follow her. They crouched down and scuttled along, Pi trying not to let the still shrinking Hammerhead bash into anything and give the game away. She checked the superword brochure Gaia had sent her earlier and could see the shortcut in her mind. It led them up a tiny wooden staircase, every step creaking noisily as they tiptoed as fast as they dared with pained expressions.

Gaia pushed open a trapdoor. "Please, please open quietly." The hinges badly needed oiling and squeaked horribly. Then, at the very moment when they should have kept going, they all stopped, temporarily stunned by the unexpected sight above them; a cathedral-like space of vaulted beams and huge sheets of suspended canvas. A breeze from the windows animated these land-locked sails, the rafters cracking and creaking as if the whole thing were a ship.

"Gor, what's this old place then?"

"Must be the original sail loft; isn't it the most magical thing," said Gaia softly.

They took one last look before leaving by a second trapdoor, shuffling down another precipitous flight of wooden stairs into what looked like a stockroom. Gaia peered around the open doorway. They were just behind Salt's counter, his back turned towards them.

"Psst," Gaia hissed.

Salt turned around, looking for the source of the noise, a mystery hand beckoning him from the doorframe. "Be that you, Tobe?" he said, shuffling over in his worn tartan slippers.

Gaia dared show her face just long enough to see Mizar still sniffing around the shop.

Salt recognised her. "Oh, it be you rascals."

Gaia put her finger to her lips, then pointed towards Mizar just as he was turning around. A look of understanding crossed Salt's face and, without being told, he surreptitiously removed a brown carrier bag stamped '*The Sail Loft, Finest Quality Chandlery, by appointment*' from beneath the counter. Hiding it behind his back, he began whistling tunelessly, walking backwards towards the doorway as Mizar approached. Gaia gently took the bag and Salt began walking forwards again, unburdened, a wide proprietor's smile on his face, Mizar none the wiser.

"Sparkin' tubes, that was a close 'un."

Gaia peeked inside the bag. "All there, now we really *do* need to run."

The girls led the way, hoping the maps in their heads

didn't hold any more surprises. They pushed open an old door, almost hidden by giant coils of rope, and emerged into the pristine tiled kitchens of the Doors.

"Hoi, you can't come through here!" hollered a baker as they dashed past.

Pi glanced at the kitchen clock. "Kicker, only ten nanos left!" She barged through a swing door, sending a waiter and his tray reeling to catastrophe, wincing as the crockery shattered behind her.

Gaia espied the elevator doors closing. "Over there – go, go, go!"

Pi leapt towards the shrinking gap. "Hold the doors!" Squeezing through in the nick of time, they discovered the elevator was thankfully empty. They'd made it! They heaved a sigh of relief, then, just as the doors were about to meet, a seven-fingered hand covered in spiral tattoos thrust itself through the gap.

Gaia stared at the others intently. "Repeat after me, *goto param pinwheel – execute random – hot.*"

The others hastily mumbled the code, Gaia's outfit changing before their very eyes.

The door hydraulics hissed, stuttered and stopped, reversing to open, and Pi quickly dropped the Hammerhead, now fully shrunk, into the nearest pocket.

Magistry strode aggressively inside and studied them intently, beholding three firsties in a *very* odd assortment of clothes, neither styles, fabrics nor colours appearing to match, their footwear bordering on the eccentric even by Leo's standards. It seemed unusually humid inside the elevator; he ran his finger down a wall, it glistened with condensation. He gave them an awkward smile, pretending to find a hair on Leo's uncoordinated lapel which he 'removed' – but they knew he was expecting to find damp clothing. The fabric was bone dry. He looked disappointed and grunted, punching a floor button with a knuckle. The doors closed, and they began to descend.

The floor indicator light raced through hundreds of numbers, for line after line around the elevator walls, until they became a blur. They felt their stomachs do a somersault, as if they were plunging into the bowels of the earth. All at once the lift shuddered to a halt, and the doors opened with the neat chime of a bell.

On the opposite wall of the corridor outside, an aged stone plaque read: *Stargazey Pi – Founded 5.14159 Billion Megaparsecs*, a smaller sign beneath in discoloured brass stating simply: *Bowsprit*.

SIXTEEN

STARGAZEY PI

Magistry left the elevator without even giving them a backward glance. They all bent double, their hands braced upon their knees, only then realising they'd been holding their breath the whole time.

"Lummy, close or what."

"Thank greenness for Trine's shortcut."

"So *that's* what that was." Pi straightened up, amused at how bizarre her clothing looked in the elevator's shiny walls.

"It's useful if you get wet and need to dry your hair and everything in a hurry," said Gaia. "But the selection leaves a bit to be desired! We'd better run or we'll miss the introductory address."

"Us can't go in there looking like a stuffed marrow, they'll laugh at I for weeks."

"You can tweak it on the move, Mottles, c'mon." Gaia led the way at a brisk trot.

Leo began playing with his pinwheel. It would take a lot to make his clothing even worse, but he somehow managed to do this with every step.

Their footfalls echoed down a vaulted stone cloister, as high as a cathedral's nave. It was filled with bright daylight streaming in from the many skylights above. Pi began to lag behind. She'd removed her binnagraph from its box and was trying to get the oversized strap to fasten securely around her tiny wrist, distracted by the enormous arches towering overhead. She paused, running a finger over the green marble of a column; it felt icy cold.

"We must be way underground, guess that's why we couldn't scan it?" Her voice trailed off, it sounded too loud in the silence. "So how come there's still daylight down here?"

Suddenly the stillness was rent from above, the light dimmed and she froze, noticing strange blue clouds scudding across the previously unblemished sky. The leaded windows protested noisily, as if they might shatter at any moment, the wind beat against them so violently. But it was not the vagaries of the air that she beheld.

Gaia turned around and walked backwards for a few steps with a knowing smile. "The reason you couldn't see it is because we're under the sea."

"You're smokin' me, right?"

Gaia shook her head. It was the watercode ocean above them, rolling over the glass. Pi ran to catch up with the others.

Gaia read her thoughts. "They won't break, you know, the coded glazing makes them the equivalent of two feet thick. I read it in the brochure they sent Dad, take a look." Gaia brushed her hand against Pi's, creating a blue spark.

"Freaks! Those things still make me jump!" Pi's head instantly filled with the elephantine halls and meritorious attributes of this strangest of structures. "Wow, this is one crazy palace."

They finally reached the end of the cloister, pausing outside an enormous pair of arched wooden doors, the words *Main Royal* in faded gold letters upon them.

"Closed. Oh dear, not a good sign, means we're late." Gaia grabbed the handle of a smaller opening inset of the right-hand door. She tried turning it, but it wouldn't budge. "Definitely locked, we'll have to try the main one." She grasped the twisted wrought-iron ring, trying to move the heavy latch upwards. The drone of a distant voice was just audible on the other side. "Please don't make any noise, please," Gaia whispered, exerting more force on the stubborn latch.

"'Un's going to give all of a sudden look if 'un's not—" Leo's warning came too late. The latch gave suddenly, a tremendous *bang* echoing all the way down the cloister. Gaia grimaced, forced to follow through and open the door, just enough for them all to squeeze through. Its hinges badly needed oiling, compounding her embarrassment. A nearby Grey quickly ushered them in, scurrying up a tiny stepladder so he could reach the door handle to close it. They bowed their heads, not daring to see the result of their noisy entrance.

"What the—" Pi lurched backwards, pinning herself against the back wall. The others did likewise. Before them lay an enormous circular chasm, its shadowy void framed by a lip of well-worn stonework barely three feet wide. Above them, a great vaulted circular skylight creaked and cracked ominously as the watercode moved over it.

"What *is* this place?" Pi frantically leafed through the palace brochure in her mind to see if they'd taken a wrong turn.

"Gor lummy, us could have fallen right in 'un, daft wuzzocks leaving a big hole like that lying around."

"This *must* be right," said Gaia, screwing up her face.

The Grey was completely nonplussed. He pointed to a small wooden sign standing perilously close to the edge which read 'Mind The Step', silently indicating for them to proceed, as if they might wish to hurl themselves into oblivion. When it became obvious that they preferred to remain in the land of the living, he walked straight over the edge of the precipice. The girls would have let out a shriek, were it not for the fact that the Grey still remained visible. He was now standing *inside* the lip of the hole as if he had magnetic feet. He gave them a tiny rectangular grin and beckoned them follow.

Gaia dared to look first, the others reluctantly

leaving the safety of the horizontal, to peek at the perilously vertical. An enormous cylindrical hall met their eyes. The chasm *was* Main Royal, for, far below them, hundreds of lumixastras could be seen seated around the vast circular inside 'wall'. This was of course the 'floor' and an endless one at that. Pi calculated the dimensions as being at least ten thousand feet deep, and another thousand across. It seemed to have been designed for a far larger gathering than the one now present.

Leo was first to state the obvious. "Some of 'un's sitting on the ceiling look."

Gaia grasped the peculiar geometry a little more easily. "I think the ceiling's that big skylight behind us; the rest is all floor, Mottles."

Pi gingerly tested the vertical 'floor' with her left foot, her sense of vertigo so disconcerted by the confusing layout she completely lost her balance and 'fell' inside, a slight exclamation escaping her lips.

The speaker continued droning away from a magnificent flying pulpit some way off in the distance. Shaped like the head of some great sea-dragon, fully fanged, and with glaring red eyes, the dark carved wood of its scaly neck snaked fully five hundred feet into the air. He paused his address; three hundred pairs of eyes turned to look at them. Gaia and Leo were now beside her as well, muted tittering dogging their every step. Gaia had meant to tweak all their pinwheels before they'd entered, but didn't think they'd be noticed. How wrong she was, although most of the attention was drawn by Leo's now incomprehensible attire.

The rotund man who had been speaking repeatedly cleared his throat, trying to regain the assembly's attention, Pi and her friends now two shades of red and one of green.

"It's only Gregius Samovar, not even a proper lumixastra really, he's in charge of processor fitness regimes," Gaia whispered, not daring to use psy; there were far too many hot receivers around.

Another Grey approached them, and the speaker finally managed to attract everyone's notice again, practically choking himself in the process. The Grey quickly noted the names on their clasps and consulted a list. "Good Inverse, Browser Mizzen-Gaff, north-east please," he said, pointing way above their heads.

Pi followed the compass bearings, marked at intervals by aged brass arrows set into the endless floor. "They're real keen on this total surface facilitation thing, aren't they?"

Gaia agreed. "Well if you think about it, ceilings are such a waste of space."

Pi quickly warmed to the unique architecture. The sheer novelty of walking all the way 'up' the 'wall' and onto the 'ceiling', in a smooth curve of ancient flagstones, couldn't help but make her smile. Every now and then, the floor was punctuated by skylights set within it, their thick glass permitting a view of the ever darker ocean outside, a shiny brass marker noting the depth in fathoms. They had apparently descended three hundred and forty-eight already.

There were thin metal bands that ran in pairs through the floor as well, in a gradual spiral right down the hall. Pi assumed these were some kind of reinforcement. Mysterious brass plaques shaped like whale flukes were set between them at regular intervals, worn as smooth and shiny as the compass arrows, by aeons of passing feet, no doubt. Leo had never seen anything like it. Even Gaia looked surprised, both gawping like tourists as they ended up walking upside-down relative to where they started.

Gaia suddenly spotted a friendly face, well, the little of it she could see. "It's Mime!"

Andomime turned and patted the vacant seat next to her, one of three that had their names, literally, written upon them, prefixed with either *Lumian* or *Lumiette* in black Indian ink on a small index card in the seat's back. It reminded Pi of the hand written name on her exam desk back at school, musing for a moment that she was still doubtless frozen in that unflattering sneeze.

Gaia sat nearest Andomime, then Leo, shuffling awkwardly and wriggling with his elbows until he was comfortable, Pi on the outside. The browser seats appeared to be arranged in boat-like pods of twenty-five, four across by six deep. A single swivel chair set within the curved 'bow' appeared vacant. Well that and the seat intended for missing lumiette Zoa Heliotrope. The venerable oak panelling of the browser's sides was richly carved with astronomical motifs and algebraic symbols, *Mizzen-Gaff* clearly visible in a glazed destination board on the stern transom. All the browsers were skewed at a slight angle towards the pulpit-dragon, in a great circle of twelve.

The seats themselves all had strange hinged cushioned headrests, well, that's what Pi decided they were, although they didn't seem to function properly as such. They were all furnished with unusual wooden desks too. They seemed quite ancient, their lids divided into three equal sections from left to right, the marks, ink stains and indecipherable symbols of countless ages covering their every surface. And there were two small raised brass signs with glass fronts at the extreme right-hand left-hand corners of each desk. They looked as if they might light up, but they were too dark for her to read the writing, although between them was a small hinged door with 'Keep Clear' stencilled upon it.

Leo, ever inquisitive, tried to peek under the lids but they appeared to be shut fast, a small eyeless brass lock for each. So he amused himself by adding to the graffiti already carved into his desk, using his Barmy-Knife to whittle his name with the first tool extracted, which wasn't exactly ideal, as it was originally designed for removing micro-meteorites from hats.

Pi tried not to let her attention wander too far from the pulpit. It was one thing to puzzle over the unique chandeliers erupting from the ends of ornate iron lamp posts, as they rose up almost to the centre of the hall, their clusters of lamps fanning out in all directions from the tops, clearly illustrating the peculiar circular gravity, but looking all the way down onto the heads of those nearly a thousand feet 'below' was a no-no. It made her feel so queasy she had to grip her desk for reassurance and stare at her feet. At the far end of the hall was a flat circular wall with four equidistant doors, its surface entirely covered by a fabulous mural. This depicted a raging sea, fantastical figures and mythical monsters that would not have shamed Michelangelo. Around the wall's rim were many more browsers, some covered by dust sheets, as if they had long been abandoned.

Samovar finally stopped talking, which was just as well, as everybody now looked extremely bored. Polite, but muted, applause rippled around the hall as he slowly stepped down the neck of the pulpit-dragon, only to be passed by Higgs-Boson coming the other way.

The head of universal affairs tucked his thumbs behind his lapels and puffed out his chest as he prepared to speak. It was only then that Pi realised how feeble Samovar's voice had been. Everybody sat bolt upright the moment the lumixastra's resonant voice boomed forth. "Well, I'm sure we'd all like to thank Mister Samovar for his entreaties regarding processor fitness regimes, although I would remind those visitors of a sporting disposition that the palace supercollider is not for the faint-hearted. Now for the first business of the day. Browser Gunwales will be escorting many of you to Topgallant, of course, for the latest meeting of the General War Council."

Leo's face lit up. "What 'un wouldn't give to be a nanobug in there look."

"Shh," Gaia hissed.

"Next, those amongst you of a more scientific bent will be escorted by Browser Meridian to Upper Topsail, where you will receive the latest updated software regarding the continuing problem of piracy plaguing our data-fleets."

"Pirates, sparkin'."

Gaia trod on Leo's toes.

"Finally, the rest of us will be escorted by yours truly in Browser Admiral to the library, whence," Higgs-Boson's voice dropped to near inaudibility, "whence we shall take up where we left off, so to speak. I need hardly add that this is all extremely hush-hush." He then fell silent and looked thoughtful for a moment. Gaia whispered in Pi's ear, "Feel that tingling in your head?"

Pi nodded. "Yeah, what is it?"

"He's using crypt, the most secure form of psy. Only a few lumixastras can read it. We just feel it as tingling."

"Love to know what they're saying."

"Us and 'un both," agreed Leo.

The tingling suddenly stopped and Higgs-Boson resumed speaking. "Well, dear hearts, there you have it. On behalf of Her Majesty, I thank you all for your attention." With that, he bowed his head a few times to acknowledge the ripple of applause, then turned and began to descend the snaking steps.

Pi's attention was suddenly caught by Peahi. He was racing up the other way, and even at this distance, she could tell he was flustered. She nudged Gaia and nodded towards the action. Gaia studied the hurried interchange between the two, but just as she was about to speak, Andomime's psy whispered in their heads.

"Most interesting, there has been a change of plan and it apparently concerns one of us."

The lumixastra turned around and puffed his way back up to the top, emerging in the pulpit-dragon once again. The assembly's chatter fell silent and they restored their attention. Higgs-Boson cleared his throat and harrumphed a few times, shuffling some papers. "Ah yes, er, one further item has just been brought to my attention by the secretary. With sincerest apologies to our modest complement of younger Inversians, I am reminded that if all lumians and lumiettes here present would kindly use their passwords to unlock their folders, they will be able to move their flick-books to their desktops. A member of palace staff will then be along shortly to conduct you all on a brief introductory tour of the palace. Well, I think that concludes matters?" He glanced back at Peahi, who could now be seen smiling and nodding. He then resumed his descent down the pulpit-dragon's neck as the assembly burst into noisy chatter.

Pi looked at Gaia. "Password, what password?"

"You know, the one they gave you with the

invitation. Don't say it out loud though, just touch the lock with your finger like this, and use psy."

"Oh *that*." Pi touched the right-hand lock with her finger and said *lumixastra* in her mind – it worked! The lock popped immediately. She opened the lid and found it was jam-packed with tiny flick-books: *Stargazey Spied, A Visitor's Guide To The Palace*, with its dazzling purple and gold cover; *Downloads For Dummies* in a rather dull shade of yellow, and finally, a curious series in equally dull brown covers entitled *The Mandlebrot Metro*, in twenty-six separate volumes from A-Z. Plus a mysterious matching twenty-seventh with no title.

Leo began prodding his brass lock repeatedly, banging it with his fist, nudging it with his knuckles, every pugilistic permutation he could think of.

Gaia paused from retrieving her flicks. "Somebody's forgotten their password, haven't they? You'll just have to request a reminder, Mottles."

Leo reluctantly stuck up his hand and a Grey was soon at his side, leafing through a little red book entitled *Password Reminders*.

"Lumian to Cydermott, ah yes, here we to are, digits please."

Leo extended his hand with a frown, several lumixastras in the next browser looking on with amusement. The Grey touched his hand.

"Gor, love a diode, how'd I ever forget 'un." Leo finally opened his desk, when his face immediately fell. "Sparkin' tubes! There's loads of 'un look. Does us have to get 'un all out?"

"Afraid so, Mottles, they're only a tenth of a nano each," said Gaia.

Leo quickly did the maths. "Lummy, that's a whole two and a half nanos' scanning that is!"

Gaia shook her head and continued arranging all her flicks into a neat rectangle on her desktop. Suddenly, a fugal fanfare echoed around the hall and the Queen herself appeared in the pulpit, flanked by various richly-attired courtiers. The whole assembly shambled to their feet.

Gaia psy'd Pi. *"It's the Universal Anthem, do your best."*

Leo flashed her a mischievous look. *"Just mime if 'un don't know the words look."*

"As if."

Then Gaia brushed her hand, and all eighteen ponderous verses came alive in her head. She was about to join in with the somewhat meandering tune, when a very distinguished voice crackled between her ears.

"Dearest Pi, I am so gratified that you chose to join us." There was no mistaking the voice, but was it a trick? An impersonation like the voice she'd heard on *Caliban?* She surreptitiously withdrew the security seal she'd been given, stealing a quick peek. The Queen's smiling face stared back at her, giving her quite a shock. The voice was authentic! Pi stared with disbelief at the figure in the pulpit. Yet, even as the Queen stood there, looking very composed and regal,

she betrayed not the slightest hint of any clandestine communication. *"You will shortly visit our magnificent and extensive library; there is something I require you to do for me there. Whatever you may encounter, fear nothing."*

Then Pi experienced a high-pitched buzzing sound and a flash of light seemed to shoot between her eyes, making her right hand feel curiously hot.

"Tell no one of this message; please remember, I am your friend."

Then before she knew it she'd snapped back to reality, only to discover that everybody was singing the last few bars of the anthem. Where had the time gone?

As the last note died away, one of the courtiers stepped forward and proclaimed, "Long live Her Majesty, lux est omnis!"

The whole assembly erupted with one shout. "LUX EST OMNIS!"

Immediately all the desk lamps lit up on the right-hand side and the words *splice the main brace* became visible, accompanied by a bell sound not unlike the one you hear in an aircraft when the seatbelt sign goes on.

A rather bedraggled-looking lumixastra shambled onto a podium beneath the pulpit-dragon and pulled a cable, firing a small brass cannon, deafening practically everybody as its noise totally belied its diminutive size, totally engulfing Browser Fore-Topgallant in choking black smoke. Straight away the whole assembly began snapping down the peculiar hinged 'head rests'. Pi discovered that the oddly-shaped device held her shoulders in place, keeping her firmly in her seat, just like the safety bars on a roller-coaster.

Greys began scooting through the aisles like cabin staff, checking all the main braces were well and truly spliced. A dozen palace staff fanned out from their shadowy seats beneath the pulpit-dragon and began taking the single swivel-seat in the bow of each browser. Gaia gave Pi a wide-eyed look as a very unusual-looking palace official bore down on them, a metallic red dress beneath her purple pockets, her slight build and delicate features topped off with a *pièce de résistance* of a hairdo. Her long red hair was plaited into elaborate coppery skeins that created a fully functional birdcage upon her head. It came complete with four colourful occupants, chirping and hopping from perch to perch.

She paused to address the browser, giving them all a slight bow. "Good Inverse, Mizzen-Gaff. My name is Amorpha Fibonacci. I am the lumixastra for unappliable mathematics to the palace and your custodian for the tour."

"Good Inverse, Lumixastra Fibonacci," they all replied in ragged chorus. Pi instinctively tried to stand up but discovered, of course, that she couldn't.

"Now then, let me see." Fibonacci consulted a piece of paper in her hand. "Lumian Cydermott, if you would kindly do the honours and look up *W* for *whale-way* in your address book, then kindly touch the index where it says *Visitors' Tour*. We shall shortly be able to enjoy a quick excursion around the palace's Upper Domains."

Leo fumbled through his pockets, going bright red as numerous incorrect (and occasionally dangerous) objects were retrieved.

Gaia nudged him and handed him her address book. "You don't have an address book, you had to give me yours, remember?"

Leo groaned, slumping forward till his forehead touched his desktop. "Needs some new valves in me short-term don't us!"

Gaia groaned with exasperation and opened the book for him. "Look, that's the one, just touch it where it says *locate*, Mottles."

Leo straightened up and reluctantly complied. As soon as his finger touched the page, a powerful engine shuddered into life beneath them, the smell of ozone suggesting it was electric. His face lit up. "Sparkin', these book things are a bit of alright, ain't 'un!"

Lumixastra Fibonacci mixed a wince with a smile and took her seat, swivelling it to face forwards, spliced her main brace and they were off.

All the other browsers began moving at the same time. Now Pi understood the purpose of the spiral pairs of brass lines that ran through the hall; they were a kind of railway. She looked back over her well-braced shoulders, as best she could at any rate, noting the train of browsers behind. Blue sparks could clearly be seen erupting from the whale flukes as the browsers ran over them. They provided electricity for the motors and, according to her superword brochure, they were made of pure virtual gold. All twelve browsers were now spiralling merrily down the hall, Mizzen-Gaff at the head of them, which made everybody on board feel very important. They had only completed two circuits when they reached the first in a series of what appeared to be pairs of tunnels, their horseshoe-shaped mouths framed by ornate gilded sculptures of stylised waves and sea monsters. Pi gripped her desk for dear life, fearing all her flicks would fly off as the browser suddenly inverted, disappearing into the first entrance with a rapid twisting motion. But the peculiar gravity ensured not a single flick was lost, and they passed quickly through a well-lit cylindrical corridor (Leo making more fuss than was strictly necessary), suddenly emerging into a great spherical room on the other side.

Lumixastra Fibonacci swivelled her seat around to face them. "First flicks then everybody, please, *Stargazey Spied,* load at will. A minor point of interest, this is your browser's namesake domain, Mizzen-Gaff."

Pi quickly located her miniature guide and readied it, flicking through the two hundred pages in a trice, only to discover she'd been holding it upside-down in her haste and had therefore loaded it *backwards.* It seemed to work just as well, her head now filled with all manner of facts, figures, maps and trivia that made the palace brochure look very terse. Leo managed to download three random volumes of *The Mandlebrot Metro* before he located the correct flick, distracted by the peculiar layout of this strange new domain.

The 'whale-way' had evidently inverted through the connecting corridor so it could align itself with the spherical interior of Mizzen-Gaff, its curious bookcases and tables following the continuous curve of the endless floor. They had no sooner completed a circuit and a half than they were disappearing into yet another corridor on the far side, emerging into an even larger spheroom (as Pi now realised they were called), named Mizzen-Topgallant.

Fibonacci began noting items of interest as they trundled by. "Looking up, we now pass the famous *Belladonna of the Rocks* tryptych, by that grand-master of the Inversian renaissance, Geometro Da Blini."

Everybody cricked their necks to behold a large, richly painted orb, apparently suspended in mid-air. It was divided by vertical gilt framing into three equal sections. It reminded Pi of a giant Fabergé egg. According to her guide, the orb remained in place without any support, delicately balanced in the neutral gravity of the spheroom's centre. The browser quickly orbited Mizzen-Topgallant and exited back into Mizzen-Gaff, all the other browsers following them. Pi noted a few familiar faces as she looked down, or was that up? In the last two, Prumiane was staring at her coldly, surrounded by her family and numerous acolytes. She looked as if she was using psy, her eyes blazed so intently, but nothing came through. Pi gave her a small wave and Prumiane scowled back, as if frustrated by something. Then Leo nudged Pi's elbow. Pi looked across and saw Gaia pointing discreetly at Andomime. Her eyeless friend's face was twitching and ticking. Pi's spam filter was working just fine!

She didn't have to worry about Prumiane for much longer. They entered the great spherhall of Main Royal again, descended another circuit and a quarter, then whizzed just as quickly through two more spherooms similar to the last, Fore-Topgallant and Topgallant. These were the destination domains for the Geights, amongst others. When they emerged back into Main Royal, the last four browsers, including that of a certain lumiesse, were no longer with them. Pi heaved a sigh of relief, as did Andomime, quite worn out by all that psy-jamming.

As they continued to spiral down Main Royal, Fibonacci swung her seat round and faced them sternly. "Best behaviour please, everybody. We are about to enter the Queen's personal domain, Seraphim, beyond which is Upper-Topsail. Strictly *no* talking and absolutely *no* psy-speak whilst we are inside. Please consult your guides for further information, as I will be similarly mute." This was not entirely true as it turned out; Pi and the others didn't know it, but they were about to undergo trial by stifled laughter, that would make the episode at the Southern Lighthouse look positively tame.

The browsers entered the panelled corridor and

inverted smoothly as before; everybody was doubly curious, poring over their guides in anticipation. The Queen's personal sanctuary was literally a labyrinth of magnificently carved bookshelves, the whole spherical floor being covered by them in an angular maze some twelve feet high. The remaining eight browsers travelled extra slowly, so as to minimise any disturbance, allowing more time for everybody to satisfy their curiosity. Lumixastra Fibonacci's birds continued to sing and twitter as normal. As there was no sign of the Queen, Fibonacci raised her hand and clicked her fingers smartly to silence them. Then the real trouble started. Gaia reached across Leo and touched Pi's arm. She'd spotted the Queen sitting at her desk; the tracks were about to carry them right by.

The birds began chirping noisily once more, Fibonacci giving them one last brace of desperate finger-snaps. The Queen raised her eyes from her work, thinking somebody was trying to gain her attention. Fibonacci nodded and smiled awkwardly, her hairdo silent for a few brief moments.

Then the birds started up again, only this time there was more to their repertoire than just chirping. "Naughty birdy, bad birdy, who's a naughty birdie then? I'm a naughty birdy." Everybody in the browser fought to keep their mouths tight as clams, muffled squeaks coming from the browsers behind, as they could hear everything too. "Birdy made a mess, dirty birdy, whoops a daisy, clean it up, clean it up. Who's a loopy lumixastra? You're a loopy lumixastra, loopy, loopy, loopy, lumixastra!"

The browser seemed to take forever to trundle past the Queen, the endless bookcases and out the other side, the birds piling up one ludicrous remark upon another without pause. Poor Lumixastra Fibonacci could hardly get out of the spheroom quickly enough, impotently wringing her hands in her lap until they reached the connecting corridor to Upper-Topsail, where she began clicking her fingers faster than a pair of castanets as they sailed through. It didn't do a bit of good; the birds began telling jokes, each trying to outdo the other, every punchline followed by riotous squawking from the other three. Fibonacci tried to ignore them, hoping they would stop if she did. At least they were out of the Queen's earshot now. They had entered the grandest spheroom yet. There was lots to see, amazing watercode sculptures and glassy holograms displayed everywhere they looked. Not that anybody took much notice; they were too busy clutching their aching ribs, tears running down their cheeks with muffled mirth.

The next four browsers slowed to a stop. They had reached *their* destination spheroom, and the anti-piracy meeting. As she passed overhead and looked down, Pi noticed Phabian in one of them. He sensed her attention and looked back up, Pi's heart skipping a beat as their eyes met. He gave her a gamma-bright smile and snapped his fingers about his head in mimicry of Fibonacci's maddening birds.

By the time they'd passed back through the hallowed silence of Seraphim, it became almost torturously impossible to contain themselves. The birds, having tired of jokes, were now singing a boisterous barbershop medley, everything from bawdy sea shanties (that would have made a Jack Tarr blush) to something that sounded very like 'Chattanooga Choo Choo' – all in perfect four-part harmony. Leo couldn't take it any longer, burying his face in his pockets, releasing his hysterics harmlessly into a tiny parallel universe.

The Queen pretended not to notice the impromptu concert as she pored over a watertext on her desk, though Pi swore she saw the corners of her mouth twitch as they trundled past. As soon as they returned to Main Royal, there was silence, the frightful feathery foursome hopping innocently from perch to perch, uttering nothing more than an occasional chirp.

SEVENTEEN

THE MANDLEBROT-SETI LIBRARY

As the remaining four browsers sped up again, Fibonacci angrily extracted several generous stalks of millet from the skeins of her hair, hurling them expertly into a passing wastebasket as the browser spiralled past.

Leo had almost managed to compose himself, although he still suffered the odd hiccup of hilarity. "Flusterin' filaments! Us thought us would burn out 'un's valves laughing."

Pi was still dabbing her eyes and trying to control her giggles. "Smartest cage birds I ever heard, they'd clean up on daytime holo back home. They took *no* notice of her; couldn't she stop them with a shortcut or something?"

"She couldn't stop them because they're her cyberpomps," said Gaia, still grinning from ear to ear. "They hold the record for being the smallest ones in Inverse, and the only ones too small for the hippodromes. They can do whatever they like and get clean away with it! You can't stop a pomp once it's been installed, you see, you can only tame them a bit and hope for the best."

The browsers had spun around another circuit and a quarter to the next spherooms on their tour, Admiral and Periscope. Fibonacci had her address book in her hands and pressed something on one of the pages. Immediately the points changed, carrying them straight past the spheroom portals.

Gaia looked back, a confused look on her face. "That's funny, I thought we were supposed to go in there?"

Pi consulted the palace brochure in her mind. The first spheroom was a common room for palace officials and the second, an observation area, complete with functional periscope as its name suggested. "Probably afraid the birds would make her look gyro in front of all the other lumixastras."

"Bit late for that!" Gaia giggled. "But she's going to have to take us into the next one, it's our first proper download."

Pi scrolled down the 'tour timetable' in her head. "Whoa! Those little guys are just gonna love this."

Leo was having trouble finding the right file in his mind, the consequence of having loaded no less than twelve flicks erroneously. "What's the next 'un then? Only me valves is all fuddled."

"Only the Mandlebrot-Seti, the largest library in

Inverse." Gaia gave him an impish grin. "Just think what they might get up to in there."

Leo was about to agree, when the browser suddenly inverted. They had indeed arrived at the universe's largest virtual repository of the written superword.

Fibonacci swung around to face them, looking noticeably self-conscious. "Due to the time lost in transiting… transiting … Sera… Sera… the Queen's study," she could hardly bring herself to say the words, watching intently for the slightest smirk on her charges' faces, "I have decided to skip our tour of Admiral and Periscope."

"Yeah, righto. Tell us another 'un."

Gaia nudged Leo in the ribs. "Not so loud, nitbyte."

"Turn to your Mandlebrot flicks, please, we will be loading all twenty-seven in alphabetical order starting with *Downloads for Dummies*." Fibonacci held the brown flick over her head for them all to see. "This is important, has anybody *not* got their *Dummies*?" A ripple of snickering went through the browser, making Fibonacci even more twitchy. "Scan – scan, come along, look sharp, we don't have much time, books don't grow on trees you know!"

At this, her birds burst into riotous laughter. "Don't grow on trees, don't grow on trees! That's a good one!" tears rolling down the cheeks of everybody within earshot.

The browsers finally slowed to a halt, literally. They had reached a place called Scriveners Halt. Here, the whale-way split into many different tracks and sidings, all seemingly controlled from a signal box up ahead. With its dark mahogany panelling and ornately carved pediment, it reminded Pi of a giant wardrobe. A couple of Greys could be seen sipping tea in the glazed interior, the enormous spherhall of Mandlebrot-Seti 'A', by far the largest spherhall they had yet seen, visible just beyond.

Two Greys in oil-stained boiler suits appeared and began walking around the browsers, banging the wheels with small hammers as they went.

"Wheeltapping, a very important safety precaution for high-speed transfers," noted Gaia, brandishing her *Dummies* flick.

The other three browsers slowed behind them. They'd been diverted to another siding, their complements seemingly comprising particularly venerable lumixastras, including Higgs-Boson (who gave Pi a discreet wave). Then a signal changed to reveal a large letter 'U' and this trio of browsers rapidly disappeared into the labyrinth of bookshelves, until there was nothing more to be heard of them than the distant clickety-clack of their progress. Mizzen-Gaff was on its own now.

Leo pulled an inscrutable face. "There 'un all goes look, give anything to know what's so secret about the letter 'U' look?"

Pi sensed that deep inside she actually *knew* what Higgs-Boson and the others were up to, but she couldn't quite put her finger on it, strongly suspecting it was something to do with the mysterious message from the Queen earlier. She desperately wanted to share this with Gaia, for her thoughts, but recalled the Queen's request for secrecy.

Mizzen-Gaff, meanwhile, seemed in no hurry to go anywhere. The main brace lights all went out and their restraints popped up, freeing their shoulders, a second light illuminating to reveal the words 'Drop Anchor'. All the firsties groaned and stretched, gratefully shrugging off the constriction.

The fluttering sound of dozens of flicks soon filled the air, Lumian Bhami Superbrahamian pausing now and again to administer eye drops. He'd stuffed over four hundred flicks into his pockets for in-flight reading aboard *Ariel*, and had rather overdone it.

Pi reached Mandlebrot 'N', noticing that both Gaia's and Andomime's flicks were fast disappearing, Andomime whizzing through hers with her braille, finger flick-reader. Pi was already in a muddle, trying to keep those she'd read separate from those she hadn't.

Gaia noticed her predicament. "You put them in the wastebasket afterwards like this, you see?" She held up an already-scanned flick and popped it through a tiny brass letterbox in her desktop. Pi hadn't noticed it before. *Dummies* didn't have a word to say about something so practical. Gaia was nearly done, she'd reached Mandlebrot 'W' and had already binned the ones she'd read. Pi became aware of the sound of running water; it was coming from her side of the browser.

It was a subject dear to Gaia's heart. "It's all about recycling. Once they're in the wastebasket, they're converted back to watercode. The desks are all plumbed together you see? Clever, isn't it?"

Pi leaned over to peek. Sure enough, watercode was pouring out of a small pipe from the browser and into a drain in the floor. Finally, she posted Mandlebrot 'Z', a little bemused that after twenty-seven flicks, her head wasn't exactly buzzing with information. "After *Dummies*, nothing seemed to happen. Did I do something wrong?"

Leo looked similarly perplexed. "Us ain't getting nothing out of 'un either, bunch of duds if you asks I."

"*Dummies* is a proper download, like the pilot flicks on *Caliban*," said Gaia. "But the others are just to format you for the real downloads in the library later. They don't actually contain any data, though why they don't *tell* you that in *Dummies* is beyond me!"

"Cos 'un was written by a proper dingleberry, that's why!" said Leo, still scanning Mandlebrot 'O', and now way behind.

Gaia posted her last flick, then gave Pi a funny look, as if to suggest she wanted to share something. She leant backwards so Pi could clearly see Andomime. She hadn't posted any flicks at all, and was secretly stuffing them into her pockets.

Andomime sensed their interest and defended her

furtive behaviour. "I collect them, there is no regulation against it."

"Whatever slides your wave." Pi studied her last unread flick. "They are kinda rad, I can see why you like them."

A rather officious-looking Grey appeared, together with another Grey carrying green and red flags.

"It's the stationmaster and guard, we'll be off any nano," whispered Gaia.

The stationmaster conferred with Fibonacci briefly and ticked something off on his clipboard. Then the guard waved his green flag, and one of the Greys in the signal box released a lever forward. A chorus of shrieks and yelps erupted from the browser as twenty-three life-sized brass hands shot out of the trapdoors on all their desktops.

"Holofreaks!" Pi yelped. "Couldn't they have warned us they were gonna do that!" She took a deep breath and tried to pluck up the courage to touch her digitiser.

Fibonacci swivelled around and looked at them intently as the Main brace lights all came on again. "Everybody pay attention, main braces spliced please, no dawdling, I want to see twenty-three hands ready for digital transfer, please."

Leo reluctantly clasped his digitiser. "Flusterin' filaments, he's a bit on the cold side."

"Oh they are to begin with," said the guard with a smile, "but by the end they'll be hot enough to bake cookies. And try not to be too terrified by the subjects in K, M, T and U. They're far less dangerous than they appear!" He gave them a tiny smile. Leo exchanged an anxious look with the others. What had they let themselves in for?

The browser quickly moved past Scriveners Halt, allowing them their first proper look at a Mandlebrot spherhall. Pi reckoned it had to be at least two thousand feet across, dwarfing even Main Royal for size, its length triple that. It looked more like a thought-wave interior than a library.

Gaia pointed at something on Andomime's side. "Look, there's one of the famous cafés, they've got branches in all the major vowels."

They quickly passed a lively, well-lit brasserie, The Justified Margin. It was cleverly built into a section of the endless curved bookcase that spiralled all the way down the spherhall. It was filled with identical-looking librarians with tweed skirts, black perms and oversized glasses.

"What's with all the clones?" said Pi.

"They're monikers, librarian functions, they clearly enjoy their coffee breaks!" said Gaia.

Leo pointed excitedly. "The lucky so-and -os, they got cookies in there they ain't even got in the Doors look! Meson-Munchies, us can't even scan the last time us had a packet of they."

"Digitiser Cydermott!" scolded Fibonacci. "I want to see digits entwined not pointed." Leo sighed and grudgingly placed his hand back on the digitiser, whilst Fibonacci used a rotary throttle to slow them all down. This was linked to a dial that was calibrated in something called B.P.N's.

"Now we shall start modestly, say, five hundred books per nano, this will give you all time to become used to the sensation, moving gradually to a full transfer speed of ten thousand. Any questions?"

Pi had a few dozen in mind, exchanging an anxious look with the others as she mimed *ten thousand*, incredulously.

The browser started slowly, Fibonacci gently easing the dial around to five hundred B.P.N. A series of bells began chiming throughout the spherhall, the last few monikers scurrying from the aisles, up wooden steps to the tops of the twenty-foot-high shelves, decoratively-banistered walkways and bridges allowing them to safely negotiate the whole library from this elevated position.

Fibonacci swung back to face them all as they rolled past the last section of the café. "We commence, of course, with the letter 'A'. Maintaining a firm grip on your digitiser greatly aids successful transfers." Something clunked into place beneath the browser; they were now locked into secure double tracking, more like that of a big-dipper than a railway.

Pi had an attack of the butterflies. "Pssst, Gaia, done anything like this before?"

"I've never gone faster than twenty B.P.N. and that

was just like scanning a long flick really. Truth be told, I am feeling a *little* nervous." Gaia took a deep breath and exhaled slowly.

Leo gave her an impish grin. "If anything happens to 'un, can us have yer cookies then?"

"My experience of high-speed transfers indicates a slight tingling sensation is to be expected," said Andomime, trying to sound reassuring.

"No talking at the back, minds clear and open everyone!" Fibonacci moved the throttle to five hundred B.P.N.

The browser picked up speed. They were fast approaching the first bookshelves. The books were large, at least two feet high, many twice that, all of them in ancient bindings with intricately embossed spines. None appeared less than three inches thick. The shelves rose up ponderously on either side, so close you could touch them, occulting the library lighting at browser level.

Pi felt the first strange sensations trickling up her arm, the books' spines sliding back out of the shelves towards her by just a few inches in ones and twos, as the browser trundled past. Her digitiser hand tingled slightly, just as Andomime said it would, a halo of blue light and the odd spark crackling around it.

"Just a little algebra to tease the circuits." Fibonacci paused, her hand hovering over the accelerator lever. "Goto read only archive – level one – upload all!" she barked, throwing the lever hard forward.

It sounded as if every last book in the spherhall was thundering outwards. They all sat bolt upright, the entire contents of five hundred holographically-encoded superwords (each one containing more information than the entire Library of Congress), filling their young memory banks in a trice. Pi's mind overflowed with theorems, conjectures, formulas, functions, sequences, tables, proofs and hypotheses. She could barely see properly any more; there were so many numbers, it felt like she was swimming in them.

They danced in innumerable ballroom pairs one minute, then spun themselves into elaborate Persian rugs that stretched to infinity the next, until they formed a vast moving kaleidoscope in fully three dimensions that would not have shamed a Broadway choreographer.

Fibonacci moved the throttle all the way around to ten thousand B.P.N., and the browser accelerated. All the books moved smartly outwards as they passed, like an army on parade, assaulting them with a barrage of facts and figures.

Geometrically impossible buildings erupted from beneath them in the *architectural* section, towering overhead in majestic marriages of the metallic and the mineral. The volcanic chemistry of beginners' *alchemy* morphed seamlessly into the fiery fusion of stars as they whizzed through *astronomy*. They found themselves in the heart of great galaxies, whirling dervishes of countless suns, nebulae in impossibly beautiful colours, star clusters like diamond chandeliers, so blindingly bright they couldn't even look at them. Soon, they were encountering crackling quasars that plunged suddenly into the endless night of black holes, rainbows of radiation from gamma to X-rays, immense G-forces pinning them firmly in their seats as the browser spiralled rapidly down the spherhall. By the time they'd reached the end of Mandlebrot 'A', their heads were buzzing like beehives – *but they had another twenty-five spherhalls to go*! Save for the briefest glimpse of a connecting corridor between the alphabetically-ordered spherhalls, they were completely oblivious to their surroundings.

They hurtled through the intensely aromatic cyphers and chilli-hot codes of Mandlebrot 'C'. They dined on *data, data-ships* and *DNA*, entertained endless examples of *encryption* and *error-correction;* filled themselves freely with *firewalls, flora* and *fauna,* and gorged gregariously on *gravity, gravitons* and *gravitars.* The fearsome folders on firewalls were bad enough, with their elaborate castles of encryption bristling with cypherous spears, algebraic arrows and calculus cannon. But this was as nothing compared to the ferocity of the universe's flora and fauna. It appeared that just about everything was trying to eat just about everything else, and that was only the plants! Giant venus flytraps, from every corner of the universe, in a myriad of variations, snapped, snipped and snarled as they passed by. There was some respite as they loaded more mundane subjects such as *hardware.* The magical properties of advanced *HTML* were far more exciting however. As were the unexpected delights of *impressionism,* as it revealed itself in curtain after curtain of the most strikingly beautiful alien landscapes, although it did leave Pi wondering what its significance was, and why it had been included, as this was curiously not explained.

Keys, keyboards and *knights* made strange bedfellows; the latter manifesting in their thousands, complete with magnificent and monstrous mounts. There were seemingly endless treatises on *light,* the subject taking up almost a whole spherhall by itself, from *angstroms* and *aurora,* to *spectra* and *wavelengths.*

They were almost halfway through when the intensity of the downloads suddenly increased to unbearable levels. *Monsters, mathematics, optics, physics, questions, quandaries, restorations, shadows, surfing, telepathy, telekinesis, unconsciousness, unknowns, vortices, waves, watercode* and *X-rays.* Then, before they had reached the final spherhalls of 'Y' and 'Z' – something strange occurred.

All the subjects began running together to produce a fearsome tsunami of the darkest, most terrifying phantasmagoria imaginable. It rose up, seemingly out of the floor, until it loomed high above them, filling the enormous spherhall of Mandlebrot 'X' and blotting out the light as it grew. A wall of deepest, darkest night, poised like a cobra, its surface alive with shape-shifting forms and ghastly phantoms riding hideous beasts.

Indescribable multi-tentacled krakens, the animated skeletons of formidable predators, the dread architecture of their enormous skulls, teeth, claws, stings and armoured plates flashing into view, then dissolving back into the maelstrom of its threatening coils.

How come they were aware of being in any spherhall at all? Surely something must have gone terribly wrong? Mysteriously, they had also come to a complete stop; even more alarmingly, they were now on *foot*, neither browser nor lumixastra in sight. They were stranded in the bowels of the universe's largest library, with an encyclopedia of a monster – and no means of escape.

EIGHTEEN

THE BATTLE OF MANDLEBROT 'X'

Andomime was the first to recognise the phenomenon as they cowered in the shadow of the endless shelves. "The data stream has overloaded, creating a mirage reality... a data-demon. We have to overcome it or we will not achieve full data assimilation."

Leo peeked nervously through a gap in the books. "Blow that for a game of cyberknights, get us on the first browser out of here says I!"

"Look around," said Gaia. "There *is* no browser."

The data-demon was already searching for them, stomping whole shelves flat but a dozen aisles away. Several enormous volumes fell in tatters at their feet, their shredded pages fluttering down like feathers. It was too much for Lumians Vaurian Thoid and Zosma Rummage; they fled back down the aisle, yelping in terror.

Pi used psy. "*Don't run, you idiots, it'll hear you.*"

"*We have to stay together, come back!*" added Gaia.

But they took no notice; worse, the demon had heard them, and immediately began moving in their direction. "Whoaaaa, it's gonna—!"

"Leo SHUTTUP!" Pi pinned him to the shelves, gagging his mouth with her pockets. "You wanna tell it where we are?" Leo made a muffled noise and shook his head. Pi released her grip.

"But it's after they idiots, that's all I was gonna say – see!"

"Yeah, so we loaded!"

There was an eerie silence. The demon had stilled itself completely and was clearly listening. Silently, it turned itself around and slithered towards the careless footfalls of the two lumians.

Pi turned to Andomime. "So what will it do to them?"

"It will completely disassemble their avatars, absorbing their firecode into itself as a terracrypt – freezing their mainframes for eternity."

Gaia agreed. "They're almost impossible to decipher. I don't think even the lumixastras could break them free."

"In other words, they're sparkin' toast!"

Until a few moments ago Pi knew nothing about terracrypts, but now she knew *all too well* about their terrible reputation as the universe's most unbreakable cyphers.

They huddled close into the shelves, watching with

horror as the demon silently stalked its prey up the sides of the spherhall. So stealthily did it ooze and pour itself over shelves and through aisles, the lumians foolishly thought it had gone, stopping to catch their breaths, hands on their knees, as it slowly homed in, directly above Pi and the others on the 'ceiling'. The demon slithered ever closer, swelling out like a great dark sheet over fully quarter of the spherhall, hiding its great bulk, practically hypnotising all those who watched.

Pi knew she had to do something, she was the host-system after all, but what? She searched her newly-expanded mind for a clue. She'd successfully loaded at least ninety-five percent of the first-level data, surely there must be something she could use? There were only a few footnotes about data-demons in her files so she decided to find out what the others knew.

"K, Mime, you said we had to 'overcome' it, so how do we do that exactly?" praying her squillion, squillion squared friend would know the answer. But Andomime didn't reply; instead she looked deep in thought, her fingers flicking the air as if it were an invisible abacus. Meanwhile, the two hapless lumians were running out of time.

Leo followed their faltering progress with his 'scope. "'Un don't stand a chance look... unless 'un can get a worm into that Dave-demon fast."

Pi looked startled by Leo's throwaway remark. "Skree! Pause everything! That's a real mountain, Mottles! We could zap it with wormcode!"

Andomime's fingers paused mid-flick. "Leo is

correct, that is the only viable solution. A wormcode would break down the demon's monolithic data-stream into harmless qubits."

Leo looked smug. "Like Anders said, it's the only way to beat 'un look – turn 'un into harmless qubits."

Pi watched the demon's ghastly progress high overhead; it was like watching a giant snake stalking two newly-hatched chicks. "But *how* are we going to create a wormcode clever enough to beat that thing? No ticklebug's gonna frag that codezilla! And what can we make it out of in here for goodness' sake? There isn't even any liquid code anywhere."

"Maybe there is." Gaia snatched up a few scraps of demon-mangled paper and handed them to Leo. "Scrunch these up, quick as you can, Mottles." She then grabbed a nearby copper wastebasket. These were large at three feet high and two feet across at the flared brim. Their perforated bottoms sat over drains in the library floor. Any book that entered the event horizon of the brim was instantly dissolved back into watercode; more recycling. She held it out for Leo and he chucked the scraps inside. Immediately the paper dissolved into watercode, ran straight through the holes in the base and made a puddle on the floor.

"Megs, there's our ammo," said Pi, "now all we need's a delivery system."

"Give me a nano." Gaia threw the basket for Leo to catch and fumbled through her pockets, quickly producing the only weapon of choice.

Leo grinned at the sight of his confiscated pistol. "Sparkin' tubes! That'd do it! But how's us going to get the code in 'un? Spiders and darts won't stop 'un look."

Andomime had been doing some calculations of her own. "Unless we overwhelm the demon with a very substantial quantity of wormcode, we will become terracrypts ourselves. I calculate that it will take at least four hundred litres to make it crash."

Leo's face fell. "Sparko, mallarko, *four hundred*!"

"We could clone the pistols with code and give one to everyone?" said Pi (consulting page forty-three thousand, eight hundred and sixty-seven of *Handy HTML Tips For The Home*).

Gaia picked up the thread. "They hold thirty litres each, pressurised. We could even have *two* apiece, that's sixty, and twenty-one of us means one thousand, two hundred and sixty litres, one drenched-demon!"

"Cryo, but we still need some bright sparks to code up the right worm." Pi tapped her index finger on her lower lip and studied them all carefully. Her gaze fell upon Bhami Superbrahamian. Gaia had already told her he was second only to Mime in the squillion-squillion-squared stakes. She grabbed him by the scruff of the neck and virtually propelled him towards their number one supercomputer. "Your task for today Superwhatchmacallit, help Mime upload some mean wormcode!"

Whilst Mizzen-Gaff Alpha's finest minds began conferring, Pi took command of an even more pressing matter. Snapping her fingers she looked at the others.

"Names, names – for Wiley and Roadrunner?"

"Lummy, 'un's bossy when 'un wants to be," mumbled Leo.

"Oh, er, Zosma and Vaurian… Izar Kornephorus, I'm a friend of theirs."

Pi declined the extended hand, there wasn't time; she focused on the imperilled twosome and sent her best psy. *"Zosma, Vaurian, listen up, Izar has a message for you."* She pointed at Izar. "Go, Izar."

"Okay, um, listen very carefully, guys, you're being stalked by a data-demon. DON'T RUN or it will hear you. You can't see it but it's nearly reached you, um—" Izar paused, confused as to what to say next.

Gaia had an idea. *"Remove several large books from the shelves as quietly as possible and put them in the nearest wastebasket. Make sure their corners are inside the event horizon, they'll create a decoy noise as they melt."*

Pi trained Leo's spyglass on the lumians. *"Take off your shoes and run, fast as you can towards category, er… X-Change. Keep to the shadows, this will bring you back to us, but don't go back the way you came. If you pass that stuff on X-rays again, you're lunch!"* She watched nervously as the pair absorbed all the messages and dithered momentarily, half afraid they'd just panic and run straight into the demon's clutches, but they didn't. Instead, they carefully removed their shoes, then quickly piled several books into the nearest wastebasket. "They did good, they're coming back, they're coming back, the demon's going for the decoy."

Everybody cricked their necks. Two tiny specks could just be seen darting silently through the shadowy aisles on the 'ceiling' above. It was just in the nano of time; the demonic sheet of darkness was homing in on the trickling sound of dissolving books. The decoy had worked.

Pi looked at the others. "You realise once it reaches the basket and sees the shoes it'll come back for us? We need to get tooled up like *yesterday*."

Andomime and Bhami remained silent, the digits of both their hands delicately entwined, Bhami's eyes closed as if in meditation.

Leo nudged Gaia with his elbow. "Sweet, innit?"

"Shhh, they're working."

Bhami suddenly opened his eyes. Pi looked hopeful. "Well?"

"There is good news and bad news, my friends. We have identified a suitable wormcode. But in order for it to be correctly programmed for guaranteed effectiveness—" Bhami's voice tailed off.

"We require a sample of the target for analysis," added Andomime.

"Cryocreeps! How the frazz are we gonna get that?" Pi scrunched up her face, then noticed the light had suddenly changed in the spherhall. They all looked up with a gasp. The demon had discovered the decoy and was on its way back.

At least the arms factory was well underway. Gaia led a team scouting around for wastebaskets, and they'd gathered eighteen together already. Some of the others were pulling out any old books they could carry, which wasn't easy by any means, petite Lumiette Mintaka Tao almost flattening herself when she tried to remove a particularly large encyclopedia on *Xenomorphs*. The books quickly grew into large piles, all in readiness to fill the wastebaskets, but how to block the holes in the base? Several of them tried their best code for leaks and suchlike, but absolutely nothing would work.

"The wastebaskets are dedicated functions, some of their codes cannot be overwritten. You will have to find another way to negate their porosity," said Andomime drily.

Hearing this, Leo produced a pack of Plutonigum from amongst the comprehensive stocks in his pockets. He grinned impishly, quickly drew out ten sticks and tore them in half. Everybody grabbed a piece and began chewing as if their lives depended on it, which in a sense of course, they did, Leo managing to attest to its miraculous properties between elasticated chomps of the liquorice and aniseed confection.

"Sticks... to anything it does... got us into... enough... trouble back home, I can tell 'un." He then blew an enormous black bubble which, for a moment, looked like a baby data-demon itself. Then he made it pop on the underside of an upturned bin, coating it with a perfect seal in an instant.

The others all disgorged (not without some difficulty) their gum in a similar manner, and in no time all the bins were tight as barrels. Well, *almost* all. There was a brief panic when Lumian Taxon Bolide's bubble backfired, sticking a bin to his face. He wasn't exactly known for being the fastest processor in the rack and Pi had to rescue him with a code shortcut.

"Goto param gum execute – undo," she whispered. The hapless lumian freed, she then invoked the gum's stickiness again so he could finish the task; the HTML handy home hints really did cover *everything*.

"K, people, listen up, let's fill those bins *wikiwiki.*"

"Some of the books are too big to fit," said Lumiette Magheera Monilon.

Pi grabbed a book. "Tear 'em up, rip the spines off if you have to, whatever it takes, this is war, people!"

"But won't we get into trouble, ruining all these lovely books?" said Mintaka.

Andomime sighed. "We are in a mirage reality, nothing we do will register in the actual spherhall itself."

Gaia, Leo and Izar had been so industrious, they'd filled a bin to the brim already.

Gaia's eyes narrowed and she fixed Leo with a stare. "We still have to get a sample of the demon somehow. Is there anything on your Barmy, Mottles?" Leo went pale.

"There *is,* isn't there? C'mon, get the manual out."

"Alright, alright, give us a nano." He fumbled reluctantly through his pockets.

Gaia grabbed the manual and started flicking through the pages, whilst Leo continued searching for his knife.

"What have we got here? Er... *data snipper, data whittler, data shredder, data sampler*, no that's not it, *data demon sampler* – yes – blade 11534. Mottles, quick, dial in the combination."

"Alright, hold 'un's cyberpomps, Inverse weren't built in a parsec." He finally located the knife, disgorging a surprisingly large pile of other items in the process. He dialled in the number using the wheeled combination set into the knife's handle (for speedy tool location), and out popped the data-demon-sampler.

Gaia looked at him and sighed. "If *only* you'd been this organised on *Caliban.*"

"You ain't still going on about he—"

Pi checked out the implement for size. It looked very small, like a miniature apple-corer or cheese sampler maybe? *"Ole wale,* we're gonna have to get real close with that thing, it's *minute*! You guys clone the pistols, I need time to think."

Gaia dropped the almost full pistol (less twelve darts worth of watercode), into the brimful wastebasket with a splash. "Goto param object fill and clone – execute." Immediately the watercode drained completely with a rude gurgling sound. She peeked inside. It had worked! There were now *two* identical red watercode pistols on the bottom, both chock full of pressurised watercode. She then cloned both clones at once and kept doing this until, but moments later, all the wastebaskets were dry. There were now so many pistols going around that some of them had three or four each, stuffing spare ones into their belts, sock tops or even clenched teeth! But was it all too late?

A shadowy tentacle suddenly appeared over the top of the bookcase and swooped downwards, as if it were searching for something. Pi put a finger to her lips and they all froze. The tentacle fixed itself to the shelves, then released its suckers, making dozens of popping sounds. The demon had employed the same stealthy tactics it had used on the runaways, giving no warning of its approach.

Leo slipped his hand slowly into a pocket and drew out his Barmy-Knife, data-demon- sampler at the ready. He tiptoed silently towards the tentacle as it continued to explore, coiling and uncoiling between every object it touched. It moved silently towards trembling Lumian Peri Helion. Everyone held their breath. Fortunately, he was strong enough to remove a large book from the shelves and use it as a shield, so the tentacle explored *it* instead of *him*.

Leo crept closer; now was his big chance. The tentacle had just begun un-suckering itself from the lumian's erstwhile shield, when Leo decided to strike. Then, *just* as he lunged forward, it coiled itself up out of harm's way. The sampler noisily struck the book instead (taking a useless sample of Inversian bookbinding in the process). There was a thunderous growl from the depths of the spherhall that made all the shelves quake, and the tentacle withdrew. They'd been discovered!

The awful sound of splintering wood rent the

air and a vast shape rose up, blotting out the light. Moments later, debris was falling like hail, forcing them to huddle close to the shelves, great tomes thudding to the ground all around them. More tentacles appeared and grasped the bookshelf in whose shadow they were hiding, effortlessly ripping it from the floor. The firsties shrieked and ran to the next aisle. Pi tried to run with them but was stopped dead in her tracks. A tentacle was dangling threateningly in front of her, poised ready to strike. It lashed downwards where it thought she was, hitting the inside of an empty wastebasket. Instantly, the tentacle dissolved in a cloud of spray. A terrible roar of pain came from the demon. *That was it*! Of course, the demon was made of *books*, it was just as susceptible to the programmed wastebaskets as they were! This would give them the edge they needed.

Gaia and Leo peeked nervously through a gap in the shelves to see why Pi hadn't joined them.

She waved them over excitedly, and immediately swung into action. "Goto param wastebasket – compact all – execute!" Fortunately, *this* code worked. Instantly, all eighteen wastebaskets scrunched themselves flat as pancakes.

Leo ran to her side, looking confused. "What's 'un *doing* for spark's sake? This ain't no time to mess around!"

Pi didn't answer. She knelt down to pick up one of the tyre-sized wastebasket discs. It was stuck fast to the floor, of course; the gum had virtually glued it solid.

"Goto param gum – execute – undo!" Immediately she was able to lift the disc right off the floor with just a few sticky strings resisting. She began frantically flipping *all* the discs over whilst Leo watched, bemused. "Don't just stand there, Mottles! Turn them over – *wikiwiki!*"

Gaia, Izar and some of the braver souls ran to help as the terrible shadow gathered itself to strike again.

"BEHIND YOU!" Izar yelled.

They looked up; all the demon's hellish weaponry seemed to fall on them at once. Pi didn't bat an eyelid. "Goto param gum restore – execute!" She whacked her left forearm hard onto the sticky black mess, immediately gluing it to her arm like a limpet, and jumped straight to her feet, just in time to deflect a tentacle lunging at Leo. The demonic extension exploded harmlessly into a shower of spray the second it touched the encoded metal. The others got the message right away.

"Shields, get yer shields while they're hot look, quick!" hollered Leo, sticking one on his right forearm, for he was *left*-handed.

As the last shield left the ground on the arm of its new owner, the full fury of the demon fell upon them.

Fast as lightning, Pi accessed all the files she'd loaded about *firewalls*. "Form phalanx, arrows incoming!"

Eighteen shields instantly locked together to form one impenetrable sheet over their heads, the formation practically knocked as flat as the bins by the terrible assault of limbs, teeth and tentacles. They rebounded back to a stumbling scrum, the demon's weapons exploding into harmless watercode, drenching them all. The demon roared with anger, its cry so loud the shields practically vibrated off their arms.

"It's going to strike again!" shrieked Gaia.

Pi cooly accessed a chapter on *emergency firewalls*. "Stand fast, everybody pool their matches!"

The three firsties who were without shields fumbled for their Firecode-Matches, shaking the box frantically in the hope of finding the single precious match inside. The others cast their matchboxes into a pile on the floor, so these torchbearers could make three bundles of seven matches apiece.

The demon fell upon them again, except this time it cleverly held its ghastly armoury short of the shields, carefully probing for weaknesses. Izar squirted a volley of watercode at an exploratory tentacle, covering it with dozens of fat hairy spiders. The tentacle recoiled momentarily, quickly absorbing the miniscule arachnids into itself, before morphing into an enormous hundred-legged tarantula with dozens of terrifying pincers and clustering eyes as big as grapes, Izar's terrified features reflected back at him a thousand times over.

"Lolo, Lumian! Don't give it ideas, hold your fire till we get the code!" bawled Pi.

"It's surrounding us!" Mintaka yelped.

A curtain of night had enveloped them, rising like a dome over their heads and plunging them into total darkness.

"Strike the matches – strike the matches!" yelled Pi.

The flickering light of the makeshift torches threw grotesque shadows all around. The demon's writhing armoury was temporarily held at bay, an assortment of serrated jaws screaming and hissing their frustration. It cleverly devised another tactic. A giant claw came out of nowhere and snipped at a shield. Despite being partially dissolved, the claw was so hard, it succeeded in damaging the improvised defence. The demon had discovered a chink in their armour, *literally*. Immediately, a hundred scaly pincers lunged at the encoded metal, making watercode explode everywhere. The demon sent more and more until the shield wall began to falter, battered and pummelled by a storm of unrelenting ferocity.

The demon replenished the destroyed pincers so rapidly, it was able to get hold of one shield and carry it high in the air, taking poor Mintaka with it. Unable to use code to release the gum, because it would make all the other shields drop off their arms, Pi had to think fast. "Lose your pockets. Take off your pockets, Mintaka!"

The tiny lumiette just managed to wriggle free and fall to the ground a split-nano before a dozen pincers tore her pockets to shreds, hurling the poisonous shield through a gap in itself, into the bowels of the spherhall beyond.

Now the demon converted *all* its spiteful limbs into pincers, brandishing them in a hellish chorus that sounded like the sharpening of a thousand knives.

"It's going to devour us, we'll all be terracrypted!" wailed Chant Pannopoly, trembling so badly he could barely stand up.

Pi was having none of it. "Hold steady there, close up that gap! You *want* we all get crypted?"

Support for the petrified lumian came from an unexpected source. "Pannopoly is quite correct; we will all become terminally encrypted unless we obtain the required sample within twenty-five nanos," said Andomime, matter-of-factly.

Pi fixed Leo with a steely stare. "Next attack, whatever it does, you *gotta* get that sample, Mottles!"

Leo swallowed hard; he didn't have long to wait. Before Pi had even finished speaking, the terrible battering began again. Leo saw his chance. The armoured pincers were a tough target compared to a nice fleshy tentacle, but Barmy-Knives were made of stern stuff. As the deafening rain of blows chipped relentlessly at the shields, losing them three more in the process, Leo seized his chance.

A pincer shot straight through a gap in the shields and struck the ground at his feet. He lunged at it, but it was not alone. Another pincer did the same behind him; instantly, they closed together and carried him high into the air.

"Woooooaaargh!"

"It's got Leo! Somebody grab his legs!" shrieked Gaia.

Leo wriggled and struggled, desperately trying to

free himself, stabbing at the pincer repeatedly without success. "'Un's too hard, us can't get through 'un!"

The demon carried him towards its mouth, the others watching helplessly as its hideous jaws readied themselves to devour him. He lashed out with his feet, kicking at the demon's teeth to save himself. Out of sheer desperation he plucked all his wave-poppers from his pockets, flicked off the safety catches with his thumb, and hurled them into the demon's maw. The demon's slavering jaws made short work of the miniatures as they stuck to its ghastly grey tongue. It was just about to add Leo as the main course, when all the poppers suddenly exploded – full size – knocking out all its teeth!

Then a brave, perhaps foolhardy, lumian, Klegg Boolean, broke ranks and ran screaming at the demon, with nothing more than a few flaming matches to his name. A tentacle shot out and wound around him, fast as a snake.

"Throw it to me!" he cried, as the tentacle snatched him skywards. Leo fumbled for a moment, still kicking at the demon's now toothless jaws, throwing his Barmy towards Klegg as best as he could. But it was hopeless. Klegg just got touch of the knife then dropped it, hardly able to see in the poor light. In a trice Gaia surprised everybody, diving forward and catching the knife, screaming with anger as she stabbed the sampler into the soft wall of the demon's underbelly before it could stop her.

Pi seized the moment. "Phalanx, attack formation – forward!" They all swarmed around Gaia, bundling her inside an igloo of shields.

"I've got it, I've got it!" She handed the knife straight to Bhami.

"Carefully remove the sample," said Andomime coolly, as the blows continued to rain down outside. Bhami tipped the tiny sample into Andomime's palm and they closed both their hands around the writhing grey sliver.

Pi peeked through a gap in the shields. Leo and Klegg were still wailing and caterwauling, kicking their legs at the demon's toothless jaws. Bhami and Andomime were now their only hope.

Andomime began processing out loud. "Demon composition: fifty-three percent *shadows*, twenty percent *monsters*, eighteen percent *cyberpomps*; the balance being?"

There was an agonising pause as the shield wall crumbled further.

Then Bhami spoke. "I am detecting eight percentage points of *vortexes*." Andomime nodded her agreement, but they were still one crucial percent short!

"One percent *unknown*," said Andomime ponderously.

Pi's heart sank. "You mean you don't know?" But this wasn't some declaration of failure – this was the *answer*!

Andomime spoke with calm authority. "Goto param

watercode pistol – embed worm – shadows five three, monsters two zero, cyberpomps one eight, vortexes zero eight, unknown zero *one* – *INITIATE ALL!*"

"Great hairy holofreaks! You mean you guys uploaded?" Pi had almost given up on the pistols. Hastily she fumbled for hers, regarding them sceptically in the paltry light. The contents had suddenly changed from transparent to opaque. There really was only one way to find out if her boffins had got it right. "All hands, draw pistols, aim around Leo and Klegg, continuous fire – *wikiwikiwiki!*"

Some thirty pistols opened up. They could hardly see what they were doing at first, their fingers pumping as fast as they could go. Then two crumpled forms dropped to the ground in front of them; it was Leo and Klegg!

"Quickly, surround them! But don't stop pumpin'!" yelled Pi, as the valiant huddle moved forwards to rescue their comrades.

Despite being dazed and exhausted, Leo and Klegg drew their pistols and began firing too. The demon still roared, hissed and clawed back at them all, but now with greatly diminished effect.

"It's retreating! Keep firing – keep firing – three-sixty, guys!" Pi let a brace of empty pistols fall from her hands, retrieving a full pair and firing again before the first had even touched the ground. Her number one supercomputers had got it right!

The demon was being well and truly drenched by a

green gunk which transformed into tiny green worms as it flew through the air. These tiny creatures were fast turning the demon's monstrous bulk into nothing more than a harmless grey sludge, its vicious limbs falling all around them and writhing impotently before melting away.

"My greenness, it's working, it's working!" whooped Gaia, the torrent of wormcode raining down on the fast-dwindling demon from all directions.

All at once, the last vestiges of it collapsed like a breached dam, a grey slurry running across the floor towards them until they were waist-deep in unspeakable slime.

Pi stopped firing, a look of disgust on her face. "Ooji! This is made of *books*?"

Leo spotted a bit of the demon that was still active. "'Un's trying to scarper, don't let 'un escape look!" He broke ranks with some of the others, administering a *coup de grâce* to a rabid remnant.

"A damn close run thing. Duke of Wellington, Waterloo, 1815. See I know *lots* of stuff now," grinned Pi.

"Behind you!" shrieked Gaia.

Pi's smile evaporated as a giant pair of shark-like jaws lunged at her from beneath the slurry; she swung her pistols round just in time to deliver a decisive volley, and the threat dissolved but inches from success, splattering her with yet more slime. "K, probably not a good idea to hang around in this demon-foo any longer, I've really had it with this stuff."

"You and me both." Gaia helped Mintaka wade

to safety, whilst Bhami assisted Andomime from the gelatinous slurry, Pi and Izar following as a rear guard, pistols drawn just in case.

Two long-lost lumians emerged sheepishly from the bombsite of bookshelves to meet them. It was Vaurian and Zosma, apparently none the worse for their ordeal.

Pi looked back at the terrible mess. Almost none of the spherhall seemed to have escaped the demon's wrath. The hallowed domain of Mandlebrot 'X' was now a wasteland of complete chaos. "I hope Andomime was right about that mirage thing?" she mused, turning back to Gaia, but she wasn't there; none of her friends were.

Then she sensed she was moving and found herself back in the browser, the familiar clickety-clack of its progress beneath her once again. She felt totally drained, so exhausted in fact, that, like waking from some epic dream, she couldn't immediately recall what had just happened.

Everything seemed so normal. Fibonacci was still sitting imperiously back to front, watching them all intently, her harebrained birds still jumping from perch to perch. Leo, Gaia and Andomime were still sitting next to her, although they looked half-asleep too, their eyes just beginning to open. The browser slowed; there was something familiar about the layout ahead. An oasis of laughter and light met her weary eyes. It was The Justified Margin; they had come full circle, and their first proper download was over.

NINETEEN

FLUTTERBOOKS

The browser finally slowed to a stop, and a cheery Grey in a smart waiter's outfit emerged from the warm amber glow of the café, his tray piled high with white towels.

"Cold to towels, nicely to chilled, delectably to damp, get your to iced hand-towels to here."

"Whassat, something about trowels?" mumbled Leo. He removed his left hand from the digitiser and rubbed his eyes, then practically leapt out of his seat. "Me hand, what's happened to me hand, 'un's red hot look?"

The Grey efficiently swept along the browser, casually draping small towels over everybody's digitiser hands as he went. Most of the firsties were still half-asleep, clouds of vapour rising from their newly draped digits.

Fibonacci left the browser, stretched her arms and yawned, casting an eye over her dozy charges. "Don't fuss, Cydermott, it's perfectly normal to experience a little thermal elevation in your digits after a download.

Come along now, wakey wakey, Mizzen-Gaff, you don't want to miss your downtime treats now, do you?" At the mention of the word *treats*, a few more pairs of eyes popped open, Leo's amongst them.

"Thermal elevation nothing, 'un's proper burnin' hot he is!" He dabbed the towel on his left hand. "Sparkin' tubes, look at the steam coming off 'un."

Pi hadn't the strength to move her digitiser hand at all, content to watch it steam the towel dry before her half-closed eyes. "Man, that feels good," she purred.

Gaia stirred in her seat. "My greenness, are we back? I had this really awful dream, it was unbelievable!"

"We all had an awful dream, ducks, 'un was awful close to gobbling I up look!" Leo delicately removed his left hand from the digitiser and waggled his fingers, suddenly realising that his right was mysteriously clasping Pi's left hand.

"So you guys scanned it too? The demon wasn't a dream?" said Pi, opening her eyes with a start as it all came back to her. She tried to use her left hand to sit herself upright, then noticed that it was not presently available. "Oh sorry, Mottles, you probably want your hand back? I must have grabbed it, you know, when things got hairy 'n' scary back there." She sensed she was blushing.

"Yeah, expect that's what it was look."

They awkwardly disentangled their digits. It was surprisingly difficult; their hands appeared to be practically welded together.

"Hey, feels like there's something in there, hope it's not a bit of you know what!" Pi carefully opened her hand to look. "Megs! Is this yours, Mottles?" She opened her palm to reveal a substantial pear-cut gemstone in a fabulous shade of green, which sparkled from a hundred facets.

Leo shifted awkwardly in his seat. "Nothing to do with I, I ain't never seen 'un before in me service life look."

Gaia became very excited. "Ooh, let me see. That's a *huge* one." She opened her left hand to reveal a smaller, square-cut version of the same thing.

Andomime wasn't nearly so excited, of course, but gamely held up her own round green gemstone and explained, "They are wisdom-stones. They are typically formed during intense downloads. The digitiser creates a powerful opposite polarity in the non-digitiser hand; perspired watercode then crystalizes into a gemstone under the enormous pressure."

"So what 'un's sayin' is – 'un's made outta sweat?" said Leo gleefully.

Gaia looked aghast. "Leo, you're just *so* unromantic. They're pure virtual emerald. Yours and Pi's is really amazing, such an unusual shape. You must have held hands really tightly to make one that size."

Leo looked suddenly bashful. "'Un's yours look, you keep 'un. Us has got me binnagraph, haven't us?" His face was now a deep shade of red.

"Megs, thanks Mottles." Before she'd even thought

about it, Pi had given Leo a peck on the cheek. Now it was impossible to tell who looked more embarrassed.

"Lummy, me poppers!" Leo frantically began checking his pockets. "Whoarr, there you are me beauties. Phewff! Us thought that mirage-munching-monster had had 'un all for brekkers." He heaved a sigh of relief, sinking back into his seat to admire his precious collection, not least his trusty Barnum-Bratt's pistol. "Downside is, 'un's still only got the one squirter look."

Gaia shook her head and raised her eyes. "Well, at least you've got your priorities right." She swapped wisdom-stones with Pi. "Second levellers make rubies, thirds, sapphires and fourths, diamonds; just imagine one of those this size! We must have loaded all the subjects after all, even 'Y' and 'Z' or they wouldn't be nearly this perfect."

Pi watched the light play on her newest acquisition as Gaia turned it. "So by beating the data-demon, we sort of loaded all that stuff in the other spherhalls anyway?"

"In defeating the data-demon, we assimilated all the blocked data, that is correct," said Andomime, climbing stiffly out of the browser.

Fibonacci appeared and swept up the line. "We have less than ninety nanos left for refreshments. If you wish to utilise the café, you had better be quick." Some of the firsties held up their wisdom-stones for her to see as they waited to clamber out. "Very nice, Io, very nice. Oh yes, a wonderful colour, Monilon, wonderful. Not to worry, Pannopoly, I've seen much smaller ones than that."

Leo felt trapped, restlessly urging the others to let him out too; they were wasting valuable cookie appreciation time!

Pi felt his elbows dig in. "Alright already, what the frazz, dude!" bundling herself out of the browser.

Pretty soon all the firsties had made themselves thoroughly at home in the café. Its polished wood panelling enjoyed art nouveau accents which were especially noticeable in the light fixtures, colourful wall tiles and windows. They excitedly swapped stories in hushed tones about their role in the Battle of Mandlebrot 'X' – as it came to be known. Several dozen lumixastras from the other browsers had evidently completed their tasks in Mandlebrot 'U' and were taking refreshments too, their secretive psy punctuated only by the solemn munching of epicurean cookies or the sipping of vintage watercode teas, the former not unnoticed by Leo, who just sat there watching covetously, dreaming of the day when he might afford such luxuries.

Lumixastra Fibonacci seemed none the wiser as to her charges' extracurricular adventures, keeping herself to herself, nursing a virtual cappuccino in a quiet corner. Pi half-suspected that her birds knew something, but if they did, they weren't telling, and neither was Mizzen-Gaff. They made a pact to keep the incident strictly secret between themselves, which was just as well, as a minor, but none the less embarrassing, phenomenon was brought to the café's attention. Lumixastra Celsia Amaranth, renowned paleocyphologist and lumixastra of history that hasn't happened yet, had received word of an unusual occurrence from one of the monikers. Apparently all the wastebaskets in Mandlebrot 'X' had been squashed flat as pancakes by agencies unknown.

Pi caught the eye of the guard on their browser as he partook of a refreshing cup of blackcurrant tea. The Grey smiled, tapped the side of his tiny nose and winked, as Lumixastra Amaranth related the story. So perhaps *somebody* had an idea about what they had been through, after all?

Fibonacci anxiously checked the café's decorative clock as she marched purposely over to them all, and they immediately fell silent. "I expect to see everybody back on the browser in forty nanos – no exceptions!"

Gaia pulled Pi out of the still excitable huddle. "C'mon, you have simply got to see this before we leave."

"What is it?"

"You'll see."

They ran out of the café and up the aisle, slowing down abruptly as they passed the enquiries desk, the monikers in attendance eyeing them censoriously through their thick pebble glasses.

Pi decided now was the moment to air something that had been troubling her since the wave-belt. "Gaia, did you hear any strange psy on *Caliban*, you know, just before that last wave crashed?"

Gaia thought for a moment as they sauntered along, then shook her feathery head. "I don't *think* so. Why, what sort of voice was it? What did it say?"

"Well, that's what freaked me out, it sounded just like the Queen. She wanted me to download something when we were trapped in that last thought-wave, you know, the restricted, classified one. She said she'd give me the restore superword for it, but I knew something was glitchy, just like 'Phabian's psy at the lighthouse. You remember? When 'he' said he could help me find my dad."

"Well, the Queen would *never* try to trick you like that, and I'm pretty sure dreamboat wouldn't have been so stupid as to go that far. This is beginning to sound like Zon-Cydes, or maybe one of Prumiane's friends? On the plane, you say? It couldn't have been them though, not in the wave-belt, no psy. Hmm." Gaia stopped in her tracks and looked pensive. "That *is* a bit creepy. I don't know what it could have been then, or whom! You have to be careful of things like that, or you could catch a virus! Did you get a chance to check your security seal?"

"Negs, I was too frazzed to even *think* straight, wish I had. What if it was, you know – *him*?"

"Greenness, now you're scaring me! I think you should tell a lumixastra about it. It sounds like what we call a 'reportable breach'. You're the host-system, that does make you a target, for, for, you know, *him*."

Pi felt a chill run down her avatar's spine. The

colour had entirely drained from Gaia's face. "So you really think it could have been, *you know who?*"

"If you suspect it's," Gaia dropped her voice to an almost inaudible whisper, "*Urizen*, then the emergency war laws insist it must be reported immediately. Don't worry, all we have to do is tell Fibonacci as soon as we get back and you will have done your bit."

"K, as long as I'm not in any trouble or anything?" Pi suddenly stopped still and silently indicated that Gaia should do the same.

"Something the matter?" Gaia whispered.

"S'funny, I'll swear somebody was following us."

"Probably just a moniker, they get everywhere," Gaia smiled reassuringly. "Nobody there now, and no, you're not in any trouble. C'mon, this'll cheer you up."

Pi looked around one last time. "Probably seeing things, I'm hyperwiped." They resumed ambling through the aisles.

Pi continued to glance back now and then. "It's just that Andomime definitely picked up on something weird too, remember? When we were approaching that last thought-wave."

"Then I think it's probably some spiteful lumixastra, maybe they know how to get around the psy thing. I'm sure Magistry knows how to use psy in the wave-belt! I wouldn't be overly concerned, bound to be a few who'll try to unnerve you now you're host-system. They're just jealous really, sweetie. Ooh look, we're here!"

A broad grin crept across Gaia's face. She'd stopped

beside a long row of wooden drawers. At twenty feet tall, these were as high as the bookshelves. Pi figured there must be hundreds of the slim, six-foot-wide drawers in this one aisle alone.

"Indexes," said Gaia enigmatically.

A moniker walked noisily along the top balustrade of the shelves above them. Gaia waited until the moniker had finished descending a flight of wooden steps in her sensible shoes, eyeing them suspiciously as she walked past.

"So what's the big *huna kahuna?*" said Pi, the moniker now well and truly out of sight. Gaia took one last peek to check they were alone, so Pi decided to open one of the drawers out of curiosity.

Gaia stopped it with her hand. "No, not like that, they're automated. This way's much better – watch and be *very* amazed. Goto param index A to Z – highlight all – reveal – execute!"

All the drawers began sliding slowly open of their own accord, starting with the lowest first, disgorging their startling contents. Pi gasped with delight as clouds of colourful butterflies billowed out of each newly-opened drawer, until the air was thick with them.

"You see, not everything in the library is scary!"

"*Kupaianaha!* Extinct! But what are *butterflies* doing in here?"

"They're not butterflies, they're flutterbooks, indexes. If you look closely at the open wings, you'll see there's one for every book. They fly to the one you want and show you where it is. But if you stay still like this, they wait for you. Of course you wouldn't *normally* open them all at the same time, but it's a shortcut a little bird told me."

"Let me guess, does the little bird have lights in her hair and chew gum?"

Gaia looked bashful. "Maybe."

By now, they were both covered in flutterbooks from head to toe. Pi carefully moved her flutterbook-encrusted arm so she could take a closer look at the ones on her hand. Sure enough, as the flutterbooks took it in turns to open their wings, she could clearly see the book index data printed upon them.

"Megs, it tells you the titles and everything! Clever little things… so why didn't it say anything about them in the downloads?"

"Because only monikers and lumixastras are supposed to use them, although third and fourth levellers are allowed to use them too, I think."

"Perhaps we shouldn't have opened so many drawers?" Pi began to feel a little uneasy at the sheer volume of flutterbooks, some of which were spilling into the other aisles.

Gaia scratched her feathery hair. "Hmm, I think we've seen enough now. I'd better stop them before the monikers notice. Goto param index 'A' to 'Z', compress all – execute!" Gaia looked around expectantly, but still the drawers continued to open.

"This is beginning to scan like the *Sorcerer's Apprentice,*" Pi mumbled to herself.

"Oh greenness, this is *not* good." Gaia took a deep breath. "Goto param index 'A' to 'Z', compress all – execute!" But still the drawers kept opening, higher and higher, disgorging clouds upon clouds of flutterbooks.

"That *should* have stopped them." Gaia looked puzzled. "I know, I'll try this – Goto param index 'A' to 'Z', *undo* all – execute!" Gaia looked around optimistically; then, when it became apparent that nothing at all was happening, she began to panic. "Oh my greenness, I really don't know what's wrong now, that should have worked! I don't know what else to try!"

"Maybe we should just scoot, they're only butterflies, I mean *flutterbooks*. The monikers will deal with them, won't they?"

"Think you're right, we'll be in trouble if we stay any longer, anyway. There's just one problem, we can't move!" Gaia looked at Pi, her arms splayed out, covered from head to toe by flutterbooks. The floor was a carpet of them also.

"Exactamundo," said Pi. "We've no choice then. They'll see us at the desk if we go back the way we came, but if we take the stairs we can sneak round to the café and these guys will fly off, won't they?"

"Okay, slowly does it."

They tried to waddle towards the stairs, but it was impossible; the ground was now so thick with flutterbooks they hardly dared put one foot in front of another. And the billowing clouds were becoming greater by the nano.

"This is lolo, all that data we just uploaded, and I can't scan a single thing to get us out of this!" lamented Pi.

Suddenly, someone cleared their throat behind them, and they realised they were not alone.

"Ahem. Ahem! I have it on good authority that one Lumiette Lightfoot was seen passing in this direction?"

Both lumiettes jumped, a squadron of flutterbooks taking to the air with surprise. They both turned slowly and beheld an ancient-looking fellow with a large hooked nose. He wore an elaborate grey wig and a long dark coat, almost the totality of his venerable personage now covered by flutterbooks.

"I – I'm Lumiette Lightfoot, Lumixastra sir. We're very sorry about all the flutterbooks."

"We tried to close the indexes but, but they just wouldn't stop opening," added Gaia.

The august gentleman waved his flutterbook-covered hand away, as if this were of no consequence to him. "Lightfoot, Lightfoot, daughter of a certain professor of the same name?"

"Yes, that's, that's me." Pi experienced a surge of adrenaline, and more than a few butterflies of the other variety inside.

"I believe you have something of mine, child – a treatise?"

Pi gave him a quizzical look.

"A book?" he added, spluttering slightly, the air was so thick with wings.

Pi was about to answer to the negative, when she suddenly recalled the *Principia*. "I can tell you have it, child. I can actually smell it, all of my books have a specific olfactory signature. I know each and every one of my bindings by heart. I discern a hint of nutmeg, sea-snake leather bindings, and indigo kraken ink in unique proportion. This recalls to me a singular book of natural philosophy. It is somewhat overdue as things stand. If you would care to return the volume, I would be very much obliged." He held out his hand expectantly.

"K, uh, a moment, er, please, maybe I, er, " Pi gave him an awkward smile and gingerly tried her pockets. Surely the old gentleman was mistaken? If it *was* the *Principia*, then it was still back in her wavesite, and he wouldn't be very pleased about that.

The old man regarded her impatiently, waving his hand for emphasis. She was about to give up the search – which was proving near impossible anyway, several hundred flutterbooks getting in the way at any given moment – when her fingers suddenly chanced upon something large, square and heavy in one of her least accessible pockets.

"Ooh, just a mo, I think," she laughed nervously, struggling to get a proper grip of the mystery object. She looking pleadingly at Gaia, who waddled over to help.

"What have you got in here anyway?" Gaia mumbled. "What does the old man want?"

"A book, I think, but I know *I* didn't put it in here – better not be one of Leo's pranks."

Finally, the mysterious object emerged, to be immediately set upon by dozens of flutterbooks. It *was* the *Principia*, with its distinctive indigo cover and gilded lettering. Perhaps somebody had put it in her pockets when they left the invitation?

The old man's flutterbook-encrusted hands looked like two psychedelic gauntlets. He blew on them hard and reached out with his momentarily unencumbered arms.

"Ah, welcome home, old friend, welcome home." He made a quick visual inspection, running his not insubstantial nose across the cover, and inhaled deeply, smiling to himself. He looked fleetingly into Pi's eyes. "Give my regards to your father."

Pi looked shocked. "My, my *father*? You know my father?"

"Why of course, child, who else do you think borrowed the book?" He rapped his knuckles on the cover for emphasis.

"But, but my, my father died over thirteen years ago!"

"Died, child?" The old man looked dismissive. "Your father was seen in Venaquise only a parsec or so ago, although nobody is entirely sure of his present whereabouts, I'll grant you." He stared briefly into her eyes and smiled. "I assumed you of all people would know the answer to the latter?" Then he turned quickly to leave, pausing momentarily to speak into the air. "The indexes require a password to close them, prefix the first singular vowel with *Ozymandius*." With that, he shuffled off, vanishing in a fog of flutterbooks, leaving Gaia and Pi both staring at one another open-mouthed.

"Whoa, did you hear that? Do you know who he was?"

"Greenness! He made it sound like your father was still alive!"

"It loads like it's lolo, but yeah, that's exactly how it sounded to me too!"

Gaia looked thoughtful for a moment. "He's definitely not one of the regular lumixastras; they're supposed to wear purple pockets at all times while attending the palace. He must be a lumixastra from Venaquise."

"Is that a planet?" said Pi, she and Gaia now little more than lumiette-shaped repositories of fluttering wings.

"No, no, it's the capital of Inverse, and where we go for the second level. Venaquise is the most beautiful and ancient spherical city, and quite the most romantic place imaginable," Gaia sighed wistfully.

Pi stuck out her tongue, daring the flutterbooks to land on it. "Thounds thovely. I'd thove to thee it, thpecially as my thad was theen there."

Gaia opened one eye and giggled. "If you could only see yourself! Sadly, I think it's time to put these little mischiefs to bed. I *really* hope the old man was right about that password."

"Thand my thad."

"And especially your 'thad'," said Gaia, giggling. "We must find out exactly who the old man was and his connection to your father. But right now, we need to get out of here!"

"Thagreed."

Gaia took a deep breath. "Goto param index Ozymandius 'A' to 'Z' – compress all – execute!"

Immediately, those flutterbooks not already airborne took to the air from every available surface, including the totality of two bemused lumiettes. "Ooh, something's happening, digits crossed," Gaia grimaced apprehensively.

"I think they're going back in – look!" said Pi, marvelling as the flutterbooks began to land back in the drawers. "This'll still take ages; maybe we should run while the going's good?"

"Floor's clear, let's try the stairs," said Gaia, discovering the stairs were now, indeed, flutter-free. This enabled them to double back over the heads of the monikers at enquiries without being seen. They had slipped back just in the nano of time; the enormous cloud of flutterbooks had alerted monikers from all over Mandlebrot 'A'. A whole posse of them were now congregating at the indexes, watching with complete bemusement as the last flutterbooks put themselves silently away.

Pi and Gaia stole back to the café, expecting to merge unnoticed into the merry throng much as they had left it; no such luck! Absolutely everybody was aboard the browser impatiently awaiting their return.

Fibonacci looked especially annoyed, spotting them as they descended the wooden stairs from their elevated escape route. "And where have you two been, may I ask?"

"Er, we had to return a book, Lumixastra, the *Principia*, to a visiting lumixastra," said Pi with a modicum of conviction.

"Newton," said Andomime suddenly. "I can see from library records that one Lumixastra Newton was recently located near the indexes." Andomime gave Fibonacci one of her rare smiles.

Gaia and Pi looked at one another with amazement and Pi leaned close to Gaia's ear. "Holy frazzballs! That must have been *the* Isaac Newton, the guy who actually wrote the *Principia?*" she whispered.

"Perhaps he's the famous lumixastra who invented the gravity boots of the same name? Greenness, wouldn't that be amazing!"

Fibonacci harrumphed to herself. "Well, I'm sure I don't know anything about *that*. I have it on good authority that *somebody* has been opening all the indexes and upsetting the monikers. Lumixastra Magistry was extremely cross! I simply do not have time to investigate such nonsense. Take your seats immediately. We should have been at Meridian X-Change thirty nanos ago."

Pi spoke sideways to Gaia. "Magistry? I didn't scan him in the library!"

"Neither did I, but he must have been there, somewhere."

"I guess," said Pi. "Wonder if it was anything to do with Lumixastra Newton? Remember I thought I saw somebody following us?"

"Greenness! Maybe *that* was Magistry!"

Pi shivered at the very thought. "But you know what the *really* annoying thing is, that Lumixastra Newton was in such a hurry. I had so much I wanted to ask him about my dad!"

Gaia sighed. "I know, I know. Like what was your father doing in Venaquise?"

"Yeah, and when was he there, exactly? Was he really seen there *after* he died? Or was the old guy getting muddled between Earth years and Inverse parsecs and stuff? Getting the timeline all wrong?" Pi sighed heavily. "This is really doing my head in. Now all I want to do is go to Venaquise!"

The whale-way warning bell started and Gaia's face brightened. "We will soon enough. I'm longing to see it too! That's where we have to go for archive training, apparently. Next, though, we're going to Meridian X-Change, so we can visit a certain host-system's mainframes, and in order to actually *reach* the Quadriga, we'll almost certainly have to go shadowsurfing!"

"Megs, so I finally get to try out my popper, right?"

"We'll *both* get the chance to try out our new

poppers. And then a certain person has to install their cyberpomps!" Gaia looked at her and raised her feathery eyebrows.

"I'm so stoked I'm actually going to see it finally, the Quadriga," Pi looked around, "although I guess we're kind of inside it already."

Gaia looked surprised. "So you've never had the chance to see where your father worked all those years?"

"Negs, Lani and I were never allowed to actually visit the Quadriga. Mum has, but I've only ever scanned holos of it. Pretty lame, huh?"

"Greenness, so this will be a first for you too? How exciting!"

"Yeah. Never thought I'd be getting a guided tour courtesy of a bunch of alien AIs, no offence!"

"Oh there's nothing artificial about an Inversian! You should know that, you're one of us now!"

"Suppose I am. That's so cryo!"

They began giggling and hastily spliced their main braces. Pi had been intending to tell Fibonacci of her 'reportable breach' the moment she saw her, but the lumixastra was in such a bad mood now she decided against it.

Fibonacci pursed her lips and cast a beady eye over her charges. "We are now ridiculously late! We have mainframes to visit and cyberpomps to install! Kornephorus, would you do the honours this time please; Meridian X-Change."

Izar nervously fumbled for his address book. "Excuse me, Lumixastra Fibonacci, do I dial 'M' for Meridian or 'X' for X-Change?"

"Oh for Inverse's sake, we'll be here a whole parsec at this rate." Fibonacci impatiently snatched up her own address book and used it instead. "They are cross-referenced, so either would have done, Kornephorus." The browser juddered forward, Fibonacci throwing the accelerator hard right to make up for lost time.

Leo was impressed by the lawbreaking lumiettes. "Well, what *have* 'un been up to then?"

"Living on the edge, Mottles. Flutterbook rustling, don't tell anybody whatever you do," said Pi, with mock furtiveness.

A look of confusion crossed Leo's face as he tried to reference flutterbooks in his memory banks, apparently without success. Pi found Leo's cognitive limitation strangely reassuring.

He quickly changed the subject to something he did understand, with professorial authority. "Well, 'un missed out on some sparkin' amazing cookies." He secretively opened his pockets and revealed they were overflowing with cookie boxes.

"My greenness! You didn't steal them, did you, Mottles?"

"*Steal* 'un! Us has been *given* 'un all by all the others look, for valiant services rendered," his voice dropped to a whisper, "you know, battling the *whatsit*.

And these were for 'un, us was just minding 'un look." Leo rapidly decanted a whole dozen boxes of Meson-Munchies onto Gaia's desk, causing her serious logistical problems as she tried to find space for them in her pockets, before Fibonacci noticed.

"But – but why me? What did I do?"

"You only got the sparkin' sample! Everybody choc-chipped in look." He laughed at his own joke.

"Well, in that case you'd better have this back!" Gaia furtively smuggled Leo's Barnum-Bratts pistol into his eager hands.

"Whoarr! Me trusty old 'un. Thanks, G!" Leo then bundled even more boxes of cookies into Pi's lap.

"*Kalikimaka!* Maybe you could give them to me later, Mottles?"

Leo turned a deaf ear, continuing to divest himself of a seemingly endless supply. "Gotta make some room look, me pockets is sparkin' stuffed!"

Pi glanced at the boxes as she hastily hid them in her pockets. "Cracker-Quarks in several flavours, megs, I didn't expect all this!" She tried out her best lumixastra-avoiding psy. "*Thanks for the cookies, er, everybody.*" Several '*don't mention it*' '*you're welcome*' type remarks came back at her by the same means. A few hands with splayed fingers shot into the air, which Gaia informed her was entirely polite, being the Inversian equivalent of a thumbs-up.

Gaia psy'd everybody else as well. "*Thanks for all mine too, innies.*" She leant across to Pi, who'd already been forced to hide boxes under her desktop while she searched for a free pocket.

"I'll trade you some of mine during downtime if you like."

"K, sure, if Cookiemeister here thinks Mesons are so cryo, then a lumiette's just gotta try 'em."

"They Mesons are sparkin' rokkerlicious, us had three packs whilst you lot were butterbook rustling."

Gaia blinked. "*Three!* You didn't!" Leo briefly held up his index finger as if to suggest they observe closely; he then retrieved three carefully flattened cookie boxes as evidence.

Gaia laughed. "You'll turn into one if you're not careful."

The browser whizzed past the portals to a spheroom named Fore Royal.

"That's where the palace usually serves refreshments. We'd have stopped there if we hadn't visited the Margin already," said Gaia.

Leo gave them his cookiemeister rating. "They got quite a wide selection look, but not the *specials* mind. The Doors is a better 'un, but you can't beat the Margin for proper rarities look." He grinned like an imp. "Bet none of 'un would do a swap for what Anders's got though?"

They looked across at Andomime. She sighed and reluctantly played along, revealing that her critical role as data-demon decoder had not exactly gone unrecognised.

"Forty-four boxes of *Conundrums* look, count 'em, and she ain't trading neither!"

Andomime decided that a split-nano's exposure of her overflowing pockets was quite long enough, and closed them. "I was most gratified to receive the gifts; they are a great favourite, it is true. But I am quite happy to *give* some away, if anyone would care to try one? But I should add, they are not for the faint-hearted."

Leo looked like he was bursting to reveal why. "'Un would have to be proper mad to eat one look, or a genius, or a mad genius."

"Let me guess, they're chilli hot or something?" said Pi.

Leo shook his head. "Nothing like that, they taste sparkin' amazing look, even better than they Madder-Lanes."

"They're supposed to be the best-tasting cookies in the universe, it's true," said Gaia. "But there's a problem with them, *literally*. Each one has a near impossible mathematical proof programmed into it. If you can solve it by the time you're halfway through, they taste, like Leo said, absolutely amazing. But if you can't solve the problem quickly, they taste so horrible you have to spit them out fast or you'll be sick! Like a certain person was last time he tried one."

"As a cyberdog look!" Leo pulled a nauseous face. "Had to try 'un though, didn't us?"

"Hmm, would be kinda interesting to try one

now I've had all those downloads," said Pi. "The mathematical proof is in the eating. Ooh, I made a smart funny, my IQ must have improved!"

Andomime allowed herself the merest hint of a smile, secretly opening a pack of the beguiling biscuits.

"Anders can eat 'un standing on her head, can't 'un, Anders?"

"I am rather partial to them, it is true, I enjoy the challenge as much as the taste."

"Have you ever had a gnazzy one, you know, one you couldn't solve?" said Pi.

Andomime looked surprised at being asked such a thing. "Never, you should try one. I believe you might get on with them." She provocatively passed no fewer than three whole boxes of Conundrums across in their blue foil wrappings. Leo nervously relayed them at arms' length, as if they were live grenades.

"Well, you're braver than me. Even after twenty-six *Mandlebrots*, I don't think I'll risk it. Maybe after the second level," mused Gaia.

Pi studied the wrapper. There was a clear warning printed on the back in black and yellow. *WARNING: may cause nausea and vomiting – do not consume if IQ below four trillion.* She had half a mind to try one now, but the browsers were slowing down again and throwing up under her desktop was not an attractive proposition. They had spun through another portal into yet another great series of twenty-six spherhalls, Meridian X-Change. They would shortly be starting their next palace tour.

So she pocketed the cryptic cookies, having decided she would definitely try one... eventually.

Then, as she withdrew her hand from her pockets, she felt something come with it. Pi puzzled over the mystery object. It was the half-eaten madeleine, for she'd only managed to take one bite before her world stopped still in its tracks.

She looked at it more closely, wondering how it had got there. She peeled back what remained of the red foil wrapper, smiling to herself as she savoured the delicious aroma, so indescribably glorious; it was all she could do to stop herself eating the rest there and then. The gold script around the rim caught her eye. She swore there was something different about it. Indeed there was, for the writing had changed; it now read *'15 milliseconds remaining'*.

End of Book One

Pi's adventures continue in:
Pi Lightfoot & The Seven Tsunamis